1

# KERALA to KAMLOOPS:

# ONE NURSE'S JOURNEY OF GRATITUDE

By Chinnama Baines

MY STORY IS DEDICATED TO

My Parents

Evangelist M.J. John & Mariyama

Appachen (Dad) & Ammachi (Mom): I am for ever grateful for your unconditional love and for your ardent prayers during times of joy and suffering. Thank you for planting a seed in me to love Jesus.

&

My Uncle

Pandit C.M. George

Achayan (uncle George): I am genuinely grateful for your vision for me and your belief in me as you helped open a door for me to go to CMCH, Vellore, and come to Canada. Thank you for your caring action.

Kerala to Kamloops:  One Nurse's Journey of Gratitude

# Table of Contents

# INTRODUCTION

*"Life is not merely a geographical journey-not just East to West, or North to South. There is also an up and down- God's way or our way."* (Zacharias 2006, 240)

After lengthy soul searching, I decided to write my journey, not because my journey was important to tell or that there would be anyone interested in reading what I had to say, but because I wanted to express my gratitude for what God had done for me.

In addition, the birth of my grandchildren has inspired me to write my story as I have no idea if they will have a chance to visit my hometown in Kerala. In fact, neither of my sons or their wives know about my upbringing in Kerala.

My sons, Anil, and Ajay were born and raised in Kamloops, Canada. Ajay's wife Joyti was also born and raised in Kamloops. Anil's wife Janice is from Hong Kong. I am in my late 70's and Ranjit, my husband, is in his early 80's now. I do not know if I will have a chance to visit Kerala with our sons and their families. Even if I do, Kerala has changed so much from when I was born and raised. Thus, I have decided to write my story for them if they choose to read it.

In addition, I have been abundantly blessed in my life, and I feel compelled to share these blessings with my family and friends. My journey is rather unique. I am considered a pioneer in my family and in my community in Kerala. I was the first one from my family to come and establish a life Canada in the 60's. In fact, I was the first one from my family to travel abroad during that period. I was also the first one to choose nursing as a career in my family. As far as I know, I was also the first nurse from India to work as a Registered Nurse in Northern British Columbia.

It is often difficult to decide what is important to say or leave out in one's own journey. I have chosen aspects that I believe are worth telling based on their significance to me personally. I came to Canada when I was 22

8

years old. I have lived in Canada for more than five decades. I became a woman in Canada and learned about life and living. Yet, the values I learned in my early years have had such a profound impact on my life. These values have guided me to stay on the right path.

My story is based on the information that I have kept in my journal, as well as my recollection of past events. In making the decision to write this memoir, I have asked myself the question, is my memory reliable? I am grateful that I still have my memory. Another question I have asked myself was, am I truthful in writing my journey? In telling a truthful story, I must admit that I have not told all aspects of my life. What I have written here are those aspects that I believe would be of worth telling. I trust that I will not offend anyone with what I have written, and through my story, I hope to pass on some of the values I hold to my children and grandchildren.

My journey is written in three parts:

Part One:      My personal journey: "Mylapra to Hazelton".

Part Two:      My professional journey: "The Hospital to University".

Part Three:    My spiritual journey: "Upholding My Beliefs in a

                Postmodern Culture "

In writing my three-part journey, my intention is also to express my gratitude to God through my story. I have included here how God has protected me from life-threatening situations, guided me to succeed in my career, abundantly blessed me in my family life, and above all, helped me to be grateful His Blessings. I am grateful for all that I have received, especially the privilege of experiencing the love of Jesus.

Three common themes have emerged as I have written my story:

Culture & Context,

Changes & Transitions

Asking Questions & Seeking Answers.

The following is a brief overview of these themes.

Culture and Context: Culture is the way of life of a group of people, and context includes the conditions that surround a situation. While growing up, I have learned aspects of culture in Kerala and in India. In Canada, I have also learned the hockey culture and the academic culture.

The basic elements of a culture in a specific society are manifested in behavioral patterns. These patterns include language, values and beliefs, shared attitudes, norms, customs and traditions and lifestyle of people which are passed down from one generation to the next. Culture can also be reflected in writing, music, style, fashion, arts, and entertainment.

When travelling from one state to another in India, one can observe these patterns of culture. Each state has its own culture as portrayed by the language they speak, the clothes they wear, the unique way in which they prepare food, the jokes they tell, the dances they perform, and so on.

Culture and context play a significant role in how people form relationships within a community. In a community, people tend to form relationships with those who share the same interests, who speak the same language, who are of a similar age group, and who hold similar beliefs and values. However, in my life, I have had the opportunity to form relationships with people from different cultures and contexts, who hold different beliefs and values, who speak different languages and who are of different societal statuses. Such relationships did not happen spontaneously. So, in addition to understanding the culture of my homeland, I have been privileged to have the opportunity to live among and work with indigenous people and nurses from the Philippines, while I was immersing myself in the Canadian culture.

Changes and Transitions: While culture has been important in my journey, so too have the many changes and transitions that I have experienced. My journey has been one of constant and continuous changes and transitions. Three components of the changes and transitions which I have experienced are: endings, transitions, and new beginnings. Endings have entailed my letting go of the past and accepting the changes. Transitions have been the periods between the changes. I have learned that transitions are difficult phases as I have faced uncertainty and confusion during those periods. The new beginnings consist of moving forward once again by dealing with the changes.

Throughout my journey, I faced constant and continuous changes, with very little time to deal with the transitions in my everyday life. For example, life totally changed for me when I landed in Canada from India. I experienced four seasons of weather, including winter with snowbanks as high as houses in Kitimat. In India, in the weather I knew, I experienced extreme heat in the summer and heavy monsoon rains. My food changed from plain rice, curried vegetables, fish curry or fish fry, to mashed potatoes, bread, roast chicken, hamburger, bacon, or pasta. These food preparations I had never even tasted before, and I had no choice as I was initially living in a residence and eating food prepared at the hospital kitchen. Once I got used to the taste of Canadian food, I started to enjoy it.

In my life, I have surprised myself by how I was able to adapt to changes at different levels. For example, adapting to changes in technology and living conditions are at one level, and I adjusted to these changes continuously. Making the transition from a large 2000-bed urban teaching hospital in India, to a small 35-bed Northern rural hospital in a Native community, was a huge adjustment.

Adapting to changing expectations in life and major shifts in culture is at yet another level. It took me a while to think like a Canadian and understand an issue the way my Canadian friend would view it. My go-to perspective was based mainly on my Indian culture and context in which I was raised and educated. Many times during this adjustment period, I asked for clarifications and tried to understand Canadian jokes and phrases. Integration into Canadian culture has been an ongoing process.

Asking Questions and Seeking Answers: When I was studying in Kerala, students were not encouraged to ask questions. Now, In Canada, I have learned that asking questions and seeking answers is a significant component of learning. Thus, I have learned to ask questions. However, at first, when I asked a question, I felt that I was exposing my inadequacy. I faced a certain level of vulnerability and humility in some situations. I needed courage to ask questions. I also learned that when I asked a question, I expected my listener to think about the question. Asking questions reminded me of the Socratic method of questioning.

Socrates, one of the founders of Western Philosophy, was famous for asking questions. His questioning technique is known as the Socratic method. He used discipline in his questioning to explore complex ideas, to uncover issues, and to make assumptions and to find out the truth. The type of questions he asked made people uncomfortable as it made them think deeply and examine their belief systems. For example, he asked questions such as: "What is justice? What is knowledge? What is love?"

These questions made people uncomfortable. In the end, he paid a big price for his method of questioning. He was put on trial and found guilty for the charge of corrupting the youth. The people of his day were not ready for the types of questions posed by Socrates. The Athenian Assembly voted to put him to death. Although Socrates had the opportunity to escape death, he chose his death sentence.

So, asking questions is part of our Canadian culture and originates in the Socratic method. It promotes thinking and learning. I know from the Socratic method of questioning that asking questions and giving answers require both knowledge and discipline. Some questions are soft and small, for example, the "why, how, what, where, and who" questions. To this end, I recall emphasizing with my nursing students the importance of knowing the "why" of underlining their nursing actions, as I believed that knowing the answer to "why" would help them in giving meaningful care to their patients.

However, to get to the hard questions, I am reminded of a ministry called "Give me an Answer" by Cliff Knechtle. (His question/answer sessions are posted on You Tube). Cliff travelled to university campuses in the US, ready and prepared to give answers to deep questions that students ask of him. Cliff met with students during their breaks from classes. I was amazed by the metaphysical questions asked by students and how Cliff was prepared to answer their questions. Cliff listened to their questions carefully and provided truthful answers, respectfully.

The questions students asked reflected different worldviews, yet Cliff answered the questions with a sound understanding of their different worldviews. I admired Cliff's patience with each student, no matter how hostile the student was. His passion in ministering to the students through answering their questions was admirable.

Moreover, Ravi Zacharias was another person that I admired for his method of answering questions. He emphasized that in answering a question, the questioner is a key person, and the focus should be on the questioner and not just the content of the question. He suggested that an answerer try to understand the worldview of the questioner. To this end, Zacharias answered the question with another question to find out his questioner's worldview. He also emphasized that answerers be respectful and humble in answering the question.

## PART ONE: MYLAPRA to HAZELTON

*"Life is a Quest for New Opportunity" (author unknown)*

And so begins my journey. I have a vivid memory of that day. I was surrounded by a small group of people in front of my home in Mylapra. Among them were my dad, mom, my two elder sisters (Annama and Ammini), my younger sister Molly, my two young nephews (Thampy and San), my two young nieces (Gracey and Laly), and a couple of neighbours. I looked around to see my home and neighbourhood one more time before I said good-bye. I saw the tall coconut trees on one side, the main road in front of our house, buses loaded with passengers going by every few minutes, and people walking on the road in both directions. It was in May 1964, and I was leaving for Canada. I was 22 years old. Who knew what lay ahead for me?

I shed tears when my mom and my sisters hugged me and cried as they did not know when they would see me again. My nieces and nephews were too young to grasp what was happening. They looked at me with wonder and curiosity. I said good-bye to my family as if I was embarking on a journey to a different planet and not a different country. I had no knowledge about the country to which I was going. I had no one within my community who knew about Canada to question. There was no internet to search for information. I could not even find a book about Canada. I was going to a country of which I knew very little.

Further, I had no idea when I would return home. My mom cried and said she would pray for me. My sisters, nieces, and nephews waved good-bye with enthusiasm. As I left, my dad prayed for my safe journey and for a safe life in Canada. I felt the love of my close-knit family. Separation from my loved ones was hard and painful. However, I had the hope that I was not alone as I believed that God loved me and His promise of being with me was comforting.

My dad and I took the train from Kerala to Madras (now Chennai). We stayed overnight at a friend's house in Madras. The next day my dad took me to the airport. I was only permitted to take $ 8 cash with me. In my

14

purse, I had my prized possessions: my passport, my credentials, and a New-Testament Bible. My dad prayed again before I left him at the airport. We both cried as we bid good-bye to each other. I boarded the 747 Air India Jet plane, my first experience of flying.

It was a long flight from Madras to New York and then to Toronto, my destination. I felt sick in the plane, but the beautiful air hostesses in their silk saris looked after me with gentle care. They provided me with a warm blanket, a pillow, and fresh orange juice. They kept checking on me. I am sure they figured out that I was flying for the first time. I remember the service on the plane was excellent, so different from what it is today.

At the time, "Air India" was a proud possession of the Indian Government. However, twenty years later, in 1985, it was a big blow to Air India's reputation when Sikh militants in Canada bombed Air India Flight 182, going from Vancouver to India via London. In the airplane were 307 passengers and 22 crew members who all perished in the Atlantic Ocean. This bombing was considered the world's deadliest act of air sabotage in history. This news spread in my Canadian hometown, Kamloops, as one of the accused was a resident of Kamloops. We watched the news with sadness for the families who lost their loved ones. Although there is more to be said about this tragedy, the trial, and the punishment for the accused, this information is not part of my journey.

The Job Offer: Back to my journey, in the 1960's, not many people from Kerala had the opportunity to travel to either the USA or Canada. How did I get this opportunity? I consider this as a blessing from God. I believe my journey from Mylapra to Hazelton was like a miracle to me. I had not travelled beyond Kerala and Madras State (now Tamil Nadu). I had just graduated from CMCH (Christian Medical College Hospital), Vellore, with a degree in nursing. I had never held a job and had not worked as a nurse in India. My ultimate destination was Hazelton, a rural area in Northern British Columbia. I got a job as a Registered Nurse in a small rural church hospital, my first job ever.

My uncle George and family

From left to right: Sam Kutty, Jose, Pandit C. M. George, (my uncle)
Santhosh, Thankama (uncle's wife) and Alice

After my graduation from the BScN program at CMCH, I was exploring job opportunities in India. To my great surprise, I received a job offer from a United Church hospital in Hazelton, British Columbia. How did this happen? I found out later that my uncle, Pandit C.M. George, had initiated this process. He approached my cousin Aleyama's dad in Kerala to enquire if Aleyama and her husband, Thampy, (I call him Thampichayan) would find out if there was an opportunity for me to travel and work at a job in Canada. They both were living in Toronto, while Thampichayan was completing his PhD at the University of Toronto.

Dr. Don Watt was the Director of all the United Church Hospitals in Canada in the 60's and 70's. Dr. Watt's brother was the United Church minister where Aleyama and Thampichayan attended church. Aleyama and Thampichayan talked to the church minister about me, regarding the possibility of a job in one of the United Church Hospitals in Canada. The church minister talked to his brother. Dr. Watt, who was a visionary and an amazing human being. He decided with the administrator, Dr. Whiting, at Wrinch Memorial Hospital (WMH) in Hazelton, to offer me a job as a Registered Nurse.

Based on the request from Dr. Watt, the administrator of the hospital, Dr. Whiting, sent me a job offer for a Registered Nurse's position. What a blessing and a dream come true this was!! I am grateful to my Uncle George, for initiating this opportunity for me. I am also grateful to both Aleyama and Thampichayan for introducing me to Dr. Watt. I am extremely thankful to Dr. Watt for providing me the opportunity to come to Canada. Above all, I thank God for making it happen.

So, I received the job offer from Dr. Whiting while I was still in Vellore. Included in the letter offering me a job, was the information that I could start my job soon after I arrived in Hazelton and that the hospital would pay my airfare from India to Toronto. As an introduction to Hazelton, Dr. Whiting indicated in his letter that ¾ of the population in Hazelton are Indians". It gave me lot of comfort knowing that there were many Indians in Hazelton.

After landing this job in Hazelton, the next step in this process was to obtain a visa to enter Canada. My dad and my eldest brother-in-law, Kunjachen (I call him Chettan), came with me to Madras (The only immigration office in Southern India in the 60's was in Madras.). Having Chettan with us was helpful because he knew the big city of Madras. I had with me my job letter, my passport, and my credentials. When I met with the Canadian Immigration officer, I was nervous, not knowing what questions he was going to ask me and if I would understand his English. To my surprise, the officer was a kind gentleman and treated me with respect. He looked at my job offer, my passport, and my credentials and seemed to be pleased. He did not ask me too many questions. He issued immigrant visa in my passport. I was ecstatic!!

Dr. Don Watt, Director of United Church Hospitals in Canada

I realize now how blessed I was in obtaining a visa with such ease, pride, and joy, in comparison to those struggling to get an immigrant visa to Canada. I have heard of many horror stories in relation to people obtaining Canadian visas, including illegal marriages, spending large sums of money, and having to wait years before a permanent residency status (PR) is issued.

No, I am a South Indian: Back to my flight to Canada, I landed at Pearson Airport in Toronto, in May 1964, carrying one suitcase and a vinyl purse, wearing a simple sari, and having my hair in a long braid. I went through Customs and Immigrations where the officer looked at my passport and asked if I was an "East Indian". I told him, "No, I am a South Indian". He smiled and said, "You can go". I did not know that people from India were called East Indians in Canada because, in India, those from the North are called "North Indians" and those from the South are called "South Indians". Now, I have come to the realization that I have been described differently through time. In India, I was called a South Indian; when I first arrived in Canada, I was called an East Indian; and now, I am called a South Asian. However, I see myself as a Canadian as I have been a Canadian citizen for over 50 years.

At the airport, I was relieved and happy to see my cousin Aleyama and her husband Thampichayan to greet me. I stayed with them for a week, and they introduced me to life in Canada and some basic Canadian customs. They took me to McDonalds and bought me a hamburger and a root beer. I told them I did not drink beer. They laughed and explained to me that there was no alcohol in root beer. They took me shopping in a grocery store, my first introduction to a super-market. I was amazed to see how the food items were packaged in plastic bags, including meat and fish. I recalled the smelly fish and meat markets in my hometown in Kerala and the markets in Vellore. Everything looked so clean and spacious in Canada. People were not bumping into each other in shopping malls. We picked what we wanted and paid cashiers at the end. The price we paid was marked, and there was no bargaining. A shopping trip without bargaining was new to me. In fact, every hour I stayed with them I was learning something new.

And even with this new knowledge, I was unprepared for the coming days. I did not have any winter clothes for life in Hazelton. Aleyama gave me a sweater and a winter coat that she owned. I had never owned a coat or even a sweater as we did not need them in South India. We only had hot summers and monsoon rainy seasons in Kerala and in Madras state, the two States that I had lived in in India. Aleyama told me about the four seasons in Canada, including the cold winter with snow. I could only imagine what it would be like in the winter season. I really enjoyed my stay with my cousin and family. They had one son at that time (Sony) who was two years old. I will always remember them and be grateful for what they have done for me.

Train Trip Across Canada: When it was time for me to leave Toronto for Hazelton, we began to search for the location of Hazelton on the map. It was a paper map; there were no Google maps in the 60's. We looked all around the big city of Vancouver on the map and finally, to our surprise, we found that Hazelton was a small rural place in Northern BC. I had no idea where I was heading to and how I was going to get there. We contacted Dr. Whiting who decided that I should travel with his 16 year-old teen-age daughter, Helen, who was attending high school in Ontario.

He made the arrangements for our trip. She was going home for her summer holidays. Helen and I travelled from Toronto to Hazelton by train.

Now, on the train, I was just amazed to see that I had my own room, a bed, and a bathroom. Meals were included in my fare. It felt heavenly, compared to travelling by train from Vellore (Katpadi station) to Kerala during my nursing education years. Then, I could only afford to travel in third class.

Reflecting on those train trips from Vellore to Kerala, the third-class compartment would be packed with people. A group of us going home during vacation would try to get inside the crowded train. One of us would get in through the window and get our luggage inside first. The rest of us would somehow push our way through the crowd. Then, we would climb up to a berth where the older women would not climb. We would make ourselves comfortable up there to the envy of the women sitting on the floor. Women had a separate compartment as I do not recall seeing any men in our compartment. We avoided using the washrooms as much as possible because the latrines were usually filthy. I was amazed at how different trains were in Canada compared to the trains of the densely populated country of India.

The train trip took three days and three nights to reach our destination. I was wide-eyed with amazement to see the vastness of Canada, miles, and miles of land with no one living on it. We passed through the lakes in Ontario. The prairies were so flat with no hills and valleys, a strange sight for me. I was used to seeing lots of mountains and thick forests in India. I was really pleased when we reached beautiful British Columbia (BC) to see the mountains, valleys, rivers, all in one province. Canada looked so big to me. I am so grateful that I had this luxurious trip as it was my first and only train trip across Canada.

Helen introduced me to a few items unique to Canada. For example, she showed me a beaver home and told me what a beaver was. I learned that the beaver was the national animal in Canada. I felt stupid because I did not know the national animal of India. I figured it must be an elephant. I had later observed when Indians travel to India from Canada, they bring back wooden elephants with them. Most Indian houses in Canada are decorated with wooden elephants. I learned later in my life that in 1973, the Bengal Tiger was declared the national animal of India. My trip across the country was an introduction to Canada for me.

I was impressed with Helen in that she was not only beautiful, but also, loving, friendly, and mature for a sixteen-year-old girl. She had blond hair and blue eyes; I just liked looking at her. I did not know that at that time she would be called a teen-ager. That was how Dr. Whiting introduced her to me, "my teen-age daughter". We met an East Indian man in the train cafeteria who came and sat with us while we were having lunch. He was smoking a cigarette and drinking beer. (I guess smoking was permitted inside the train those days.). He told us he "drank like a fish and smoked like a chimney". I did not understand what he was saying. Later, I asked Helen what he meant by what he said, and she explained it to me. I was rather dismayed and realized this was another introduction to Canadian culture.

First Indian Nurse in Hazelton: I arrived in Hazelton in mid-May 1964. Life in Hazelton was totally different than I ever imagined. All the people I worked with were either white or Native Indians except for a couple of nurses from the Philippines. I was the only person from India. (Please note, in the 60's, the "Indigenous" people were called Native Indians. Now, they are also called Indigenous, Aboriginals, or First Nations. I learned later in my life that the Indigenous people do not like to be called Indians or Natives).

Hazelton was a rural town surrounded by mountains called the Seven Sisters and by valleys, the main one called the Kispiox Valley. There were many lakes and rivers, and fishing was an important job for the local population. The hospital was in the middle of two small towns, Old Hazelton, and New Hazelton. The few stores were small. There was a Royal Bank in Old Hazelton, and I opened my first bank account. Fifty-six years later, I am still a Royal Bank client.

The food I had in Hazelton was totally different from what I had eaten in India. The climate was cold for me even during springtime. The hospital was way too small (35 beds) compared to CMCH with over 2,000 beds. The way of life was totally different, too. I was trying to adapt and learn this new way of living. I was fortunate that the people around me were loving and caring and accepted me for whom I was. I lived in the Nurses' Residence with a residence mother and other nurses. All the nurses were single women. There were no men in the residence, and no male nurses in the hospital.

In his letter to me, Dr. Whiting had indicated that ¾ of the population in Hazelton were Indians. Yet, I was considered the first Indian woman who came to work at the hospital. So, I asked Dr. Whiting, "Where are the Indians that you told me about in your letter"? Little did I know that the Natives in Hazelton were also called Indians then.

I learned in school about the expedition of Christopher Columbus to find a passage to Asia. He arrived at a land, he thought was India. The people inhabiting the land looked red in colour, and he called them Red Indians. I realized later that the Indians Dr. Whiting was referring to were the "Red Indians" that I had learned about in school. I wondered if he referred to them as Indians to make me feel at home in Hazelton. I only knew the Indians from India. I am glad to note that there was little confusion between an Indian nurse among the Native Indians.

I must admit that the opportunity to work with the "Native" (Indigenous) people was an enriching experience, both personally and professionally. Since that time the status of the Indigenous people in Canada has improved greatly. At the Wrinch Memorial Hospital (WMH), the staff, the doctors, and the nurses worked for and with the Indigenous community in Hazelton and surrounding villages. Dr. Whiting and his family showed much love for them. In fact, the Whitings adopted an Indigenous boy and raised him like their own son. I found out later in my life, beautiful Helen with blond hair and blue eyes, married an Indigenous man from Hazelton.

I am sad to say that Dr. Whiting and Mrs. Whiting both died together in a car accident in Summerland, the place where they lived after they had retired. Fortunately, Ranjit and I had an opportunity to visit them in

Summerland prior to their deaths. Their adopted son was also living in Summerland at that time.

My Canadian roots are in Hazelton where I began my life in Canada. My initial experience with the Indigenous population in Hazelton created an interest in me to learn more about their culture. Later in my life in Canada, I had the opportunity to learn and work with them in my role as a nurse educator and administrator at Cariboo College.

## Humble Beginnings

This section may be of interest to my children and grandchildren as it focuses on what my life was like growing up in Kerala compared to their lives in Canada. I will begin with my birth and my early years.

An Untimely Birth:   My parents told me that on the day that I was born my six-year-old sister Mary had died.  My uncle came over and looked at me; he told my parents not to worry because God had given them another daughter in Mary's place. Did I diminish the grief of my parents from the loss of their daughter Mary?   Another death or one more birth was, common events in our large family.

Later in my life, I came to realize that the place where I was born was called Rajagiri, a rural village surrounded by a thick forest with wild animals. Many people who lived in Rajagiri were stricken with malaria during that period. There were no schools in that community and no suitable roads for buses or other vehicles. Land was cheap to buy and so that was the main attraction for my dad. I am glad to note that my dad moved us from there three or four years later to a place where we children could attend school. I have never returned to my birthplace, and I have no recollection of it.

Namesake / What's in a name? My parents named me, Chinnama. It is strange that they named all my siblings with English Christian names and gave me a traditional South Indian name. Years later, I asked my mom why I was given a traditional name. She told me it was a modern name when I was born. They had no "book of names" or google to find modern names.

In India, people knew how to say my name. When I first came to Hazelton, the Indigenous children giggled and called me "Chim, Chimney". Some people had difficulty saying my name and called me, "Chimna". Another experience with my name was when I was living at the hospital in Kitimat. I ordered an item from the Sears catalogue with my maiden name: "Miss. Chinnama John". The parcel from Sears was sent to me with the name: Mr. John Chinnama. Only women nurses lived in the residence, so the mailman was looking for a man in the women's residence. Another experience with my name was one day when I received a phone call when I was at Cariboo College, and I answered, "This is Chinnama Baines". The caller responded, "I am looking for the man, "Chinmaya". That was another instructor in another department. Apparently, he went to India and came back with a changed name: Chinmaya. I had to tell him I was not Chinmaya, but Chinnama.

I grew up with a name, Chinnama, which I did not like. Surprisingly, everyone liked my name at my workplace. I am retired now, and I want to make my name easier for the "old folks". I am thinking of if I go to a senior's facility. I have shortened my name to "Gina" for those who have difficulty saying "Chinnama". That is enough about my name.

Now, my date of birth was not registered with the municipality. My mom told me I was born in 1943. However, my school certificate states that my date of birth was 1942. I found out later in my life that my eldest brother registered my elder sister Rachel and me together in grade one with the same year of birth. The school certificate was my legal record of birth which was used when I applied for my passport. I have since learned that many people who came from India to Canada have different dates of birth in their passports than their actual dates of birth. It seems registering births was not mandated in India at that time.

One of Eight Siblings: My mom was around eighteen years old when she was married to my dad. Of course, it was an arranged marriage. She was a beautiful and healthy young girl. My parents did not practice family planning. As a result, she had twelve pregnancies with thirteen children. Each pregnancy was around two years apart. Of the thirteen children, eight of us survived to adulthood. The following is an account of those who did not survive to adulthood.

Her first birth was twin boys, but they were still born. I found out the reason for still birth. My mom had a fall when she was eight months pregnant, and she went into labour soon after her fall. The twin boys did not survive. Thank God, my mom was all right. My elder sister Mary died at the age of six. My mom's next pregnancy was full term, and she gave birth to a boy. However, he died soon after birth. The youngest in the family, Babu (a boy), died around the age of three. He was the darling of our parents, so his death was very traumatic to them. I was around ten years old when Babu died. That was my first experience with death. Babu had dysentery (I figured it later). If he had had proper medical care, his dysentery could have been prevented or treated. Thus, my mom gave birth to seven boys and six girls, a total of thirteen children. Three boys and five girls survived.

I learned later in my life that, my mother never saw a doctor or a midwife for any of her pregnancies or childbirths. All children were born at home with an untrained midwife in attendance. There was no prenatal or postpartum care available to my mom. Newborn babies were cared for at home by my mom and older siblings. I am amazed that eight of us children grew up to be healthy adults without any interventions from doctors or nurses.

Where are my siblings now? As I am writing this book, my parents are deceased, as are my two elder sisters (Rachel and Ammini) and three brothers (George, Samuel, and Thomas). My eldest sister (Annama) is currently suffering from diabetes and other age-related illnesses. My younger sister Molly and I are in good health thus far. We are all in different parts of the world. I am in BC, Canada; Annama is in Kerala; and Molly is in Florida. Life is a mystery in that once we all lived together under one roof under the guidance of our parents, and now, we all have our own families and are living apart. Thus, the family cycle continues.

My siblings and me: (My sister Rachel had died before this photo was taken) Back row from the Left: Samuel, George, Thomas. Front row from the Left: Molly, Annama, Ammini, Chinnama

At the age of 39, my sister Rachel died on February 13, 1980, from renal failure (I have included the story of her suffering and death later in this book). The next sibling to leave us was my brother Samuel. He died on December 21, 2011, in Vancouver Hospital after a short illness. He was around 84 years old. He was blessed during his illness and death as he received excellent care from his daughter-in-law, Juji. I have witnessed the genuine love and care, Juji provided for my brother. I have nothing but praise for Juji for her unselfish and tireless care until my brother's last breath. I was glad to be able to attend Achayan's funeral-service with my immediate family and with a large presence of family and friends. My eldest brother George and wife (Susama) came from India to be with Samuel (Achayan).

My elder sister Ammini died on May 1, 2014, in Pathanamthitta Hospital after a short period of illness at the age of 83 years. She was also blessed to have her daughter Laly with her during her entire time of illness to care for her. Her entire family, relatives, and community were in attendance for her funeral-service which was held in Mylapra.

My eldest brother George died in July 2018, after a lengthy, age-related illness. He was bed-ridden during the latter part of his illness. He died at home in his own bed with his family by his side. His grandson Shon, was his main caretaker, attending to his comforts. I admired Shon who was a young boy to have such love and care for his grandfather whom he called Appachen. Thampy, his eldest son, conducted an elaborate funeral-service in Achayan's hometown, Ottakkal. The place was packed with family, relatives, and friends. Ranjit and I had an opportunity to visit Achayan before his death. He was very fond of Ranjit. I was touched when I saw Ranjit giving a kiss to my brother on his cheek. That was our final visit to see my brother.

Most recently, my brother Thomas died after a lengthy illness with Parkinson's disease in his late 80's. Achayan was the hub of our extended family in Canada. Although he had problem with his mobility, his mind was sharp, and his memory was amazing. I miss him now as I have no one to ask questions that are related to our extended family history.

Although he was chair-bound most of the day when his disease had progressed, he loved visitors. He lived a blessed life because of his loving children, his grandchildren, and his devoted wife. They took care of him until his last breath. Another example of the love and care by his children was how his eldest daughter Mercy and her husband, Rusty (of German ancestry) accommodated Achayan and Kochama for over eight years in their home.

His children understood that their mom and dad did not wish to live in a facility. To this end, their son James (Saji) built a new home with an adjacent, spacious suite with an elevator for Achayan and Kochama to live in. Achayan lived there until his death. He died on February 26, 2019, in the Grey Nuns Community Hospital in Edmonton with his wife, children, and grandchildren by his side. My sister Molly and I were also able to spend the last few days of his life with him. He had a beautiful funeral service to celebrate his life. As he was a founding member of his church, the pastor and church members were a big part of his celebration of life.

Away from Home: During my school years, our family moved to four different places. My dad was looking for fertile land for cultivation. Schools were far away from where we lived. My sister Rachel and I had to walk about four miles each way to go to school when we started in secondary school. Therefore, my dad decided to place my sister and me with relatives. I was placed with my uncle and his family for the last two years of high school.

It was the first time I was away from my home, and it was tough. I was not prepared for this change. I was a teenager. Adolescent years were not recognized in Kerala culture as we recognize them in Canada. It seems that I grew from childhood into adulthood while skipping the adolescent phases. I was a child and then, I was an adult. Thus, the needs of a teenage girl, going through puberty, did not seem a family concern. My mom or my elder sisters did not talk to me about how I would cope during menstrual periods. I did not discuss it with my friends in school either. So, when it really happened, I was totally unprepared, nervous, and scared. I felt something bad happened to me. I was embarrassed and ashamed. Girls usually stayed away from school during their menstrual period. We had no access to sanitary pads. I struggled with not knowing what to do. I was away from home.

I learned that in 2009, Arunachalam Muruganantham, a welder by trade from Tamil Nadu, pioneered sanitary pads for menstrual health. He is now known as the "Pad Man". He was humiliated in his village for his innovation because menstruation was a taboo subject. At that time in India, only 12 per cent of women had access to sanitary pads. Pad Man set a goal to make sanitary pads available to all those who needed it. I really admire Arunachalam for his innovation and courage.

Being the seventh child and having older sisters and a mom, I never had to cook or do housework. However, this was not the case when I stayed with my uncle and family. My uncle was running a hostel by a college. I had to help with housework. At my home, my focus was to study. I was good in my studies and wanted to do well. At my uncle's house, I did not get enough time to do my schoolwork. I did my studying as I walked to school each day. The school was still two miles away from my uncle's house. As I walked alone to school, I had a book open, and I read as I walked and learned by heart.

Those two years were difficult, but I had the desire to study and do well in my final year of high school. I wrote the provincial examination, and the result was published in the provincial newspaper. I was filled with gratitude when I found out that I passed the S.S.L.C (Secondary School Leaving Certificate) with First Class Honours.

Parents: My Role Models: In contrast to the violence I have witnessed as an adult, looking back I realize how fortunate I was that I was brought up in a home surrounded with love and joy. While my mom and dad had arguments, I had never seen my dad beating my mom. My dad loved us children, both sons and daughters alike. This is unusual, as in many Indian homes, sons are loved more than daughters. This is inherent in Indian culture. I do not recall my mom or dad beating me or my siblings in a brutal manner. We had been disciplined with love.

My sister Rachel and I fought a lot. We were closer in our ages, and we played together. I used biting and throwing stones at her as my defensive weapons. I did not know any better at that time. I felt bad later in my life when she became ill with renal failure. We both were disciplined by our eldest brother George when we were children. We called him Kunjchayan, and we feared him although he loved us.

My Ammachi and Appachen (Mariyama and M. J. John)

His discipline technique was rather unique. He would call my sister and me to stand in front of him with feet close together and hands down. We would have to tell him what exactly happened. Then, he would have each of us stretch our right hand forward with palm open. Then, he would give us one hit each on our palm with a small stick. He would tell us not to fight any more. We would fight less when he was around. This strict method of discipline was nothing compared to the beatings that some of our friends had to endure, mostly inflicted by their parents. At that time in India, beating was the main method of discipline of children at home. "Time-out" as a punishment was not known to us.

Just like the "time out" for punishment was unknown, so was the idea of a family vacation. In Canada, we, as a family, went on vacations. It was always a fun time. Many of our trips were to watch Ajay play hockey. Whereas in India, we never had a family vacation when we all went on a trip together. A few of us did go together to attend a wedding of a relative or to attend a funeral. That was the extent of a family trip. In Canada, parents take their children on vacation and see different places.

Christian Heritage: "The two most important days in a person's life are: the day you were born and the day you found out why." (Mark Twain)

What is my Christian heritage? I was born and raised in a Christian family. My parents and grandparents were Christians. In fact, I was not able to find out how many generations our family had been Christians. India is a Hindu Nation, so Christianity was brought to India. Christians are scattered throughout India; however, in some parts, they are found in much larger numbers; for example, in Kerala and Tamil Nadu as well as in some North Eastern parts (Nagaland and Manipur).

Perhaps one of the reasons for the strong Christian influence in Kerala was a result of the influence of St. Thomas, an apostle of Jesus. In A.D. 52, he founded seven churches while on a missionary journey to India. Correspondingly, a large population of Christians in Kerala trace the origins of their churches to St. Thomas. The Kerala Christians were called Mar Thomas Nasrani. The word Nasrani is derived from the Hebrew word for "branch". My mom's side of the family once belonged to the Mar Thomas church group. Thus, the Christian heritage in Kerala is different when compared to Christians in other parts of India.

Although my family hailed from the Mar Thomas Nasrani branch, I was curious to learn why we call ourselves Syrian Christians. The word, "Syrian" is used to recognise the authority of the Nestorian Patriarchs of Babylon rather than the Bishop of Rome (Keay. 1999). In Kerala, there are many branches of the Protestant churches, and it seems, the number of these churches is growing steadily in Kerala.

As part of the Christian heritage, being raised in a Christian home, I attended Sunday school and church regularly on Sundays. Reading the Bible at home each day was an expectation. When possible, attending Christian conferences and conventions was a treat. Thus, from a very young age I was exposed to the Gospel message. I learned the Ten Commandments, The Lord's Prayer and many verses from the Bible. Although, I had a Christian heritage, I believed that my relationship with God was a personal matter.

In India, we had the right of the freedom of worship; therefore, it was easy for me to pursue my Christian faith. I grew up with friends who were mostly Hindus. We were friends, and religion did not play a part in our friendships. However, I understood that if one was born a Hindu and converted to Christianity, that individual was often persecuted and disowned by his or her family. Kerala is one State where people of different religions and faiths live side by side harmoniously and, for the most part, have become tolerant of each other. I was fortunate to have parents who modelled their Christian faith for us children to follow.

When my father accepted Jesus as his personal saviour, he left his business and became an evangelist. When we were young, he left home many times to preach in different parts of Kerala. This absence was hard on my mom who was left to raise us small children. My mom was a very hard-working woman. She took care of us children, did housework, and helped with vegetable farming. She was physically, mentally, and spiritually strong. My dad did not like hard physical work. His passion was in business and evangelism. He was a smart businessman. I remember him having a business in carpentry where he hired carpenters to build beautifully carved cabinets made of rose wood and teakwood. Eventually, he gave up business and focussed on evangelism.

As an evangelist, my dad was a dynamic speaker and delivered his message with charisma and emotion. Fortunately, when my dad preached in my hometown, I was privileged to attend the service and hear him preach. He recited poetry during his sermon and occasionally sang a couple of lines of song and clapped his hands. No one would fall asleep when he spoke. Needless to say. I enjoyed listening to him when he gave a sermon.

When I was in middle school (Junior High), I was walking with my dad, and I heard him talking. So, I asked him whom he was talking to. He said he was talking to God. I took it for granted at that time. Later, I understood that when you talk to God, it is called a prayer, but if you say God is talking to you, it is perceived to be delusional. My dad was a man of God.

I have a vivid memory of the day I promised to follow Jesus as my Saviour and Lord. It was at a Sunday service in a different town. Only my dad and I were in attendance from our family. My dad was the preacher. During the time of testimony, I stood up and gave a testimony saying that I would commit my life to following Jesus and requested everyone's prayer. I was around 12 years old. My dad was happy to see that I committed my life to follow Jesus. I did not have a dramatic conversion experience. It was simply my commitment to follow Jesus. Four years later I was baptised in a river, by my dad's older brother, Pastor M.J. Thomas. There was no baptism pools in churches that I was aware of.

As a Christian, my dad showed love and compassion for the poor and needy. He was a man with a kind heart. Our home in Plachery was facing a main road. Thus, some of those walking on the road, hungry and thirsty, stopped at our house. My Dad made sure they were at least given something to drink to quench their thirst and if available, some food to eat. He did not keep more than three or four shirts for himself. The rest he would give to the poor. He understood the plight of the poor. I think I learned from my dad to have love for others, and the act of giving to the poor and needy. For me, it has always been better to give than to receive. Both my mom and dad paved the way for me to grow in Christian faith, and for that, I am grateful.

My parents were blessed as they were able to make a trip to Canada when they were healthy and able to travel. In 1974, they came to visit us in Kamloops. My dad wore pants, a shirt and a suit jacket, and my mom wore a sari, a change for them from their local Kerala outfits. They spent almost four months with us and were able to travel to different places in BC and to Seattle in the US. It was a pleasant time for us siblings and our parents. They were able to spend time with my sister Rachel who was on dialysis. We children took turns in hosting my parents. My mom would have liked to spend more time with her children in Kamloops, but my dad was restless and wanted to get back to his familiar place, Kerala.

## India, My Motherland

As I grew up in India, the country itself becomes part of my story. Thus, I will include an overview of my Motherland in my story. India is a diverse country of extremes and contrasts. Although India is a newly independent country, its civilization is many thousand years old. It is a vast country of many states with its own unique culture. Some aspects of Indian and Kerala culture that had an impact on me are the caste system, the influence of major religions of India, and the British rule.

Indian Culture: In my estimation, India is the most complex country in the world. I am amazed at how over 1.3 billion people belonging to all the major religions, speaking many languages, and hundreds of dialects live together fairly harmoniously in one country. The few thousand years old culture of India is complex, and it is tarnished with the culture of the caste system which is deeply rooted in Indian culture.

When a person visits India, he or she will see people everywhere: walking, running, on bicycles, scooters, carts, rickshaws, trucks, buses, cars, and trains. Now, airplanes are becoming a mode of transportation for those who can afford it. People live in luxurious mansions, ordinary houses, huts, and slums, and many are homeless. People value cleanliness, yet pollution is a huge problem with garbage on public roads, sewage in rivers used for drinking water, and dirty latrines (toilets) in train and bus stops. Indian food varies from the sweetest dish (jalebi) to the spiciest curry, pleasing to people around the world. India's tropical climate is ideal for poisonous snakes of different kinds to thrive. I was alarmed to learn that over 100,000 people die of snake bites annually in India (Wolpert, 1999).

India houses the poorest and the richest, the highly intellectual and the most illiterate, of the world. Middle class Indians are the most computer literate in the world. India is a country of origin to most major religions. Hinduism is the predominant religion producing many mystical gurus. It is also the largest democracy in the world yet, known for corruption as its number one problem. India is also known for the most movie productions per year and celebrates Bollywood fashion. India is the second largest in its population (next to China), with almost 1.3 billion people (2016) and is growing steadily. India is not just a country as such, it is an experience (Wolpert, 1999)!

Pollution in India is a major problem. Delhi's air is the foulest on earth. During a visit to Delhi, I do recall that the air was so dense with fog, that the visibility was practically nil. Water pollution is also a big problem. The River Ganges has the most polluted water in India, yet it is the sacred river for Hindus. Walking through a city street in India, one cannot avoid the pungent smell. When I was in Agra city a year ago, I could smell both jasmine flowers and the urine while walking on the street. The smoke of cigarettes and beedis combined with the aroma of Indian spices was rather unique on the streets of Agra. I had to be extra careful not to step on a pile of cow dung before I entered a shop. Latrines were scarce. I saw a man peeing in a gutter by the city street. It also reminded me of what I had seen on my train trip from Delhi to Agra of many squatting on the open field. It seems, privacy was not a concern for those who were squatting in the open field, close to the Taj Express railway track. These problems are widespread across the country.

During my visit to Calcutta, I learned that the streets of Calcutta were the most crowded in the world. In India, Calcutta was known as the first modern city and the city of palaces. It was a shocking experience to walk through streets in the city of Calcutta (now called Kolkata). Just the sheer number of different types of people was overwhelming. The streets of Calcutta were littered with animal and human remains. I was excited to walk on the Howrah Bridge and to look down to see the Hooghly River. I understood the city of Calcutta a little bit better when I watched the movie, "The City of Joy".

Similarly, visiting the big city of Bombay (now Mumbai), as my nephew's wife Gracey drove me to the shopping mall, I saw uncoordinated chaos on the streets. There were no traffic lanes with all sorts of vehicles (cars, trucks, bullock carts, rickshaws, scooters, bicycles, and animals, mainly cows and buffalos) travelling in both directions as Gracey was trying to navigate through this chaos. In the midst of this chaos, I was confronted with many beggars pleading for alms.

Another occasion, when I took a taxi from the airport to my nephew Thampy's place, I passed through a slum. The sight of the slum was quite disturbing, when I saw the children, some naked and filthy, sitting in dirt looking lost. Again, I learned more about the slums in Bombay by watching the movie, "Slumdog Millionaire".

While pollution and uncoordinated traffic in big cities were major problems, poverty was still another major problem in India. Poverty was predominant in the land of the rural poor in the North. Eighty per cent of India's population lived in villages, of which 75 per cent were illiterate (Wolpert, 1999). Often, I would hear alarming stories of rural ignorance, superstition, and brutality making news across the Nation. Now, I am glad to note that poverty in India has declined drastically, and there is enough food now to feed the poor.

Another major problem I experienced during my trip to India was the lack of clean toilets in public places such as bus depots and railway stations. This was a problem for tourists visiting India. When I travelled by car from Dholpur to Delhi recently, I had no choice but to use the public toilet facilities, and they were filthy. Most public rest rooms were filthy in cities and in towns. I think the main reason was that people did not know how to use these toilets. Hopefully, this will change as toilets become available to those living in villages, replacing the use of open fields as toilets.

The rape culture in India really saddens me. The number of rapes, especially gang rapes, occurring in India is astonishing. India's rape culture tends to blame the victim rather than the perpetrators. The horror stories about rapes in India haunt me, for example, the torture and gang rape of Jyoti Singh, the 23-year-old physiotherapy intern, while she was

36

travelling in a bus. Ninety rapes a day are reported in India. As a result, India is considered one of the worst countries for women to live in. The rape culture, although prevalent throughout India, is worse in big cities.

India is divided into 29 states (This is changing as new states are being formed). India's population speak 22 recognized languages (written and spoken) and hundreds of spoken dialects. Sanskrit is the classic language, and Hindi and English are the two official languages. Growing up in India, one cannot help but learn more than one language, for example, one's mother tongue and at least one or both of India's official languages. I am glad to have learned five languages: Malayalam (my mother tongue), Hindi and English (two official languages), Tamil (language of Tamil Nadu) and Punjabi (language of Punjab). One of the states that is important to me is the Kerala State.

Kerala State: I was born and raised in Kerala State in the deep South-West. Each state in India has its own distinct culture. Kerala is surrounded by the Arabian Sea on the west and the Indian Ocean in the South. Kerala is a network of canals, beaches, and backwaters with heavy monsoon rainfall and extremely hot summer months. It is also known as a tropical paradise. I love visiting my homeland; however, I find the summer too hot. November and December are cooler months to visit Kerala.

In Kerala, coconut is plentiful, and no part of a coconut is wasted. The coconut oil is used for cooking, and most Kerala dishes contain coconut as a flavoring ingredient. Toddy made from the coconut tree is an alcoholic beverage and sold in toddy shops, similar to a pub. Rice and tapioca are staple foods. Fish is prevalent in Kerala State from the sea and the many rivers contributing to the cooking of delicious fish curry and fish fry. Although, cow is considered a sacred animal by Hindus, I have observed that beef is eaten by people of all religious groups in Kerala.

Though Kerala is densely populated, most people are well- educated. In general, I have found that f Kerala is cleaner than other states in India; however, I was disappointed to see the litter along the main road during my recent visit two years ago. Kerala has the highest literacy rate in India. However, the state is politically unpredictable. For example, the first communist party in the world, democratically elected to power was in Kerala. The Marxist Communist party leader won the election in the 1950's and formed his communist government in Kerala. The political parties in Kerala seem to be in turmoil.

In Kerala, Hindus, Muslims, Christians, and Jews seem to live in harmony. The Jews of Kerala have been happily accommodated for so long without persecution. There is a cosmopolitan atmosphere while one walks through the Bazar of Cochin. The Church of St. Frances in Ernakulum, a British War Memorial, and a tomb of Vasco da Gama are a few of the many tourist attractions. Along the Malabar Coast, Muslims control the trade routes of the Arabian Sea. The 30 per cent of Muslims in Kerala are closer to the Arab world than to Pakistan.

As a woman and a nurse, I am proud of Kerala where the literacy rate is the highest in India. Education is highly valued by Keralites. Kerala has the highest percentage of Christians compared to other States in India. These factors have resulted in the fact that women have a higher status in society compared to other Indian States. Historically, Kerala has been the state that has produced the most nurses, and the majority of them came from Christian homes. I am privileged to be one of those Christian nurses from Kerala.

## **Major Religions**

Contrasting India to Canada compels me to discuss my experience with the major religions in India. Growing up in India, I was exposed to most major religions of the world. India is the land of where all the major religions in the world are found. These are Hinduism, Buddhism, Islam, Christianity, and Sikhism. Jainism is another religion that originated from Hinduism, and it is considered a sect of it. Hinduism is the primary religion, and India is called a "Hindu Nation" by the current ruling party. More than 80 per cent of India's population belong to Hindu religion. Islam is practiced by around 10 per cent of the population; two per cent of the population practices Christianity, scattered throughout India, and two per cent practice Sikhism. (the majority of Sikhs live in Punjab). The remaining population form all the other minority groups, such as,

Buddhism, Jainism, and other religious sects. In some parts of Kerala, Christians form around 25 percent of the population.

India is a land of temples, mosques, and churches, and one sees them in every nook and corner. Some of the buildings are magnificent. I had a chance to visit the famous Meenakshi temple in Tamil Nadu. It is a sacred and historic temple dedicated to the goddess Meenakshi. It is a pilgrimage destination, and it is visited by millions of people. The building itself is magnificent.

When India was under British rule, people had the freedom of religious worship. When India became an independent democratic nation, the first Prime Minister was Jawaharlal Nehru. He was an aristocrat and a foreign educated democrat. Nehru respected the rights of people to worship the religion of their choice. Thus, the Indian constitution allowed freedom of religious worship. However, changes are taking place in India now with a different political party (BJP) in power which promotes the idea of a pro-Hindu constitution. The minority religious groups are nervous about the consequence of this change. For example, in certain parts of India, Hindu extremists persecute Christians.

Further, India's parliament has recently (2019) passed a contentious bill called CAA (the Citizen Amendment Act) which offers amnesty to non-Muslim illegal immigrants and provides citizenship to religious minorities from Pakistan, Bangladesh, and Afghanistan. One purpose of this bill is to provide sanctuary to people fleeing religious persecution. Because Muslims are omitted from the religious minority, this move is seen as an anti-Muslim law. People who oppose the bill say faith cannot be made a condition of citizenship. In fact, critics claim the Citizenship Amendment Act is discrimination against India's 200 million Muslims, and it is in violation of the country's secular constitution. So, the new bill is of grave concern for minority groups in India.

Caste system: Another major issue is India's caste system that persecutes the low caste and untouchables in India. Caste is an integral part of the Hindu religion. The caste system is over 3,000 years old; it is a tradition in India, and it is deeply rooted in the Indian culture. Following is a discussion of the caste system based on my experience and exposure. The caste system divides Hindus into hierarchical groups based on the work they do. The four main categories are: Brahmins, Kshatriyas, Vaishyas, and Shudras. Brahmins are at the top, and they are the priestly class. Kshatriyas are the warriors and rulers, and Vaishyas are the farmers, merchants, and traders. Shudras are the labourers. These Shudras are further divided into many sub-castes based on their specific occupations. For example, carpenters, tailors, goldsmiths, and cleaners form a few thousand sub-castes.

Finally, there was a group called the Dalits, or untouchables. They were outside of the caste system. They were the street sweepers and latrine cleaners. The untouchables were the real victims of the caste system, as they were not allowed in public institutions, including schools. Thus, they remained illiterate and unable to defend their plight, while the upper castes enjoy many privileges. Mahatma Gandhi called the Dalits, Harijan, which means children of God (Wolpert, 1999). I was rather dismayed to learn the many names to address the untouchables: Dalits, Scheduled castes, Harijans, Backward class, and Depressed class.

Based on Hindu beliefs, untouchables were condemned by their sins in their previous incarnations, and so, they were born as untouchables. They were characterized by the darkness of their skin, their submissive natures, and their ragged dress. In the caste system, Brahmins did not share their water wells with the lower castes, nor accept food or drinks from them. A Hindu Brahmin could not eat in the presence of an untouchable. Hindu temples were not open to untouchables. Their children were not allowed in schools. Even in death, untouchables were not allowed to use common cremation ground. Mostly, they could not afford to buy firewood to burn their corpses; they were usually consumed by vultures rather than flames.

There are no arranged marriages between different castes. The tenet of the caste system is that people are born into their castes, so there is no escape from the caste system. One belongs to a caste by his or her birth. A caste is more pernicious in that, for an "untouchable", the "dharma", (the right way of living) of caste is a menial one, and one has no desire to oppose it. "It is good to ignore a sweeper because it humbles her, she wears a faded sari, and moves as she does because that, too, is humbling. Her status is a humble one, and her aim in life is to live down to it" (Keay, 1999, p. 131).

In 1950, an independent India's constitution banned discrimination on-the-basis of caste, explicitly prohibiting its practice in any form. Since this constitution, the "untouchables" emerge as "ex-untouchables", "Harijans", or "Scheduled caste Members" (Keay, 1999). Accordingly, today, untouchables are permitted to attend public schools. Further, it is against the law to discriminate against people based on their caste. Despite this law, the practice of the caste system is still prevalent in India, as these practices are deeply rooted in the Indian culture (customs and traditions). Deep-rooted, irrational prejudices die slowly.

Dr. Bhimrao Ambedkar (1891-1956), India's greatest untouchable, and the most respected leader of the untouchables in Indian history, chaired the committee that drafted a policy to abolish "untouchability". He was a British barrister, received his PhD from Columbia University, and served as the Minister of Law under Nehru's government. In the end, he was disheartened with the deep-rooted tradition of "untouchability" in Hinduism and converted to Buddhism (Keay, 1999).

In his argument, Dr. Ambedkar had refuted what Gandhi and the Congress had done for the untouchables. He believed Gandhi and the Congress deceived the untouchables in order to keep them under the control of the upper castes. An example of such deception was when Gandhi did not support the proposal for Scheduled castes to select their own legislators. Further, Ambedkar went onto say that, Mahatma Gandhi succeeded in ensuring that the lower castes remained subservient to the upper castes. Dr. Ambedkar had pointed out that Hindus oppress the lower castes because it is part of their religious worldview.

I was saddened to observe that Christians in India also practice certain aspects of the caste system as it was deeply rooted in Indian tradition. For example, the lower caste people did not enter inside our home. They were served food in different dishes outside the home. This practice is inconsistent with what Christ taught us (We are created equal in the image of God). Yet, the deeply rooted customs and traditions in Indian culture were entrenched in daily practices.

Moreover, when marriages are arranged, parents will determine if the boy or girl is from a newly converted Christian background and which caste they once belonged to. A Syrian Christian family would not arrange a marriage from a family of the lower castes or untouchables. Growing up, I, too, had supported this system because I could not see an escape from it. Only a person born and raised in that culture would understand the gravity of the caste system. Now, I find this system offensive and against what Christ has taught. This is another example of how strong culture and traditions are within a community and society.

Living in a rural community in Kerala during my childhood years left me with two haunting memories. One was the death of a low-caste servant and the other, the abuse of a neighbour woman.

The Death of a Low-caste Servant: In Kerala, I witnessed a dead person hanging on a tree in front of our neighbour's home. Our neighbour was a rich Hindu businessman, belonging to a higher caste, who employed many servants who belonged to lower castes. The dead man was one of the servants belonging to a low caste who worked for the rich family for many years. The news of this death spread in our neighbourhood. It was common for people to go and see this unusual event. Thus, I also went with my family members to see the dead person hanging. It was an unforgettable sight as I saw the family of this dead person crying loudly and helplessly standing around the hanging dead body.

Rumour had spread in the neighbourhood that the rich man and his son had killed this servant (the reason unknown to the public), hung his body, and then reported to the police that their servant had committed suicide by hanging. It seemed the rich man had bribed the police, and there was no criminal investigation. I was too young to analyse what had really happened. However, the memory of this event still haunts me. In my later life, I questioned the helplessness of the poor and illiterate low caste people and how they were at the mercy of their rich master. In addition, I learned that the justice system was corrupt, as no justice was served for the poor man and his family. It was heartbreaking.

Beating of Our Neighbour Woman: I was still in my pre-teen life when I witnessed family violence. A middle-aged Hindu couple was one of our neighbours. The wife was from his second marriage, and no children lived with them. The couple mostly kept to themselves. Every now and then, we would hear the cry of the woman at night pleading with her husband to stop the beating. The beating would continue for a long time, and her crying would keep us awake. In the morning, we would see the woman with a swollen face, bruised hands, and bruised legs. Frequently, my dad, being an evangelist, would talk to the man about the beatings, and he would not show any remorse. Although such beatings would happen on a regular basis, the woman continued to live with him.

I did not understand why this happened. Again, I was too young to analyse the situation except that I knew it was wrong. Looking back, I understand that in our community at that time, family violence was considered a personal matter, and it was not reported to the police. An abused woman had no place to go, and thus, she continued to live in the abusive relationship. Moreover, men had more power and control over women, and this seemed to have been accepted by society. I am glad to note that change is taking place in Kerala. Yet, I still hear horror stories of family violence and other heinous crimes in India.

Schooling and Corporal Punishment: I believe, opportunities for the poor and low castes, including untouchables, for learning and education will open doors for their liberation. This leads me to my experience of learning in the school system in Kerala.

In Kerala, the government made primary education compulsory for all children and youth in 1958. However, it wasn't until 2009 that the Indian Government passed the Education Act for Right of Children to Free and Compulsory Education. As a result, free primary and secondary education for children from low castes and untouchables is now made possible. Thus, when I was in primary school, children from low caste families were allowed to attend public schools. Yet, I do not remember any children from the Scheduled caste attending the school where I went. I wonder if they just did not send their children to school.

It was amazing that our literacy rate in Kerala was high compared to the other states in India. (Kerala State had achieved the total literacy rate in 1991). The main method of learning in schools was by rote memory. We took notes from information given in the classroom, memorized what we were taught, and wrote examinations from what we had memorized. Written examinations were the main method of evaluation. We seldom asked any questions of our teachers. Writing papers, class presentations, and individual or group projects were not assigned as part of teaching/learning process.

There was little opportunity to apply critical thinking skills in the classroom. Reading mainly included the required textbooks, as books from libraries were not accessible to us. Moreover, there was no television or internet to find out what was going on around the world as it happened (no "Breaking News"). We relied on reading newspapers and listening to radios. Thus, our knowledge was limited to what we learned from our teachers, textbooks, and conversations at home.

By contrast, in Kamloops in 2020, we have breaking news on TV, access to the internet, and the good fortune to be able to borrow books through the public library. How different it is now!! My granddaughter Mila is just three years old, goes to the public library in Kamloops with her parents, and signs out books. Both of my grand-daughters, Mila and Alea, have their own collection of books at home. Children are exposed to reading at a very young age now, and they grow up to love reading books.

Discipline was a big part of learning in the Indian school system of my youth. Corporal punishment was sanctioned in Indian schools, and teachers had the authority to beat students. Many teachers abused this authority. Where I attended school, teachers used a cane to beat students. Pinching students under the upper arm was another form of punishment. Teachers also humiliated students by ridiculing them and by punishing them in front of everyone in the class.

My husband Ranjit told me that he was punished by his teacher when he was in grade three because he forgot to bring his geometry box to class one day. The teacher beat Ranjit with a cane several times very hard. He quit that particular school as a result. Another example Ranjit told me was how his teacher in primary school had told the students to beat the student sitting next to him. When it was Ranjit's turn to hit his classmate, he refused to do it as he believed it was wrong. I admired his courage for standing up for his principles. Such beating of students was irrational, yet it was not scrutinized by the system.

In those days, students seldom told their parents or anyone else about teachers abusing them because of the belief that students were to respect teachers, and teachers did have the authority to punish students. These practices have changed over the years. I had a positive experience in secondary school, which was a private Christian school, and did not notice unusual corporal punishment in that school.

## The British Rule

Since the British ruled India for almost 300 years, the influence of British rule is also part of my story. I was born in a British India. In 1947, (I was five years old) India became an Independent Nation. The jubilation and celebration of India's independence at a young age was exhilarating and remained a significant part of my story. So, I was eager to learn about the British rule and subsequent independence of India.

The British came to India looking for trade opportunity and found India was a land of wealthy Maharajas (kings) with rich culture. The British established the East India Company in the 1600s and the British Parliament took over the responsibility of governing India, in 1858 (Mangalwadi, 1997). The British had colonized many countries around the world and was a powerful Nation. During the British rule, Indians were treated as second class citizens. While making friends with the Maharajas (kings), the British exploited India's wealth, gold, and aromatic spices. Yet there were some British who did care for the Indians. For example, Dr. William Carey was one of the influential persons who contributed a lot

45

towards positive changes in India. Following is a brief account of his contributions.

Rev. Dr. William Carey (1761-1834) was born in England and died in India. He was highly regarded for his contributions to India. He was a Christian protestant missionary, a social reformer, a translator, and a cultural anthropologist. Inspired by his vision, he crossed the oceans to go to India and never returned home. His contributions to India are celebrated by all Indians regardless of caste or religion.

During his lifetime, Carey translated Ramayana and other Indian Hindu classics in English. He also translated the Bible in many Indian languages. He worked hard with an Indian activist known as Raja Ram Mohan Rai to prohibit "Sati" (burning of wife in the pyre with her dead husband). In 1828, the practice of sati was abolished. The practice of widow burning might have originated to solve the problem that a young widow may had created for the joint family. The problem was, what would happen to the dowry she brought? Sati eliminated that problem by eliminating the widow (Mangalwadi, 1997). Further, Carey also opposed the ritual killing of infants and child marriage.

Carey, not only abolished Sati, he also started the first degree-awarding university in Serampore, India. Known as the father of vernacular education, Carey started first Indian Newspaper and championed for the free press in India. He was the professor of Sanskrit and Bengali at Fort Williams college in India. To add to his accomplishment, he introduced the steam engine in India. In addition, he led a campaign for humane treatment of lepers. He was also deeply moved by the injustice in treating the poor labourers working in the fields. His mission was in teaching the labourers how to earn their own living, which led him to start the Allahabad Agricultural Institute.

William Carey's work was inspired by the "Christian presupposition, that liberating power comes, not from the barrel of gun but from the Truth" (Mangalwadi, 1997, p.186). To honour Carey, the Government of India, released a stamp on his bicentenary (1973-1993).

Despite William Carey's contributions to India, the Indians fought for India's freedom from the British. For example, a group of people worked hard to fight for India's freedom. Following is a brief account of the popular freedom fighters of India.

Freedom Fighters: Not only Carey worked for justice, so have many others worked for justice in different ways. I will introduce the four main leaders, known as the quartet. They were: Mahatma Gandhi, Jawaharlal Nehru, Sardar Vallabhbhai Patel, and Mohammed Ali Jinnah. They were quite different in their personality and political approach, but one thing common to them was, they were all barristers educated in London. They worked with the last viceroy to India, Louis Mountbatten to make final arrangements in the realization of an independent India.

While growing up in India, after India's independence, I had heard about these freedom fighters. Both Gandhi and Nehru were popular in political sphere and I had learned about them in school. I have a better understanding of these men as freedom fighters after reading the book, 'Freedom at Midnight" by Larry Collins and Dominque Lapierre (1991).

Mahatma Gandhi (Mohandas Karamchand Gandhi) 1869-1948). Many books have been written about Gandhi. He was known as an unlikely revolutionary and the gentle prophet of the world's most extra ordinary liberation movement (Collins & Lapierre, 1991). In a country fraught with violence, Gandhi had offered an alternative, his doctrine of ahimsa (non-violence). His message was simple, yet he spoke to India's soul. He used fasting, as his main strategy to achieve his goal. He carried with him the religious books of Bhagavat Gita (sacred book of Hindus), a Koran (sacred book of Muslims), a New Testament Bible and a book of Jewish thoughts. Gandhi wandered the villages of India talking and praying with its inhabitants

After completing his law degree in London, Gandhi went to practice law in South Africa. Twenty-one years later in 1921, he returned to India and assumed the role of Indian National Congress Leader. The next quarter of a century he campaigned using various strategies to achieve the goal of India's freedom. He was arrested and jailed many times for civil disobedience. Thousands of Indians followed him and went to jail. One example of civil disobedience was the 'Salt Satyagraha'.

Growing up in India, I could not escape but revere Mahatma Gandhi for what he had done for India. He was talked about and worshipped by many even in Southern India. I have come to know later in my life, not all Indians revered Gandhi. In fact, some people had hated him and hold him responsible for the partition of India. He was killed for the very reason. Many did not like his non-violent approach to seeking India's freedom, although it has gained admiration around the world.

Pandit Jawaharlal Nehru (1889-1964). The second important figure was Nehru, a Kashmiri Brahmin. Nehru was the first Prime Minister of independent India. At the age of sixteen, he went to England to study. After seven years of study and completing a law degree at Cambridge University, he returned to India. He worked along with Gandhi to fight for India's freedom. He was a superb orator and writer. He was jailed and spent nine years of his life in Indian prison. For Nehru, Gandhi was a genius and his "Guru". They both differed greatly in their belief system. Gandhi was a devout Hindu and Nehru was an atheist and a socialist. Of the four leaders, Nehru was able to work closely with the last viceroy Mountbatten. The viceroy saw his relationship with the gracious and elegant Jawaharlal Nehru as the prime support of his own policies in India.

On a side note, Nehru became the first Prime Minister of India. His daughter Indira Gandhi and grandson Rajiv Gandhi also assumed the role as India's as Prime Minister. Both Indira Gandhi and Rajiv Gandhi were assassinated while in power.

Sardar Vallabhbhai Patel (1875-1950). The third influential freedom fighter was Patel. He was the first Home Minister of Independent India. He was known as India's quintessential politician. When Patel talked, people listened. He was the toughest among the four leaders. Patel went to London to study Law when he was 33 years old because he had to earn his own money to study abroad.

Patel was an Indian Nationalist, and an activist. He was highly respected for his leadership. Patel and Nehru were natural rivals and their idea of an independent India was vastly different. Nehru argued for a socialist society while Patel argued for a capitalist society. Patel dismissed Nehru's vision of building brave new Socialist world. Patel came from an industrial town, a center for machines, factories, and textiles, while Nehru came from a place where they grew flowers and fruits. Patel was underestimated, his importance was undervalued as most were looking up to Gandhi and Nehru (Collins & Lapierre,1991).

I was curious to learn that, in 2018, the current Government of India (Narendra Modi, the current Prime Minister) erected a statue called, "Sardar Vallabhbhai Patel Statue" (the Statue of Unity) in the State of Gujarat. It is the world's largest statue (597 ft or 182 meters) high. I am curious to learn that both Patel and Modi hailed from the State of Gujarat.

Mohammed Ali Jinnah (1876-1948): The fourth freedom fighter was Jinnah. Although Jinnah worked along with the three freedom fighters of India, his interest was focused on the Muslims in India. He served as the leader of All India Muslim League from 1913-1947. In 1947, he became the newly formed Pakistan's first Governor general. Jinnah was also a barrister, educated in London. Quite the opposite of Gandhi, Jinnah loved champagne, caviar, and oysters. He drank whisky and smoked cigarettes. He was both a successful and a natural politician. He did not believe in civil disobedience and going to jail for it. He was always impeccably dressed and detested the jail garment. He told Gandhi, Civil disobedience was for the "ignorant and for the illiterate".

Jinnah despised India's crowds and detested the dirt and the heat. Gandhi travelled in filthy third-class trains to be with the Indian people, while Jinnah rode in first-class to avoid them. Among his Muslims, Jinnah had no friends, but had followers. Jinnah was scornful of his Hindu rivals. He saw Nehru as an English professor not a politician. (Collins & Lapierre, 1991). Among the four leaders, Viceroy Mountbatten had the most difficult time with Jinnah.

The following three unlikely heroes who fought for India's freedom were different from the four influential leaders mentioned above. These three were revered as heroes in Punjab and my husband had talked about them.

So, I researched to find out who these men were. I was not able to find any books about them, thus resorted to information available online. I watched a video on Udham Singh, his life and his bravery in action. The following three freedom fighters were different in that they tried to overthrow the British Government by violent means. They were disillusioned by Gandhi's non-violence approach, for this they paid a big price. These three brave men were: Subhas Chandra Bose, Bhagat Singh and Udham Singh.

Subhas Chandra Bose (1897-1945), an Indian Nationalist and a patriot, was admired by people of India. He was the president of the Indian National Congress. However, he left a troubled legacy as he sided with Nazi Germany and Imperial Japan to get rid of British rule. He advocated violent resistance and established a separate political party. He held a political view that combined national socialism and communism. His slogan was, "Give me blood, I will give you freedom". He wanted full and immediate independence of India from British rule. He was imprisoned and expelled from India. Growing up I had heard of his name but was not aware of his strategy of embracing Nazi policy. (Subhas Chandra Bose 2020)

Bhagat Singh (1907-1931) was born in Punjab, also a controversial figure, a handsome young man with a mission. He was identified as a socialist revolutionary. In 1928 Bhagat Singh fatally shot a 21-year old British police officer. He also witnessed the Jallianwala massacre when police killed many unarmed people. It occurred under the order of British General, Dwyer, where thousands of unarmed people gathered at a public meeting.

Bhagat Singh was disillusioned with Gandhi's philosophy of non-violence. Bhagat Singh joined the Young Revolutionary Movement and began to advocate for violent overthrow of the British Government in India. Singh was an atheist and a socialist. He was imprisoned and executed at the age of 27 after a questionable trial. Supporters of Bhagat Singh were against Mahatma Gandhi for his policies in achieving independence through non-violence means. (Bhagat Singh 2020)

Udham Singh (1899-1940) was a revolutionary known mainly for his assassination of Michael Dwyer, Lieutenant Governor of Punjab in 1940. The assassination was in revenge for the Jallianwala massacre in Amritsar, Punjab in 1919. Dwyer ordered to open fire where thousands of men, women and children were gathered at Jallianwala Bagh. As a young boy Udham Singh witnessed the massacre. He took the revenge 21 years later. Udham Singh shot Dwyer at a joint meeting of the East India Association and Central Asian Society in London. Singh did not flee and was arrested and was hanged after four months. Apparently, Udham Singh had said after he shot, "Dwyer crushed the spirit of my people, and I crushed him"- a true revenge. Bhagat Singh was Udham Sing's hero. Today in India, especially in Punjab, both Bhagat Singh and Udham Singh are hailed as heroes (Udham Singh 2020).

With the efforts of all the above-mentioned freedom fighters, India achieved its freedom from British rule in 1947. I was passionate to learn about India's independence and partition, the two most significant events in Indian history.

**Freedom at Midnight**

For all the work of political activists, on August 15, 1947 at midnight, India became an independent nation. I have recollection of my dad talking about it and the jubilation and celebration all over India during the time of independence. The news had spread mainly by radio and newspaper. India's independent movement was brought on by nonviolence, which gained international admiration. The last British Viceroy in India was Lord Louis Mountbatten who was assigned to mediate a peaceful transfer of power. India's population at that time was only about 450 million compared to current population of 1.3 billion.

Louis Mountbatten came to New Delhi with his beautiful and intelligent wife, Edwina. They both were likable and did not hesitate to mix with the Indians. They visited the home of Nehru. They invited Indians to their dinner parties in their home. As a couple they went around without escorts. The Indians began to like them. Edwina ordered to prepare Indian vegetarian meals for the guests. These gestures won the genuine affection, respect, and confidence of the Indian people.

The Viceroy's first task was to study the four men, the quartet of freedom fighters, whom the viceroy would be mediating with for the transfer of power. He met with each leader individually: Nehru, Gandhi, Patel, and Jinnah.

Viceroy and Nehru had a good relationship. For the viceroy, Nehru would be one person, who would be able to maintain a link between India and Britain. He saw his relationship with gracious Nehru as the prime support of his own policies in India. He showed his transfer of power plan to Nehru before he showed it to the other three Indian leaders. Nehru suggested changes before he presented it to the Congress.

Viceroy planned to meet with Gandhi next. He sent him a plane, but Gandhi declined and travelled by train in third class as he always travelled. Viceroy wanted to get to know Gandhi better. In their conversation, Gandhi pleaded not to divide India. Mountbatten assured him that, dividing India would be the last option. Gandhi said, if we ever had to divide India, he would be prepared for a "Solomonic judgement", give the Muslims the baby instead of cutting it in half (Collins & Lapierre, 1991).

The Viceroy met with Sardar Vallabhbhai Patel next. Patel had a reputation for toughness. Viceroy made it clear to Patel that he was seeking cooperation in working together and not confrontation. They both seemed to have a good understanding of each other, and viceroy knew he could win his cooperation.

It was lot more difficult for the viceroy to get along with Jinnah. Mountbatten commented after his first meeting with Jinnah that he did not realize how difficult his task in India was. It took a while to get to know Jinnah on a personal level. Mountbatten and Jinnah held six critical meetings to convince Jinnah of a united rather than a divided India, but without success. Jinnah said in the end, there was only one solution, a speedy "surgical operation". Otherwise, India would perish (Collins & Lapierre, 1991).

Mountbatten expressed concern about the possibility of a bloodshed. Jinnah assured him that once the division had taken place, we would cooperate and would live in harmony and happiness. A solution was, the one country India was divided into two countries, the Hindu majority, India and the Muslim majority, Pakistan. Gandhi had no option but sign the "divorce paper" as Gandhi's option of giving the "whole baby" to Jinnah was denied. India was divided into two separate countries.

Partition of India: The Divorce Settlement: Collins & Lapierre (1991) called the partition of India as the "most complex divorce in history". Louis Mountbatten worked mainly with the four Indian leaders (Gandhi, Nehru, Patel, and Jinnah) to make this happen. His most difficult task was winning the cooperation of Jinnah, in transferring the power without dividing India. This is where Mountbatten failed, he could not convince Jinnah.

Mountbatten had 73 days before August 15th to draw up divorce papers. He had the responsibility for preparing the gigantic, unimaginably complicated property settlement accompanying the Indian divorce (Collins & Lapierre, 1991). The division of cash and gold in the bank resulted in bitter arguments between the two parties. There were minute details of dividing assets, for example the books in India's libraries. India refused to share their national identity of postage stamps and currency. The Muslims wanted Taj Mahal broken up and shipped to Pakistan because it had been built by a Mughal (Muslim).

Another major challenge was, dividing of the Indian Army involving 1.2 million Hindus, Sikhs, Muslims, and Englishmen. In addition, there were the vast number of public employees (thousands of human beings). Each one was given a choice of serving India or Pakistan. Mountbatten had pleaded with Jinnah to leave the Indian Army intact for a year under the British Supreme Commander responsible to both India and Pakistan. Jinnah refused (Collins & Lapierre, 1991).

While dividing up the army was difficult, so was dividing Punjab and Bengal. Viceroy had to come up with a plan, where to draw the line, what goes to Pakistan and what belongs to India? This task was given to Cyril

Radcliffe, the most brilliant barrister in England. Radcliffe had never been to India and knew very little about India as a Nation. The assumption was that Radcliff could do an impartial job as he did not have previous knowledge about India. Radcliffe was a man with a deep sense of duty. He drew the line with great precision, a line through the homeland of 88 million people (Collins & Lapierre, 1991).

Finally, Viceroy Mountbatten had to resolve what to do with the "Prince rulers", once Maharajas in India. There were, a total of around six hundred and sixty-five princes left in India. They still had their private armies and air forces. The Viceroy was not aware of the intensity of the problem. The Princes looked up to Mountbatten to save them from their impending demolition. Mountbatten saw their only course was to go quietly and un-protesting into oblivion (Collins & Lapierre, 1991).

Thus, with the described difficulties, papers were prepared and given to both parties. Nehru made a final and an extra ordinary offer to Mountbatten to stay as independent India's first Governor-General. Mountbatten would stay if the offer was for both India and Pakistan. However, Jinnah did not see him as Governor-General, but only as a supreme arbiter, just to make sure that Pakistan received its fair share. Jinnah himself wanted to be the first Governor-General of Pakistan.

In learning this "great divorce" between India and Pakistan, I had come to realize that I had not understood the complexity and risk involved for the people of India when it happened. In hindsight, I wonder, what could the Viceroy and Indian leaders have done to prevent the bloodshed and suffering that occurred after the partition. I hold Jinnah responsible for the bloodshed to some extent, as he was most resistant in accommodating and cooperating with the Viceroy. I am also saddened by the lack of insight and vision on the part of the Viceroy and the Indian leaders in foreseeing the disaster ahead during the greatest migration.

The Greatest Migration in History: I did not experience this tragedy on a personal level as I was living deep down in the South. However, Ranjit's extended family in Punjab had to endure the tragedy. It had become a family tragedy. I read a vivid account of what really happened from

Collins & Lapierre (1991). It was heart wrenching and devastating. I will only cite few excerpts from their book. They coined the phrase, "the Greatest Migration in History".

Although viceroy Mountbatten was tough and strict in his approach to ensuring security for the people most affected by the partition and migration, it seems to me it was beyond his control and ability to protect the innocent victims. He was most perturbed by what was happening in Delhi and stated, "If we go down in Delhi, the whole country will go down with us" (Collins & Lapierre, p.318). So, he placed protection in Delhi as the top priority. He ordered additional troops for the capital city. The other two cities that required immediate attention were, Punjab and Bengal. They did not get the protection and they paid a big price.

The human misery and tragedy occurred in Punjab was unparallel and the enormity of anguish and suffering endured was beyond human imagination. About 800,000 refugees were involved in a mass migration. The authorities hastened this mass migration and finish it before winter arrived. They had to walk 100-200 miles with dust in their eyes and throat, feet bruised by stones, tortured by hunger and thirst, enrobed in a stench of urine, sweat and defecation. The crippled, the sick, and the dying hung in slings tied to the middle of a pole, the ends of which rested on a son or a friend. The women carried cooking utensils, a portrait of Shiva, or Guru Nanak or a copy of the Koran. They faced, exhaustion, starvation, cholera, and attacks they could not defend. Worst of all were those who could not make it, children whose parents could no longer carry them left them behind to die and the elderly resigned to death. The forty-five miles from Lahore to Amritsar became a long open graveyard (Collins & Lapierre, 1991).

There was bloodshed across Northern India as Muslims were trying to flee from newly formed independent India to Pakistan and Sikhs and Hindus from the newly formed Pakistan to India. Nine million Muslims migrated from India to Pakistan and five million Hindus and Sikhs migrated from Pakistan to India. During this migration thousands of people were killed on both sides of the boarder. Punjab, a majority Sikh state paid a big price from casualties during partition. The tension that began between these two countries is still growing. I was curious to learn that the Muslims in Kerala did not migrate to Pakistan. It would be a long way for them to travel. They must have believed that, there life was not in danger in Kerala. For me, they were Keralites Muslims and they had the right to live in Kerala.

Although, I did not experience this tragedy on a personal level, I could not help but question the lack of foresight from the leaders. Why was arrangement not made to transport people safely to their destination? Why was there more security provided to protect the innocents? At least the tragedies could have been minimized! I believe this was the ultimate downfall of partition.

Although the impact of partition was minimal in Kerala where I grew up, India's independence gave the educated and progressive thinkers in Kerala State an opportunity to adopt socialistic and communist ideology. The disparity of wealth and the separation of the rich from the poorest was echoed by many writers, poets and influenced the minds of thinkers. I do recall the election in Kerala State and the communist party winning the election. My dad, although a Christian in his faith, was sympathetic to the plight of the poor. He was opposed to the rich having enormous power over the poor. I wonder if my dad really understood the Marxist ideology of communism and socialism!!

Regardless of the political party and where we lived, our life in this world is unpredictable. We can be faced with threats, accidents or even death. The following is a recall of life-threatening situations in my life.

## Life is Unpredictable

Before I begin to describe the life-threatening situations, I must admit that it seems a miracle that I survived these events. Because of my faith in God, I believe, I was protected and spared. This does not mean that I am immune from accidents, suffering and death. I am just grateful to God that I am still alive and well. I have learned to count each day of my life as a gift from God. I believe that God can protect us from danger and harm. I also know that life is suffering, and I must be prepared to face it with courage. The first incident was being chased by a cobra.

Chased by a Cobra: My sister Rachel and myself were chased by a cobra. The cobra did not bite us. I was around ten years old. I was walking home with my sister after we went to have a bath in a canal. We had to walk by a thick bush (kavu), and we saw a cobra coming behind us with its hood spread. We had heard that there were snakes in that bush and once a cobra had its hood open, it was sure to bite. We ran as fast as we could and barely escaped from the cobra. Apparently, cobra could run faster than humans. We could not see the cobra anymore. Did it go back to its home, the kavu? We believed that God saved us from the bite of that cobra. We came home, told everyone and we all just thanked God. Please note that cobra is one of the most venomous snakes and those bitten by a cobra rarely escape death.

A Serious Car Accident: In the second situation, I survived a serious car accident. In October 1964, I went with a friend in her car from Hazelton to Kitimat. It was the first day of snow fall, and I was delighted to see snowflakes for the first time. She was driving a Volkswagen and the car skidded. I was thrown out of the car. There was no seat belt in the car and wearing seat belt was not mandatory. I had a compound fracture of my left elbow, a fractured jaw, and injury on the right side of my face. I was unconscious and was taken to Kitimat General Hospital.

The surgeon who operated on me was Dr. Gordon Mack, who was not only a competent surgeon but, truly a man of God. He took care of me with love and compassion. He had to use a pin and wire to fix my elbow. My arm was in a cast for a few weeks. My jaw was wired by a competent dentist. I lost a tooth in my lower jaw. Thank God, I suffered no head injury.

While I was recovering in the hospital, to my surprise I had a phone call from Ranjit expressing how sorry he was to hear of my accident. I was pleased to receive a call from Ranjit and realized that he was a kind and loving person. I had briefly met him for the first time through friends in Hazelton. This was the start of our friendship and relationship.

My parents were extremely concerned about me but could not do anything except pray. For the first time my mom wrote a letter to me. I could not even phone them as I did not have a phone and there was no phone at home of my parents. As a newcomer to Canada, I did not know I was eligible to collect money from the car insurance company for the injuries I had incurred. I did not sue my friend to collect money from her insurance agency. Here I am left with permanently fractured and repaired elbow and jaw and scar on my face, my life was spared. I am grateful to God for sparing my life again.

The Notorious Kettle Bomb: The third situation involved a kettle bomb. The breaking news in BC in 1972 was that a young couple, Gurmail Singh Sidhu and Paramjit Sidhu, were victims of a kettle bomb tragedy.

What really happened? It was in 1972, Ranjit was working as a Realtor in Kamloops and I was enrolled in the master's program in nursing at UBC in Vancouver. Ranjit came to know a young, good looking Punjabi couple who wanted to sell their condo in Kamloops and buy a house in Vancouver. Ranjit noticed they were so much in love yet frightened of something. They disclosed their fears to Ranjit and told him that their father was against their marriage and he threatened them with a death penalty.

They had to leave their home in Merritt and went to Alberta and got married secretly and moved to Kamloops. In India this would be called a 'love marriage'. The girl's father was against his daughter marrying the man she was in love with. His plan was to arrange a marriage for his daughter with a doctor from India. Such an "arranged marriage" would bring honour to his family. Whereas his daughter falling in love with Gurmail Singh, who belonged to the same culture, religion, and caste, but did not have a white-collar job, would bring shame and dishonour to his family! The father threatened to kill them both. They were afraid to live in Kamloops and moved to New Westminster.

They had trusted Ranjit and requested him to visit them in New Westminster. One evening, Ranjit decided to visit them and took me and Anil along. When we got close to their house, we noticed, police cars were parked in front of their house. We got out of the car and walked towards the house. The next thing we knew that we three were in a police car and were taken to the Royal Columbian Hospital in New Westminster. We found out that a few minutes before we arrived at the house, the couple we were to visit were killed by a bomb. Since Ranjit knew the couple, the police took him to the hospital to identify their bodies.

It is hard to believe that Ranjit, Anil (2 years old) and I could have been victims of this notorious kettle bomb killing if we had arrived fifteen minutes earlier.

The kettle bomb story was published as follows: on October 23, 1972 at 10PM, a kettle bomb blasted in Gurmail Sing Sidhu's basement suite in New Westminster. An electric kettle rigged with dynamite exploded when it was plugged into an electric outlet. The kettle was sent to the couple by Lewis, a co-worker of Tatlay, Paramjit's father. Lewis mailed the parcel in Kamloops. Lewis's handwriting was traced, and he was arrested and sentenced to serve a few years in jail. The murder was not solved until 1976, four years later.

The culture of shame and honour: For the father, his daughter's marriage to the mans she loved, brought shame and dishonour to the family, so Tatlay's sympathizers called it an honour killing. The couple were killed by a cowardly act by her father, Santa Singh Tatlay. Paramjit was pregnant at the time when she was killed. Tatlay was sentenced to seven years in jail after a lengthy trial. Ranjit had to testify in court as he identified the bodies of Gurmail Singh and Paramjit. How could such a heinous crime happen in Canada? Gurmail and Paramjit, although Canadian citizens were killed based on family values, culture, and traditions.

I had a chance to visit Paramjit's father and mother before the tragedy. They owned a motel in Merritt and Ranjit went to list his motel and took me along. During the short time I was there, Paramjit's mother took me to her bedroom and showed me Paramjit's photo (a beautiful young woman) and started crying. She would not tell me why she was crying. I later found out that Paramjit had already left Merritt with Gurmail Singh and her father was planning to kill both Gurmail and Paramjit. It seems the mother was also afraid of her husband and could not share the secret murder plan with anyone.

A close friend of Tatlay told us that the daughter had disobeyed her father and brought shame to the family and that drove him to commit the murder. He was in fact, justifying for his friend. This murder still haunts me as I believe that true justice was not served as the father got off easy. The culture of "honour killing" is still thriving in Indian communities.

Now it is time for me to introduce Ranjit, the first man I dated in my life and I ended up marrying him.

## Meeting Ranjit: A New Chapter

Ranjit, when I met him in 1964

I came to Hazelton in May 1964, before the cold winter began. I was homesick and missing my family. So, I was glad to see a couple from India who recently arrived in Hazelton: Hans and Meena Gautham. They heard about me and visited me in the residence, where I lived. Meena was a nurse from Kerala and Hans, a military officer from Kashmir, now a school principal in Hazelton. They were very friendly and invited me to their home. They cooked Indian food, which was a special treat.

A few weeks later they told me they had a friend visiting them and they wanted me to come for dinner at their home. Their friend's name was Ranjit. Meena and Hans introduced me to Ranjit, who drove over from Merritt to Hazelton. He came to get his car, a big Chevy impala. Hans and Meena had borrowed his car when they moved from Vancouver to Hazelton as they had only a small Volkswagen. Thus, Ranjit and I met at Meena's house in Hazelton on October 3, 1964.

Ranjit was well dressed and handsome. He was very friendly and nice to talk to. I was happy to meet him. I had no idea that he would be my husband one day. I had just come from India with goals and ambitions and was not thinking of forming long-term relationships. We had a good visit and Ranjit went back to Merritt. However, Ranjit phoned me and wrote to me after our visit, the beginning of our friendship. Ranjit made several visits to Hazelton during my stay in Hazelton.

Dr. Whiting and my friends in Hazelton really liked Ranjit. Whenever Ranjit came to Hazelton, I would have one of my friends (Eleanor, a white nurse or Elma, a Filipino nurse) accompany me to go out with Ranjit. My friends enjoyed Ranjit's company and it was a treat for us, as none of us owned a car in Hazelton. Ranjit also came with me to Dr. Whiting's cabin at Seeley Lake in Hazelton. Dr. Whiting and his wife Marjorie used to invite us nurses to their cabin on weekends. It was a lot of fun at the lake, cooking food outdoors and singing country songs and hymns by the campfire in the evening.

The Seeley Lake water was cold and deep. I never swam in that lake. One day to our surprise, Ranjit jumped into the lake and swam across. We all were impressed with what he did. I had no idea he was such a great swimmer. Nurses in the residence asked me, if Ranjit was my boyfriend. I did not know how to answer that question. I said, he was a good friend. In Kerala and Vellore, in the 50s and 60s, we did not use words like boyfriends and dating. It is different now, back home. Young people in cities in India go on dates. They are influenced by the social media and the

Bollywood culture. They seem to be competing with the Western Hollywood culture and fashion. I told those who asked me about Ranjit, "he is my friend".

## Who is Ranjit?

The following information about Ranjit, although from my perspective, has been vetted by Ranjit. He was raised in Dholpur, Rajasthan. He was the second oldest of seven children to Sadhu Singh and Dhanti Kaur Bains. Ranjit's dad was educated at a college in Amritsar, Punjab. He was also a professional soccer player in Punjab and served as Captain of his team. After the wedding, his parents moved to Delhi and lived there for about five years. Ranjit was born during this time.

Ranjit's parents moved to Dholpur, Rajasthan State when Ranjit was around five years old. Ranjit's grandfather, Basant Singh Bains fought in the First World War, with the British Army in Iraq. Upon his retirement from the Army, he was given 80 acres of land in Dholpur by the King of Dholpur. Ranjit has fond memories of his grandfather living with him during his childhood years.

Ranjit' only sister (Jeeto) was the eldest in the family. She got married to an educated man from Punjab, Sansar Singh Heer. The marriage was arranged by Ranjit's dad and grandfather. After the marriage, Jeeto and her husband immigrated to England where they lived and raised their family. They have three sons (Georgie, Billy, and Baby), and today they are well settled with their families, in England. The time of writing this memoir, Sansar Singh Heer had died. Ranjit's three nephews are married and living with their families. Ranjit's sister Jeeto, is living with his son Billy and family.

In School and at College: As a young boy, Ranjit attended a local school (grade one and two) at Village Pachgaon. Starting in grade three, he had to move to a school in Dholpur and had to walk from Pachgaon to Dholpur, a two-mile walk to attend school. In grade three, he studied English, Math and Hindi. While he was finishing grade three, an unexpected change took place in his life. Ranjit's uncle (Thayaji), Maluk Singh Bains of Gondpur, District Hoshiarpur in Punjab, came to Dholpur for a visit. He just returned from Canada, where he had applied for his immigration status. Thayaji saw the condition of how Ranjit and his family were living in Pachgaon, in a small house with two families (Ranjit and family and his dad's brother and family), without adequate space for children to focus on their study. Thayaji knew Ranjit was a good student with potential and needed a better environment for him to focus on his schoolwork.

Thayaji checked with Ranjit's mother, if he could take him to Gondpur, Punjab where he had a big two-storey home with a guest house and a nearby school for him to attend. With his parents' consent, Ranjit went with his Thayaji to Gondpur to begin his grade three in a new school. He soon realized that he had to learn a new language, Urdu instead of Hindi and English. He had to learn Urdu in a hurry for grades one to three. He successfully completed the language requirement and was promoted to grade four. In the meantime, Thayaji got a letter from Canadian Immigration that he was qualified to immigrate to Canada. He decided to go back to Canada. He also decided that the family situation in Gondpur was not ideal for Ranjit to live without him around, as his wife did not treat Ranjit with love in providing him with his basic needs. So, he took Ranjit back to Dholpur, where he had to complete grade three again.

In grades four, five and six, Ranjit stayed with a loving family of Mr. Kartar Singh, his wife and two little children, in Dholpur. They cooked good food and provided a room for him, in their spacious home. Ranjit was able to excel in school because of Kartar Singh and family. He moved in with a different family to finish grades seven to ten in Dholpur. It was the home of Dr. Narayan Singh, a Rajput family. He was the dentist to the King's family in Dholpur. He provided a room for Ranjit to stay and food to eat. He took care of Ranjit like his own son for almost four years, while he completed high school. Ranjit often wondered what would have happened to him if these two loving and generous families did not help him to complete his schooling. Ranjit stayed at Dr. Narayan Singh's home until he completed high school.

After completing high school in Dholpur, Ranjit went to Balwant Raj college in Agra and completed his BA degree with three majors, English literature, Philosophy and Economics. The standard of education was much higher when Ranjit went to high school and college, compared to education in high school and college now. In college where Ranjit studied, most professors were educated in England with doctoral degrees from Cambridge, Edinboro University and London School of Economics. Ranjit is very proud of the education he received in high school in Dholpur and at college in Agra.

While in College, he took part in sports (track and field). Ranjit excelled in long distance running and track and field events (shotput). He was the captain of the sports team at his college for three consecutive years. The rule at the Balwant Rajput college was that whoever won the championship, became the Sports Captain of the college. Ranjit was hard working and was dedicated to his sports and studies. He spent very little time with his own family in Dholpur, as he was away attending school and college.

To England, Then, to Canada: Upon completion of his B.A. degree in 1958, Ranjit left for England by ship. It took almost a month to reach England from India. Ranjit was just 22 years old. After one year he was able to immigrate to Canada. Ranjit believed, he would have better opportunity in Canada to get ahead in life.

Ranjit's uncle was working in British Columbia. Although Ranjit had the goal of furthering his education, he had to find a job initially, to support himself and his family in India. Looking for jobs, he landed in Merritt. Initially he worked in the office at Craig Mont mines Ltd. During this time, he became a good friend of the mining engineer, Mr. Ross Duthie and his wife Betty and their three sons. Mr. Duthie recognized Ranjit's potential and encouraged him to go to university in Canada. However, his responsibility towards his family to help them financially, forced him to continue working. Although Ranjit had left the mines in Merritt, he kept his friendship with Ross and Betty Duthie for years to come. I remember going with Ranjit to visit the Duthies few times, in their mansion on Granville street. Years later we visited them in their senior's residence in Vancouver. I was touched by the love and affection the Duthies had for Ranjit.

Ranjit worked very hard at his job as he wanted to make money and build a new house for his parents in India.

A New Home for Parents: In 1966, Ranjit returned to his motherland, India, after seven long years. His main purpose for the visit was to build a new house for his parents. It took one year for him to build the house. He had to work very hard to get the house built in the village as he had to get the building material from different far away places. Ranjit's mom was very proud of him for what he had done and was happy to be living in a new big house.

During his visit to India, he also visited my brother (Thomas) and his family, who were living in Sindhri, Orissa. My brother was working at a big steel plant as an assistant Engineer. Since Ranjit and I had become good friends and was making plans for our future, this was an opportunity for him to meet my brother and family. Ranjit really enjoyed his visit and the hospitality shown by my brother (Pappachayan and wife, Susy Kochama). He really enjoyed the food prepared by her. He also enjoyed playing with my brother's three daughters (Mercy, Lizzy, and Daisy). So, he stayed an extra day with them. This was the first introduction of Ranjit to my family other than my sister, Rachel and husband, Mathew (Ponnachayan).

To University – Then A Realtor: Although Ranjit worked at a mine initially to make some money, his goal was to pursue further education. Thus, before he went to India, he had completed the process for admission to Simon Fraser University (SFU) and was admitted to its teacher training program. Upon his return from India in 1967, Ranjit began his course work at SFU. After completing one year of full-time study he returned to work, and studied courses, on a part-time basis. He explored the options of becoming a teacher or a social worker. In the end he chose to become a realtor.

He worked as a realtor and investor for 25 years in Kamloops. Block Brothers Realty was the first company he worked for and its manager Ron Lemke and Ranjit became very good friends. Their friendship lasted over

40 years until Ron died in 2016. This was a shock as Ron and wife Lorene had become great family friends.

Ranjit was a hardworking and successful realtor and an investor. In the 80s, the housing market was down, and it was hard to sell houses. Since then, the market has improved over the years. Ranjit was a smart investor and had bought properties wisely. Ranjit and my brother Thomas, who was a builder (TJ Homes) worked together. The many years my brother and Ranjit worked together, they had not ruined their relationship over money. I loved my siblings and families who lived in Kamloops and got along well with each one of them.

Our wedding photo, 1969

## Our Wedding: No Parents

Since moving to Canada, I had become more westernized in my thinking regarding dating and getting married. Growing up in India, my older siblings' marriages were arranged by my parents. In Canada, far away from parents, I felt I had more freedom to make decisions regarding my goals in life including finding a suitable husband. As a new Canadian, I had become an independent woman, working, and making my own money. However, I was reminded of my foundational beliefs, and my obligations towards my parents and the rest of my family.

My parents had not met Ranjit. Thus, I was torn in making my decision. My marriage with Ranjit would be called a "love marriage" because in a love marriage the couple "fall in love" first and then marry. Whereas in an arranged marriage, the couple get married first, and then they "fall in love". Arranged marriages have changed. In a modern arranged marriage, the couple is introduced by the family and then the couple make the decision to marry or not.

I asked my parents for their permission to marry Ranjit. They told me; if I married Ranjit, it was my own decision, and I could not blame them if I had any problems in my married life. They knew Ranjit was from North India, raised in a different culture and religion. In an arranged marriage, it is the responsibility of the parents to choose a suitable husband for their daughter, from a family of similar religion/faith and cultural background. I was breaking these traditions by marrying Ranjit.

Ranjit and I discussed our faith in God. Ranjit told me that he had attended church in Merritt before he met me. I was open with him and told him that my faith was important to me. Ranjit was fully supportive of me and encouraged me to continue my faith after marriage. We both met with Pastor McCarthy in Alliance church in Kamloops and discussed with him our plans to get married. He blessed us and prayed for us.

We got married on April 5, 1969 at the Kamloops Alliance Church by Pastor McCarthy. I had no family in Kamloops in 1969. My only family in Canada was my sister Rachel and her husband, Mathew. They were living in Vancouver. My friend and colleague, Marilyn and her husband, Jim

White were a great help. I got dressed in their home and they drove me to the church. I wore a simple white silk sari for the wedding. I had no make-up, did not get my hair done by a hairdresser. I had no manicure, or pedicure done in preparation for my wedding. There was no rehearsal, no party or dance or alcohol served at our reception.

We had a total of around 125 guests attended our wedding. Most of them were our friends and a few family members from Ranjit's side. From my side of the family, I was fortunate to have my sister Rachel and her husband Mathew. My sister was seven months pregnant and was suffering from hypertension and renal failure. From Ranjit's side of the family, we had his brothers and a few cousins attended our wedding. In addition, Ranjit's uncle's (Sohan Singh Bains) wife Bibi and daughters Mohinder and Ajmer also attended the wedding. Mohinder and Ajmer were of great help to us during this time. I was pleasantly surprised when my friend, Anna David from Toronto came to attend the wedding. We were friends from CMCH, Vellore, India.

Our wedding reception was at the Stockman's Motor Hotel (Now called Delta Hotels) on Victoria street. The MC for our reception was Mr. Marvin Phillips, a founding member of Alliance church. The cost of our reception was $217. in total. We spent our honeymoon at the same hotel and the cost for one night was $11.50. We travelled to Honeymoon Bay in Vancouver Island for our honeymoon and stayed at Ranjit's cousin's place.

We had no professional photographer or videographer to take pictures. Thus, we do not have any photographs of our wedding ceremony or reception. After our wedding we went to a studio in Vancouver. Ranjit and I put on our wedding outfits again and got our wedding photograph taken. The total cost of our wedding was under $300, significantly a small amount compared to the cost of elaborate Indian weddings now. The wedding gifts we received were all boxed items, no cash or cheque. This was how gifts were given in the 60s. Wedding invitations did not indicate "no boxed gifts please".

I often wonder, if I had not met Ranjit when I met him, what would have been my life in Canada? Ranjit was wise and practical and helped me when I needed help. I had been richly blessed in my married life and established our home in Kamloops.

The Married Couple

Our Home in Kamloops: Our first purchased home was on 943 Schubert Drive. We had rented out the top floor of the house. Ranjit renovated the basement floor where we began our married life. Before long, we moved upstairs where we had a lot more space and comfort. Fortunately, Ranjit and I shared similar values in relation to helping our family members in India. We both had family responsibilities towards our siblings and parents. This responsibility was part of our culture and tradition. Girls from Christian homes in Kerala, once educated, went out of province or country to work and contributed in helping family financially. Nursing was a popular chosen career for Christian girls in Kerala.

## Family Obligations

Just as my parents and brothers supported me to obtain an education, I felt the obligation and responsibility to support my family back home in India. As per Indian custom, parents make sacrifices in educating their children with the expectation that, once the children got jobs, they would help parents and other siblings financially. When I was in Vellore studying, my family supported me with my financial need. Both Ranjit and I acknowledged our obligation to help our family in return.

I do recall when I first started working in Hazelton hospital, a portion of my monthly salary was sent home to my parents each month. I continued this practice until I was married. My parents really appreciated this help as they were caring for grandchildren. In addition to financial help, both Ranjit and I sponsored our siblings and their families to obtain immigrant visa to come to Canada. I believe, helping my family and sponsoring my family members was a purpose in my life. I did this not merely to fulfil my responsibility, but out of love for my siblings and family.

Loving the family as I do, it would only make sense that I would want to have my family back at home also brought to the land of milk and honey. We considered Canada and USA were two countries as the lands of milk and honey: land of opportunity. We knew the life in Canada would be a lot better in the long run. So Ranjit and I, through the legal processes, tried to bring our family members to Canada. With Ranjit's help, I was able to sponsor my siblings and their families.

Because Ranjit had already sponsored his brothers, he was knowledgeable about the immigration process and had made connection with the immigration officer in Kamloops. Ranjit had an amazing ability to make friends with good people. In the 60s and 70, Kamloops had an immigration office. During this period the immigration law permitted us to sponsor parents and siblings and their young families. The few we had

70

sponsored, in turn, brought many more to Canada and the number increased far beyond what anyone had expected. The number of family members who came from India and established themselves in Canada with spouses and now with their children and grandchildren, is a real success story. Following is an account of those who came and established themselves in Canada.

Rachel, my had completed nursing diploma and was working as a graduate nurse. In 1967, Dr. Watt, gave a job offer for Rachel to work in Hazelton hospital. Thus, Rachel was able to obtain an immigrant visa and arrived in Hazelton. Before long, my sister sponsored her fiancé, Mathew, who also arrived in Hazelton. In 1967, they got married in Hazelton. Through their connection with Rachel and Mathew, two more nurses (Janet and Mariyama) from Kerala also came to work in Hazelton hospital.

Thomas, my brother and family were sponsored with Ranjit's help. My brother arrived in the summer of 1969. A few months later, his wife, Susy and three daughters (Mercy. Lizzy, and Daisy) joined him. Sponsoring family members involved assuming responsibility for those, in providing accommodation and other living expenses until they were able to support themselves in Canada. My brother was able to get a job before his family arrived. As a result, he was able to support himself and his family. My brother was blessed with their only son James (Saji), who was born in Kamloops.

My brother eventually became a builder (TJ Homes) in Kamloops and built many houses in Kamloops before he settled with his family in Edmonton. Susy sponsored her brother Philip Samuel (Baby), who brought his wife Lucy. They lived in Kamloops for a while before they settled in Calgary.

Molly, my younger sister was sponsored next and she arrived as an immigrant in 1970. She studied nursing in Canada and established herself with a long and successful career in nursing. She married Jose Kadavil. After a short stay in Kamloops, they were established as a family in Calgary. Jose sponsored his parents and siblings. Eventually, all members of his family (two brothers and five sisters) came to North America and are now well settled with their families in Canada and in the US. The Kadavil family multiplied in numbers and are blessed financially and spiritually. Molly and Jose moved to the US and now are retired and living in a resort at Fort Lauderdale, Florida.

Samuel, my brother Samuel was the next person I tried to sponsor but was not successful. In 1972, Ranjit and I took a risk and brought him as a visitor to Canada. To our pleasant surprise, the federal government made an announcement that those who were living in Canada with a visitor`s visa could apply for permanent resident status. My brother applied and got his immigrant visa. He later applied for his wife, Mary and three children (Gracey, San and Babu). They all came to Kamloops and lived here for few years. Eventually, all three children got married and settled in Calgary, Windsor, and Vancouver respectively.

It was my desire to bring Thampy, my eldest brother's son. He was single and attending college. I applied to bring him as a student. It was far more difficult to get a student visa in the 80's compared to the present. Thampy was denied a student visa. Now, students are coming in large numbers across Canada to study as international students with the goal of becoming permanent residents. Thampy went on to become a very successful businessman as the Founder and President of Riya Travels and Tours.

Sheila, my sister Ammini's daughter came as a visitor with the hope that she would be able to obtain her immigrant visa. The immigration process became stricter and it was difficult for a visitor to even obtain a student visa or a work permit. Sheila had to leave the country before she could apply for any permit to stay in Canada. She got her visitor`s visa extended a few times. Eventually she went to England and was able to obtain work permit to come back to Canada. With a work permits she could take courses at Cariboo College. In 1981 she got admission to the nursing program at Cariboo College and completed the program in 1984. Sheila was the first international student at Cariboo College. There were no policies in place for admission and tuition fee for international students. The college registrar was a good man and allowed Sheila to study as a domestic student status.

Upon graduation from the nursing program, Sheila was not able to get a job without a permanent residency status. In-order to apply for permanent residency, she needed a job offer. Again, Dr. Watt gave Sheila a job at the hospital in Bella Bella in 1984. Thus, she was qualified to apply for immigrant visa and finally obtained her immigrant visa. Sheila is currently residing in Richmond with her son, Rahul, and daughter, Jasmine.

Sheila's children Rahul &Jasmine with Ajay

Sheila applied for her parents (George and Ammini) and three siblings (Joemon, Jolly and Santhosh). Ranjit`s connection with the immigration officer helped to clear the visa for Joemon and Jolly who were over age at the time of sponsorship. Sheila was unable to sponsor her one remaining sibling Laly, as she was married and had three children. Sheila's dad, mom and three siblings came together from Mylapra to Vancouver. It was truly an unusual event that five adults from one family got immigrant visa to come Canada. Eventually, Laly`s three daughters (all completed BSc degree in nursing) came to Canada and settled in Edmonton. Laly was also sponsored by her daughters. Thus, Laly joined her family in Canada. Sheila and her siblings and their family are well established, living in Richmond, Delta, and Edmonton.

I am not the only one who sponsored family members to come to Canada. My eldest sister's (Annama) daughter Rosie also helped her siblings. As a nurse, Rosie came to Dallas, US with a work permit. Once she was settled, she sponsored her younger siblings (Sherly and Biju) who joined her in Dallas. Eventually, Rosie's sister Susan and family also joined them in Dallas. They all are well established in Dallas.

Rachel Samuel, my aunt's sister, a RN also came to Canada by the generosity of Dr. Watt, who gave her a job offer to work in a rural hospital in Newfoundland. After a year, she joined us in Kamloops. She lived with her family, husband (Thomas) son (Cyril) and daughter (Been) in Kamloops.

With all the family members Ranjit and I had sponsored during early years of our married life, I do not recall a time when Ranjit and I were alone in our home. We always had one or two family members living with us. I was able to love and get along with all family members from both Ranjit's and my family. However, I must admit, it was not easy always as we had our own personal struggles to deal with. It was a period of working hard and making money to survive, fulfilling family obligations, gradually building up a decent life in Canada. I could not have done it alone. God has been with me throughout.

A Kerala Community in Kamloops; In 1966 when I came to Kamloops, I was the first and the only person from Kerala in Kamloops. Once my family members began to arrive, there was a group of us from Kerala living in Kamloops. Thus, my extended family was the first Kerala community in Kamloops. Of course, there were people from Punjab and other parts of India settled in Kamloops long before I came.

Most Indians who settled in Kamloops were from Punjab, belonging to Sikh religion. Some of them came to Kamloops as early as 1900 and became well established in Kamloops. They owned large pieces of farmland and were successful farmers. In fact, two streets in North Kamloops are named after two successful Sikh families: Singh Street and Ollek Street. Ranjit also had his extended family in Kamloops. We celebrated our kid's birthdays and special occasions by gathering as a large group. This had all changed now as most of them had left Kamloops, while Ranjit and I had made Kamloops as our home. Kamloops looked quite different in the 60s and 70s.

Kamloops in the 60s and 70s: In the 1960s in Kamloops, there was no college. Students graduating from grade 12 and pursuing post-secondary education had to leave town and move to the Lower Mainland. There was however a diploma program in nursing at the Royal Inland Hospital. In Kamloops, Nursing was the only post-secondary education offered.

In the 70s, a few prominent doctors from India arrived in Kamloops to practice medicine. These doctors were specialists and were a real asset to the community of Kamloops. Among them were Gur Singh, neurosurgeon; John Chacko, General Surgeon; Gautam Parghi, Urologist; Raj Joneja, neuropsychiatrist; and Bas Gowd, Obstetrician. I was the only Kerala nurse in Kamloops. It was a privilege for me to work along with these physicians and surgeons from India. As far as I knew, I was the only Registered nurse from India working in Kamloops, during the 60s and 70s.

Royal Inland Hospital was a Regional Referral Hospital with over 400 beds. In Kamloops there were no separate senior's facilities or mental health facilities. The hospital accommodated the older population and the mentally ill patients. There were no senior's home or long-term care are facilities to accommodate growing number of older people who needed healthcare. They ended up in the acute-care facility (Royal Inland Hospital). There was no hospice in Kamloops. People mostly died in acute care hospital or at home.

Today there are independent living homes, assisted living facilities, intermediate care facilities and long-term care facilities for older people. The demand for these facilities is still on the increase. So more private facilities are being built to accommodate the increase in the numbers of older population.

In 1970, the current Thompson Rivers University began as Cariboo College in a building in the "Indian Reserve". It offered mainly university transfer courses. A year later Cariboo College moved to its current location. At that time there were only two or three buildings on campus.

There were no international students admitted. Now the Thompson Rivers University has attracted international students from many countries. The campus now has quite a diverse look. Today Cariboo college is called Thompson Rivers University. It offers many baccalaureate and graduate degree programs including a Law program.

Not only are there changes in the demographics but also the shopping facilities. In the 70s the main shopping mall was the Thompson Park Mall, without London Drugs and Save- On-Foods. There was no Aberdeen Mall, no Winners, no Wal Mart, no Home Depot, no Super Store, and no Costco. For coffee drinkers, there were no Star Bucks or Tim Hortons either. There were also no Indian restaurants. We took our kids mainly to McDonalds or KFC for treats.

Kamloops was mainly a cowboy town. The smell of the pulp mill was very strong. Since the 80s Aberdeen, Sun Rivers, Juniper Ridge, Rose Hill, Bachelor Heights, Dufferin Terrace, Barnhart vale, all developed to its current capacity. Looking back, we have come a long way in making Kamloops, a welcoming city.

Consistent with the growth of shopping Malls, the population has also increased and has become more diverse. In 1980, we moved from North Shore to South Kamloops (708 Chaparral Place). At that time there were only a few houses on this street. Now there are no more vacant lots left on Chaparral Place. The demand for houses and the price of houses have been on the increase steadily.

Now that I have settled into a new home, I felt it was time for me to make a trip back to India to see my parents and the rest of the family back home. I suddenly realized it had been six years since I left India for Canada.

Returning to My Motherland: In January 1970, I made the trip back to India. When I left India six years back, I was a single girl. I was going back as a married woman and five months pregnant. Ranjit was studying at Simon Fraser University and could not go with me. So, I made the trip alone. First, I went to England to meet Ranjit's sister and family. From England I flew to Delhi to visit Ranjit's family in Dholpur.

76

Ranjit's brother Darshan and his wife Keval were newly married and were in Dholpur at the time of my trip. Darshan was supposed to meet me in Delhi and take me to Dholpur. However, I missed the flight from London to Delhi because the car broke down on our way to Heathrow airport. I rebooked my flight to Delhi for the following day. I had no means of contacting Darshan, as I had no cell phone. There was no mobile phone then. So, Darshan came to Delhi airport to meet me and went back to Dholpur as I as I did not arrive. The next day when I arrived at Delhi airport, there was nobody from Dholpur to meet me.

So, I had found my way to Ranjit's home. I took an express train from Delhi to Dholpur. The train conductor who came to check passengers checked my ticket and noticed that I was going to Dholpur. He told me that this was an Express train that did not stop in Dholpur. I pleaded and told him my situation that I had never been to Dholpur, I was coming from Canada and going to meet my husband's family in Dholpur. I requested if he could stop the train in Dholpur station. He looked at me and told me I was a brave girl, going alone to meet husband's family in Dholpur. He recognized I was a South Indian girl. He was kind and pulled the emergency chain and stopped the train for me at Dholpur railway station. I thanked the conductor and thanked God that I arrived in Dholpur station safely.

Dholpur railway station looked small and there was no one around, except a young boy on a rickshaw. He asked me in Hindi, where I was going. I did not have a street address as I was supposed to go with Darshan. There was no google map to search the address. I just knew Ranjit's dad's name, Sadhu Singh. I told the boy I had to go to Sadhu Singh's house. The boy told me he would take me to their store in town. In a small town, everybody knew each other.

The boy took me in his rickshaw to the store owned by Ranjit's dad's brother. It just happened that Ranjit's dad (Papaji) was also at the store when I arrived. Of course, I had never met Ranjit's dad or his brother before. I also knew that their house was couple of miles away in a village from Dholpur town. Papaji made arrangement for a car and took me to his home. I was happy to reach Ranjit's home in the village and meet his family. Ranjit's mom was such a loving person. I was greeted with a warm welcome. Everyone in the family treated me with love and respect and I soon realized how much they loved and respected Ranjit, the eldest son in the family.

I spent two or three days with Ranjit's family. The village culture was different from Kerala culture. All at Ranjit's home talked in Punjabi or Hindi. Fortunately, I knew those languages. The villagers who came to the house spoke Hindi in a different way. I later found out it was "village Hindi". It was different from what I learned in school. Village ladies kept coming to see the new bride, Darshan's wife (Keval). She was dressed in new outfits with jewelry, makeup and hair well done and looked beautiful and colourful. I looked plain with a simple sari, no jewelry, and no makeup. Ranjit's family had servants for cleaning and washing dishes. Ranjit's home was in the middle of many acres of fertile land. There were different kinds of animals (dogs, buffalo, chicken, and monkeys) around the house.

My visit to Dholpur and Pachgaon village, was joyful and a learning experience. The town itself was dirty and congested with litter and polluted water flowing through the alleys on both sides of the roads. Rich people in town lived in big mansions and didn't seem to be bothered by the filth. It seemed to me the rich lived in comfort and luxury and the poor lived in dirt and poverty. There were no community programs to improve the city. I said goodbye to Ranjit's loving parents. Darshan and Keval took me back to Delhi.

I flew from Delhi to Trivandrum, Kerala. My dad was at the airport to meet me. Just seeing my homeland, I was emotional when I landed at Trivandrum airport. So much had happened in six years since I left Kerala for Canada. I was almost killed in a car accident, got married, pregnant with our first child and became a working woman and a Canadian citizen. Yet, my love for my homeland was something special. With great joy, I went with my dad to our home in Mylapra by car, where my mom and other family members were waiting to welcome me home. I experienced love from everyone at home and the community. People appreciated if you gave them something I brought from Canada. Relatives and neighbours came to see me at home. I enjoyed my stay and time spent with my parents, siblings, nephews, and nieces.

Things have changed since my first visit back home. I have been back to India several times since then. Now, many people from my family and community have left and many young people from extended family also have left Kerala looking for jobs elsewhere. People now are prosperous and rich and the love they once had for each other seems to have vanished. I am sad to note that when people become rich, relationships are of lesser priority. People become too busy in their lives, doing things for themselves and have little time to foster relationships.

Since my first visit back home my perspectives have also changed. I now realize that money and wealth cannot protect us from pain, suffering and death. In reflecting on my family history, I cannot forget the suffering and deaths we have faced. And through these experiences of suffering and pain I have been able to find positive meaning in life. Following is my experience of suffering and deaths involving my loved ones in my family.

## Suffering and Deaths

Jordan Peterson has asserted that life is suffering, and one must accept it voluntarily and bear it. Moreover, death is inevitable. Throughout history, religious people have also said this. Common questions people ask in relation to suffering is, why good people suffer, especially why children suffer. We still do not have answers to such questions. I see so much suffering all around us. I think suffering is more bearable if we assume responsibility in caring for the one suffering. If not suffering takes a toll on everyone.

Suffering can be either bearable or unbearable. For example, the suffering of Christ on the cross was the ultimate suffering and unbearable. (The suffering and agony of Christ's death on the cross is described in part three). Also suffering of Job in the Bible was also unbearable. It is the pre-cursor to the suffering on the cross. Job lost all his possessions, his family and he developed sores all over his body. All alone, he suffered with pain and agony. Even his own family left him. He felt even God had forsaken him. Yet, Job bore the suffering and kept his faith in God. Even during unbearable suffering, he was able to find positive meaning in life as he was able to praise God and never lost his trust in God.

It gives me comfort in that, I believe in a God who has suffered brutally on the cross, and thus understands our suffering. I still ask the question "why there is so much evil and suffering in this world"! Although I have been spared from unbearable suffering, I have watched loved ones suffer. Death is inevitable, often we experience untimely deaths. For example, the death of a child, death of parents of young children, and death of those in their youth, are called untimely deaths. We also face suicidal deaths and deaths from malevolence. Malevolence amplifies the suffering. Regardless of where we live, we see suffering and evil. People in depth of despair sometimes commit suicide. I find it unbearable to witness torture and people being beheaded. Such types of deaths amplify the suffering for those who are left behind.

I had encountered suffering and deaths of my family members. They were untimely deaths. Although I was better able to cope with death and suffering, but it was never easy. My first encounter with death was the death of my youngest brother Babu. He was only a toddler when he died. I was around ten years old. He was a healthy and happy child, who had diarrhoea (I figured it was dysentery) and died within two days. Reflecting on Babu's death now, his life could have been spared if he had received immediate medical intervention. My dad was away and there was no one to take him to a doctor or hospital, which was a few miles away. We did not own a car and we did not have access to a car. Thus, medical help was beyond our reach. Such deaths were common occurrence in our community. My mom and dad were grief-stricken by the loss of their darling son. I remember seeing my dad cry with so much sadness.

The following two deaths in our family were much more difficult as there was lot more suffering involved before death occurred.

Loving Nathoon, Pennama: The second death was my eldest sister-in-law whom I called Nathoon. Her two children Leelama and Thampy might be interested in this story. I remember my Nathoon well. She was slim, tall and of fair colour. There were no wedding pictures or photos taken and we had no photographs of her. I recall her as a loving and caring sister-in-law. She loved her husband dearly and loved and respected my parents. Above all she loved the Lord. I do recall her giving a testimony during a church service. She would sing a hymn first and then would tell her testimony. She had a beautiful voice.

She had to work very hard in our home helping my mom with cooking for a large family. She gave birth to their first child, Alice, who died before she was a year old. A year or so later, she gave birth to Leelama, a precious little girl. In 1954 my brother and Nathoon moved to a place called Ottakkal with their daughter, Leelama. There they were blessed with their son Thampy. He was the pride and joy of her life. Both Leelama and Thampy inherited their mom's fair colour and some features.

Six months after the birth of Thampy, Nathoon became ill, and her disease progressed rapidly. She was diagnosed with late stage of cirrhosis of the liver. I assume that, her liver failure might have resulted from hepatitis she might have contracted years earlier. As we know excessive consumption of alcohol is another cause of liver cirrhosis. I can confidently say that she never had a sip of alcohol in her life. In the hospital, to ease her breathing, the Doctor removed some fluid from her abdominal cavity. "There is nothing more we can do for her": Doctor told my brother. Thus, he brought her to our home to die. This was the practice then. Patients were sent home to die as keeping them in hospital would be too costly for the family.

My Nathoon was dying. I remember vividly this occasion. I was around 12 years old. Before she died, she said good-bye to each one of us by calling us by name. She was lying in a bed, sad and sick, and we all were sitting around her. I only recall what she told my mom and my sister Molly. She told my mom to raise her children, Leelama and Thampy. She told Molly not to fight with Leelama. They both were closer in their age. She told us she loved us all very much. I have realized now it must have been a lot more difficult for Nathoon. She had to say good-bye to all of us. She was dying and leaving all her loved ones behind. My Nathoon wanted to live so badly to see her children grow and spend time with her husband and her two children. Yet, her life was cut too short. This was an untimely death.

Even though their mother was not there, both Leelama and Thampy grew up to be two amazing persons. Now they each have their own families with children and grandchildren. The blessings both Leelama and Thampy have in their lives, to some extent, attributed to their mom's faith and love for God. I can only imagine, if she were alive today how happy and proud, she would have been of her daughter and son. I regret to this day, my Nathoon, such a loving person, suffered and died. She had so much to live for as she loved her husband, daughter, and son so much. She would have been extremely proud of her son, Thampy's achievements in life. However, her life was cut short at a very young age.

Left to right: My sister Rachel, sister Molly, myself and my nephew Thampy

Sister Rachel: Dialysis, Transplant and Death: The third death was sad and tragic for me. It was the suffering and death of my sister, Rachel. She was only 39 years old when she died. This story might be of interest to Rachel's son, Jaison. I was very close to Rachel and her suffering and

82

death had a lasting impact on me. However, I gained peace and comfort in realizing that I did whatever I could do to help and support my sister and her family. Over a period of ten years before she died, she suffered significantly. I would only dwell on certain significant aspects of her suffering and death.

In1967 Rachel came to Canada with dream and hope of pursuing a career in nursing, get married and have children and live a comfortable life in Canada. However, her dream and hope were shattered. Her first job was in Hazelton hospital. She sponsored Mathew Thomas (Ponnachen), her fiancé. When he arrived in Hazelton, he was seriously ill with type two diabetes. Eventually, he recovered from severe hyperglycemia. They got married in Hazelton. Her married life started knowing that her husband had advanced type two diabetes. To make the suffering worse, the same year, Rachel was diagnosed with chronic renal failure. Hypertension was identified as the cause of her renal failure. Thus, both Rachel and her husband had to cope with major health problems from the start of their life in Canada.

Most immigrants who came to Canada, start with nothing, but had to work hard to establish their new life in Canada. Accordingly, both Mathew and Rachel had to work to survive. However, with their failing health, each day was a struggle for them. Moreover, Mathew had difficulty finding a job. So, their life in Canada started with suffering. Rachel and Mathew moved to Kamloops to be closer to us, family.

Renal biopsy: It seems to me, each step they encountered added more suffering to their life. For example, to confirm the diagnosis of renal failure, the urologist at Royal Inland Hospital decided to do a kidney biopsy. The biopsy was done under general anesthesia and he had to take one or two ribs out by making a long incision. I went to see my sister at the hospital after her biopsy. I found her very ill and struggling for breath. The nurse called the surgeon on call, Dr. John Chacko, who came and inserted a chest tube, and her breathing became easier. Apparently, during biopsy the urologist had (accidently) nicked the pleura and thus the air leaked into the pleural cavity caused breathing difficulty. She was nursed in the intensive care unit for a few days. I must say, Dr. Chacko saved her life. If we had known the biopsy was going to be this extensive, we would not have consented. To this day, I regret that I did not advocate for my sister.

In search of a job, Rachel, and Mathew moved to Vancouver. Rachel was pregnant and her kidney failure gradually progressed. They were faced with a difficult decision: whether to carry her pregnancy to full-term, knowing full well that it will damage her failing kidneys faster. They decided to have their child rather than her own health. Rachel had to be admitted in the hospital during the last term of her pregnancy. She was on bed rest for her high blood pressure. On June 20, 1969 Rachel gave birth to their son, Jaison. Rachel knew her kidney failure was progressing and before long she would require dialysis to live. She wanted to make that first trip back home to India and see everyone before she started dialysis. Rachel and son, Jaison made that trip, her first and last trip to India. Her life on dialysis began when she got back from India.

Rachel and Mathew with Jaison moved back to Kamloops. I do recall Rachel bargaining with God for healing of her damaged kidneys. She bargained saying, said she would live the rest of her life doing God's work. We just must trust in God totally as we do not comprehend God's plan for our lives. Rachel was emotionally distraught when her doctor made the decision to begin dialysis. She realized that her life would be dependent on a machine. I was at RIH with nursing students. I was paged to go down to see Rachel. When I visited her, Dr. Joneja, a Neuro-Psychiatrist, talked to Rachel and had just left her room. When I saw her, she was crying. I shed tears with her. I did not know what I could say to her to console her. She was hoping that God would perform a miracle in making her kidneys function again.

We noticed Dr. Joneja had left a note for my sister on her locker. We opened it, and it was the:

*The Serenity Prayer:*

*"God grant me the serenity to accept the things I cannot change, the courage to change the things I can - And the wisdom to know the difference". (Reinhold Niebuhr)*

84

Life on hemodialysis three days per week was suffering for Rachel. She became ill, prior to dialysis from the build-up of fluid and toxins in her blood. Then she was ill again after dialysis from the dialysis itself. Yet she was happy to be alive and see her son grow up. Her desire was to see Jaison grow to be at least, 10 years old. She told us that.

In 1973, her doctor decided to start Rachel on a home-dialysis program and sent her to Vancouver for training. I was studying at UBC at that time. One day she came to see me where I lived on campus. During the evening, she became short of breath and I knew she was building up fluid in her lungs and needed dialysis to ease her breathing. It was evening time and there was no vacant bed in any of the dialysis units to admit her for dialysis. The only option for us was to take her to Royal Inland hospital in Kamloops. It was almost 12 midnight and I left Vancouver with Rachel sitting in front seat with breathing difficulty. My son Anil (three years old) was sleeping in the back seat of the car.

I drove through Fraser Canyon for six hours on a foggy night. The visibility was poor, and I tried to follow a car in front of me, most of the way. I reached Kamloops at six in the morning and took her to the renal unit. It was a relief to see her being dialysed that eased her breathing difficulty. Not able to breathe, is a scary feeling and my sister was scared that she would die.

Renal Transplant: Rachel was a candidate for renal transplant and her doctor placed her name on a kidney transplant list. This meant, she had to be ready twenty-four hours of the day, to leave for Vancouver when the call came. So, the donated kidney could be transplanted as soon as possible. One day the call came for Rachel. She was taken to Vancouver by my brother Thomas and her husband, Mathew. We all prayed and said good-bye before she left. She survived the transplant surgery and her new kidney started functioning and she passed some urine. This was a thrilling experience for my sister and the rest of us rejoiced with her. (I suddenly realized that I ought to be grateful to God for the ability to pass urine. I could not take it for granted).

However, my sister's joy did not last long as the transplanted kidney was rejected. Rachel was devastated. A week later, she had to have another surgery to take the transplanted kidney out. She was back on dialysis again. (I had a lingering question: Should I have donated a kidney of mine to Rachel?).

Desperation: I recalled visiting my sister at Vancouver General Hospital (VGH) dialysis unit. She was desperate and told me with tears in her eyes that her new kidney failed and now her renal shunt was blocked and unable to have dialysis. She was waiting to see the specialist. I cried with her helplessly and just looked up to God for help. I felt her suffering and pain. I was so helpless as I could not do anything for her other than just be with her. May be that was what she needed at that moment and I was glad to be with her. A shunt revision was performed, and once again dialysis was resumed.

Rachel's death: She lived almost 10 years on dialysis as she desired. She was able to see her son grew to be 10 years old. On February 14th, 1980, she died quickly during a minor surgical procedure of revision of her shunt. She was only 39 years old when she died. We all were shocked as she was doing well when she went for her shunt revision. Did she have a cardiac arrest on the operating room table? We did not know. My sister's suffering and death make me grateful for each day I have on this earth. It brings me peace to know that we as a family cared for her and supported her during the years of her suffering. Her husband Mathew cared for her to the best of his ability. Mathew (Jaison's dad) also died seven years later from type two diabetes complications. He was blessed to have his wife Annama by his side to care for him. Jaison, (my nephew), now a successful Realtor, lives in Calgary.

I must mention here that how grateful we ought to be living in Canada, where essential health care is free compared to those who live in India and in many other countries where only the rich can afford proper health care. I am grateful for the healthcare system we have in Canada.

The next tragic death for me was the death of beautiful and loving Ajmer.

Ajmer and her Shattered Dreams: The sudden accidental death of Ajmer, Ranjit's cousin, brought such sadness and shock to Ranjit and I. She died in the prime of her youth. She was a beautiful young woman with a promising future, who was preparing to become a teacher in Canada. She got married to Bahadur in 1973 and a few months into their wedded life they both decided to drive from Vancouver to Kamloops to visit us. On the way, they met with a car accident near Ashcroft.

Ranjit and I were waiting for them at our home with lunch ready, when we received a call from an RCMP asking if we knew Ajmer and Bahadur. The police told us about the accident and informed us that Ajmer was killed, and Bahadur was admitted to hospital injured and disoriented. We were called to the hospital to identify Ajmer's body. How could this be? A beautiful and loving young girl, coming to visit us, now we had to witness her body in the morgue!! It was shocking and tragic. Life is suffering! Ajmer was such a loving person and we miss her forever. Both Ranjit and I will always cherish sweet memories of Ajmer.

Ranjit and I were close to Ajmer's family: Papaji, Sohan Singh Bains, wife Bibi and her sisters; Pal, Mona, Jessie and Babu. This was the first family I met in Canada from Ranjit's side. They welcomed me with love. I have enjoyed the time I had spent with each and everyone in the family. I will be always be grateful for their love and the enjoyable time I had with them as a family.

Death of parents, no matter at what age it happens, is an emotional and sad occasion. Following is a brief narrative of my parents' death.

Final Good-bye to My Parents: My mom had a massive heart attack and died quickly. My brother, Samuel Achayan was with my mom during the time of her death. He was a great help to both my mom and dad during this most difficult time. My dad was too distressed to be of any help to my mom. It was almost a miracle that from Canada a group of us made it to Mylapra, just in time for the planned funeral service. According to my journal entry and my memory, following is an account of my trip to attend my mom's funeral service.

On September 9, 1992, I received call from my nephew, Thampy from Bombay stating "Ammachi died suddenly, are you able to come?". I was stricken with sorrow as it was such an unexpected event. I decided I must go to my mom's funeral. First, I obtained leave from my workplace, Cariboo College, then plane ticket and visa, all in one day. My brother Pappachayan and kochama left Edmonton for Vancouver. Jose and Molly (my sister) drove from Calgary to Kamloops. Ranjit drove us to Vancouver the next day. We all met in Vancouver and went to Indian consulate to obtain our visa. Our flight to Singapore was two hours late, thus we were able to obtain visa and catch the flight on time.

Flying Home: Our flight from Vancouver reached Singapore after a short halt in Saul, South Korea. We had a ten hour stop in Singapore. We reached Bombay the next day. Thampy met us at the airport and we stayed overnight with him. We left with Thampy and Gracy the following day's flight to Trivandrum. My nephews, Babu and Saji were waiting at the airport with cars. We left Trivandrum for Mylapra, a two-hour drive.

The funeral service was to begin at 2 PM. We got to Mylapra at 1:50 PM. How could this be possible? a miracle and a blessing! The service was conducted in our home: the living room, porch, a pandal in front and other rooms, were all packed with people. We, six siblings were present to celebrate my mom's life. Her only living brother (Kunjachayan) and her two sisters were sitting in the front row. My mom looked peaceful in an open casket. My Appachen was sitting with his brother (Thomas) and many others. I looked at my Ammachi and then, hugged and kissed my Appachen. We both shed tears. The service was beautiful with singing and words of praises of my Ammachi. Thampy spoke with emotion and tears. We said good-bye words to our Ammachi.

I had come prepared to spend a few days with Appachen, as I knew he would be lost without his wife. I soon realized how frail he had become. He wanted my help to hold him to walk inside the house. He was grief stricken. Ammachi was his soulmate and caretaker. They were together for 68 years. I felt Appachen would not live much longer without Ammachi. He died 19 months later (1994). He was 93 years old. I missed my dad's funeral and still regret it to this day. I was glad to know he had a blessed celebration of his life with his family and friends.

Now that I have talked about my experience with death and suffering in my extended family including my parents, move on to my children and my role as a mother.

## Love and Responsibility:

Speaking of love and responsibility, I believe a mother's love for her child is unconditional and she is responsible for raising that child. Of course, the father is equally responsible for loving and caring for the child. A child deserves the love and discipline from both parents. However, we know that there are times when this responsibility is passed onto others. It is unfortunate when this happens.

In raising my children, I am reminded of God's love for children. It is written in the Bible, "Let the children come to me, do not forbid, for such is the kingdom of heaven" (Mathew 19: 14). It is comforting to note that Jesus acknowledged children and promised that heaven belonged to children. Implied in this promise is that Jesus loved children and admired their attitude of receptiveness of Jesus compared to the stubbornness of religious leaders.

I do have concern about how today's postmodern culture has the potential to corrupt the minds of youth. (This is discussed in Part Three). Bible also guides us parents how to discipline children: "Fathers do not provoke your children, lest they become discouraged" (Colossians, 3:21). Implied in this verse is the advice that children must be handled with care and need firm discipline administered with love. Don't alienate them by nagging or destroying their self-respect. Ranjit and I raised our two sons with lots of love.

Raising Our Two Sons: "To raise a child who is comfortable enough to leave you means, you have done your job. They are not yours to keep but to teach them how to soar on their own" (author unknown).

In raising our children, the main challenge we faced in falling back on our experience of how we were raised by our parents. Because Ranjit and I were brought up in different cultures in India, we adopted a common approach in raising our sons in Canada. The social setting, we lived was totally different from the setting where we were raising our sons. Thus, we could not fall back on our past experiences. In Canadian culture, technology was advancing, communication through internet and social media was the norm and music and television programs had a great on impact on children and youth, especially.

The values I learned in my early years are important to me as they laid the foundation for my life. These values are: love and respect your parents, love one another, and above all love God. Love is the supreme ethic as it can overcome hate. Another value I have internalized is to help those who are in need, also work hard to get ahead in life. I also value learning, and for me learning has been a life-long process. Another value I cherish, is to be grateful for all the blessings I have in my life. As a mother, I have tried to pass these values on to my children, Anil our first born and Ajay, our second son.

Anil, Our Precious Firstborn: Although, I am a nurse, a midwife, had taken care of pregnant women and had delivered babies, it was different when I became pregnant with Anil, my first child. I did not have my mom or any family around to talk to or seek support. Anil was born on May 16, 1970 at Royal Inland Hospital in Kamloops. He was delivered by Dr. McDougall, an experienced General Practitioner, with an obstetric nurse assisting him. While it was a GP who delivered Anil, GPs are no longer delivering babies in Kamloops hospital. Instead, the mother has the choice to have a midwife or an obstetrician.

It was a natural birth and Anil weighed six pounds, one ounce. During delivery Ranjit was present at the hospital but not in the delivery room. It was not a practice to have husbands participating in the birthing process. Today husbands become partners in birthing process. There was no epidural administered during labour, so I had to bear the labour pain. I forgot all about the intense labour pain when I held Anil in my arms.

90

Parents can now find out the sex of the baby before birth. This technology was not available to us in the 70s. Having a son as your first child was considered a real blessing to an East Indian family. Thus, our relatives were all pleased and celebrated Anil's birth. Ajmer, (Ranjit's cousin) was Anil's first visitor in the hospital.

When I was pregnant with Anil, I was working fulltime at Royal Inland Hospital School of Nursing. In the 70s maternity leave was only for three months as opposed to one year now in Canada. I worked until a few days before Anil was born and had to go back to work three months after Anil was born.

At the time of my maternity leave, Ranjit was going to Simon Fraser University. So, decided to live in Burnaby during my maternity leave. It was difficult to find a place to rent as we had a newborn baby. Fortunately, we found a one-bedroom apartment. There was no crib or car seat for Anil. When we drove with Anil, I held him in my lap. Car seats and seat belts were not required. At the apartment Anil slept in a small bassinet. I nursed Anil and did not need formula for the first three months. Disposable diapers were also too expensive for us, so we used cloth diapers without liners which were washed and re-used.

When Ranjit finished his semester at SFU we moved back to Kamloops and I went back to work full-time. We had to seek help from extended family members to care for Anil until he was two years old. In Kamloops there was no daycare facility that took children under two years old. When he turned two, we placed him in Cariboo Day Care at college campus.

Anil and I at UBC Campus: In 1972, I decided to go back to university to study for a Masters' degree in Nursing. I got admission to University of British Columbia (UBC) MScN program. The program was for two years full-time study on campus. This was a brave move on my part, at least that was others told me. I was just doing what I had to do to achieve my goal. I was at UBC campus without Ranjit with a two-year old. During the month of November that year, it rained just about every day. Each morning, I put on my raincoat and rainboot, carried an umbrella, would drop Anil off at daycare and then attended classes.

Anil was a toddler and the family co-op day care program on campus was a good place to keep Anil occupied. Since it was a co-op day care parents had to volunteer four hours per week to clean the day care and help with childcare. I was able to do my share after classes in the evenings. The day care provided lunch and snacks for children. I had to organize and plan my study as I did not have evenings or weekends free to go to the library.

I had a 1967 Chevelle Malibu car, which I drove from Kamloops to Vancouver and back on weekends when possible. Ranjit also came down to Vancouver on some weekends. My car was not equipped with a seat belt and wearing seat belt was not mandatory. Thus, when I took my two-year old son in my car, he was neither in a car seat nor fastened with a seat belt. He would sleep in the back seat of the car. It was a six to seven-hour drive through Fraser Canyon. I did not even pack snacks for my son. I had something for him to drink. There was no Tablet for him to watch. Looking back, how we survived the driving without accidents was a miracle. I thanked God for watching over us.

Ajay Our Pride and Joy: Eight years after Anil's birth, Ajay was born. Things were easier when Ajay was born. Anil was eight years old and he played with Ajay even as a baby. We had Sheila with us, and she was a great help. Ajay was born on March 25, 1978. He was delivered by Dr. Ian Findlay, an experienced GP. It was a natural birth and Ajay weighed seven pounds and two ounces. Again, I had to bear the labour pain again, as epidurals were not given. We were ecstatic by the birth of our second son, a play mate for his older brother. The maternity leave was still only three months. When Ajay was two years old we moved to South Kamloops (708 Chaparral Place), where Ajay grew-up.

Although, Ajay was eight years younger than Anil, he was a close buddy to his older brother. Ajay looked up to his older brother and tried to participate in games Anil played with his buddies, for example, road hockey. Even as young as a four-years old, Ajay would play road hockey with Anil and his friends. He showed his emotions by crying if things did not go his way. Ajay's close buddy growing up, was Phillip who lived close by. They both went to the same day care and same school until their high school graduation. Philip's mom, Sharon and I worked together at

Cariboo College. I really valued the loving relationship between us two families.

Immigrant Parents: Canadian-born Children: The culture of parents plays a significant role in raising children. Ranjit and I were immigrant parents from India and were influenced by our cultural background in raising our children in Canada. We worked hard to provide the best for our children. We wanted to compensate for what we did not have in our childhood. However, we were cautious in not spoiling them. We had observed immigrant parents buying expensive sports cars for their sons upon graduation from high school and giving excessive amount of money to spend without rules and discipline. I believe, such parenting could lead boys to taking drugs, and participating in gang violence, a huge problem among the Indian youths in Canada.

When our sons were born, Ranjit and I were well integrated into Canadian culture. Moreover, we both valued education was significant in living a meaningful life. I was raised in a family where parents pooled their resources to educate their children. We also believed that keeping children involved in sports would keep them occupied and active.

Since we had to start our life in Canada with bare minimum, we learned to live a frugal life in the beginning. Eating out in restaurants was not part of our everyday life. There was no time or money to eat out. McDonalds and KFC were our big treats for Anil and Ajay. Our extended families got together on special occasions and enjoyed home cooked meals.

We decided to send our sons to public schools over private school or home schooling. We wanted them to be part of the public-school system and learn to cope and adjust to the mainstream life. We were fortunate that both Anil and Ajay were good in their studies and they made friends with similar interests and values.

Anil was restless and naughty in kindergarten. We realized later that he was bored in the classroom. What he was doing in kindergarten, he had already learned at UBC day care. He needed to be challenged. Both Anil and Ajay were honour role students throughout their school years. They neither smoked nor got into drugs and did not drink alcohol in their school years (to our knowledge). We took them to church with us on Sundays. Ajay had an opportunity to attend the Eagle Bay church camp, for kids.

I do not recall having any problems at school with Anil or Ajay. I was aware of bullying and drugs as two major problems in public schools. Fortunately, both Anil and Ajay were not victims or perpetrators of these problems. Since then, major shifts have been occurring in sexuality and sexual identity. However, during Anil and Ajay's school years this was not a major issue. They both loved sports and were naturally good at it. As parents we tried to provide them with opportunity to play sports in addition to focusing on their studies.

## Love of Sports

Two major sports were a large part of our family: hockey and soccer. As a family we also enjoyed watching tennis. Anil and Ajay displayed athletic talent and interest in playing sports. They both played soccer and hockey. Anil also played volleyball and basketball through school. Both enjoyed playing tennis and excelled in the sports they played. I also loved the game of tennis. I even took lessons one year and learned that playing tennis was hard, so resorted to watching tennis.

It seems, Anil and Ajay inherited their athletic skills from Ranjit who was very good in track and field. Anil was a great soccer player and played the game of soccer throughout his school and college years. He played with the prestigious team, The Riverside Auto, in Kamloops and won provincial championships. He also had an opportunity to play in the "The Nations Cup" in Vancouver for the East Indian team. This provided him an opportunity to play with other East Indian guys from the lower Mainland.

Anil's Love of Hockey: When Anil was seven years old, one of Ranjit's friends (Jerry and Connie Kline) suggested that we let Anil play ice hockey. They told us it was a great game for boys in Canada and we should let our son play. Although, we both knew very little about ice hockey and could not even skate, in our desire to provide opportunity for our son to play hockey, we registered Anil in minor hockey. We did not even know what equipment was needed to play hockey.

Anil was two years behind and had to catch up to the rest of the boys on his team. He showed promising skills in playing hockey and became quite good at it. We were not serious about Anil pursuing hockey as a career, although we were surrounded by parents who took hockey seriously. We had disrupted Anil's hockey by taking him with us to India when we went on vacation. We went to India in the winter during hockey season. Anil loved the game of hockey and excelled in playing the game.

Anil had his ups and downs in hockey. As a Bantam player, he tore his knee ligament during a tournament in Vancouver. We did not realize how serious it was. We took him to the Kamloops hospital and realized the ligament in his knee was fully torn and needed surgery. When the surgeon told Anil, his hockey was over for the season, Anil had tears in his eyes. He was looking forward to the season and had been playing well. It was another setback for him in getting ahead in hockey. Anil was a goal scorer and he played as a winger. He had good reach with his long arms and was great in passing the puck. He had the right size and the skills for playing hockey.

Anil was made captain of the team in Bantam and the team did exceptionally well in the North Shore Winter Club tournament. Anil was awarded the MVP (Most Valuable Player) of the team. The following year he was cut from the Rep team by his coach. This was a devastating experience for Anil. I believe, these experiences made Anil a stronger person. In Minor hockey, coaches played a big role in deciding who makes the team and who gets cut. Both Ranjit and I believed that Anil played well enough to make the team. Through these tough experiences we learned the real hockey culture.

Anil, Hockey Team Captain

Amidst setbacks, Anil continued to play hockey on the Midget Team. His coach really liked Anil. After graduation from high school, Anil attended Cariboo College for one year and played hockey with the college team. For second year of university, Anil went to University of British Columbia (UBC) in Vancouver. He tried out for the UBC hockey team but dropped hockey to focus on his studies. Anil continued to play hockey as a recreational sport. His passion and love for the game of hockey continues today.

Although Anil is no longer playing hockey, he remains an ardent Vancouver Canucks fan. It was tough for Anil when Vancouver Canucks lost to Boston Bruins in the seventh game of Stanley Cup final in

Vancouver. Anil was one of the spectators. He was broken hearted when a riot erupted on the streets of Vancouver. That was the year Vancouver was expected to win the Stanley Cup. Both Anil and I are still waiting for the day to see the Canucks hoisting the Stanley Cup. I am not sure if it will happen in my lifetime!

With his hockey career over, Anil focused on his education. He was enrolled in a Science degree program at UBC. Anil completed his BSc degree in Biopsychology and then worked for a couple of years and went back to UBC and completed a MA in Counselling Psychology. He is now practising as a Registered Clinical Counsellor and a Clinical Supervisor. We are proud of his achievement in establishing his own counselling practice.

Even though Anil has a successful counselling practice his love of hockey did not fade. So, Anil played a significant role in Ajay's hockey career. As his brother, Anil encouraged his younger brother to pursue hockey career seriously.

## Ajay's Hockey Career

Ajay in Minor Hockey: When Ajay was old enough to play hockey, Ranjit and I knew more about hockey and its culture in Kamloops. Ajay started his minor hockey in a team called "Peanuts" at the age of five. It was amazing to watch these young kids trying to take the puck and score a goal and falling down several times on their attempt. It was also incredible to watch how fast they learned to skate and score goals. After a year as a "peanut", he was skating with his teammates and one father asked me "Is that boy who's skating funny, your son?". I didn't even know he was skating funny. I took him to a skating teacher to have a look at his skates. She told me Ajay was wearing skates that did not fit his feet. Ajay had flat feet and needed special skates. We got him a pair of better skates but not the special skates he needed. I guess we were not serious enough about him playing hockey.

Ajay was promoted to the next level in minor hockey, Novice, at the age six and seven. He showed a lot of enthusiasm and love for the game of hockey. He made significant progress in puck handling and skating. From

Novice he moved on to the next levels: Atom, Pee Wee and Bantam. Ajay made the rep team in each hockey team. In the 80s this was a real achievement for a kid with brown skin. He was the only brown kid on his team.

Kamloops Minor Hockey Association (KMHA) was one of the premier organizations of its kind in BC, as some players, who came through KMHA, had made it to the National Hockey League (NHL). Most parents place their boys in minor hockey with the hope that their sons, one day, might become an NHL player, sign a big contract, make millions, and become famous. Thus, each parent would like their son to play in the "Rep Team," in minor hockey. Making the cut to play on the Rep Team was challenging and political.

Mickey Fritz was the head coach for Ajay and his team for four years (Pee Wee and Bantam) in minor hockey. These players had the chemistry to play together and they excelled as a group and won most games they played together. They became a winning minor hockey team at tournaments and provincials. As a team they were unbeatable. The coach would treat them with donuts, cakes, steak BBQs and pops. The players loved the winning, the treats and the friendship they shared with one another. Mickey's son, Brent Fritz was the Captain of the team for each year they played together. He became and still is a very close friend of Ajay to this day.

We parents had fun travelling with the team to tournaments in Western Canada. Those were fun times especially when the team was winning most games. Ranjit, myself and Anil would travel with Ajay and watched him play most of his games. To accommodate these games into my fulltime work schedule was a challenge. I had realized then. I had become a "hockey mom". This was an unusual title for me being a woman of brown colour (I think I was the only brown mother among the parents). I was really into hockey. Enjoyed watching the game, curious in learning the hockey culture and politics and took time to travel to watch the out-of-town games. Ranjit was also really enjoyed watching Ajay play hockey. We made friends with most parents in the team.

Winning the KIBIHT: In 1991/92 season, Ajay's team under coach Mickey Fritz had over 80 wins and one loss. The one loss was during an exhibition game and thus their competition record was unblemished. They became the provincial champions that year. It was reported in the media, "Jardine Blazers Pee Wee AAA Team was simply the best". Ajay was fortunate to be a big part of this winning team. From Pee Wee, the boys moved on to the next level in minor hockey: Bantams. Ajay played two years as Bantams (1992/ 93). Again, the team kept winning.

One of the significant wins in Bantam level was winning the prestigious KIBIHT (Kamloops International Bantam Ice Hockey Tournament) title. No team from Kamloops had won this tournament from its inception, 26 years ago until 1994. There were teams from a few selected countries. The defending champions were from Red Deer. The Detroit Compuware, a team from the US was expected to win the championship that year. On April 6, 1994, the Kamloops team played the Detroit Compuware in front of an estimated crowd of 3,800 and Ajay's team won the game and made history. We were all proud of the team, and especially our son, Ajay.

Ajay was a goal scorer and was named MVP at major tournaments. Ajay was gifted at taking faceoffs, blocking shots and being a playmaker. He was considered an important player in the team. Ranjit, Anil and I went with the team to most to most games. Ranjit's dad (Papaji) and uncle (Chacha) also had the opportunity to watch Ajay play during their visit to Canada from India. They also loved watching Ajay play hockey. Depending on which city they played, our relatives would join us to watch the game. My brother (Thomas) and his family and Ranjit's cousin, Babu and husband, Harjit and family were frequent spectators. Ajay brought home many trophies of different categories.

Team Canada: Making the Cut: Ajay was selected for a tryout camp to play for Team BC. The tryout camp was for one week in Osoyoos, BC. At the end of the camp, we were ecstatic to find out that Ajay had made the cut. Ranjit went to pick him up from Osoyoos and noticed that Ajay had lost weight. Ajay was so happy that he made Team BC, he did not pay attention to his weight loss. On his way to Kamloops Ranjit had to stop the car several times as Ajay had to pass urine. In addition, Ajay had a sore throat.

We took him to a doctor in Kamloops for his sore throat and mentioned to him about the frequency in urination. The doctor ordered a fasting blood sugar. We were in shock when the doctor told us that, Ajay has Type 1 diabetes. Having Type I diabetes meant that his life would depend on taking insulin for the rest of his life. I shed tears as I knew what this meant for Ajay, especially as a hockey player with a big dream. Ajay tried to be positive. When the nurse told him about what food he could and could not eat, he stated, "This will force me to eat healthy". I knew he was not fully aware of the impact of living with Type 1 diabetes. Our life began together in learning to live with Type 1 diabetes. It was in August 13, 1994.

Ajay Playing Hockey with Type I Diabetes: To survive Ajay had to take insulin injections daily. As a 16-year-old, playing hockey at the Rep level, he had to keep his blood glucose at the optimum level to play his best. Both Ajay and I learned together how to test blood glucose, take insulin injections, and eat a healthy diet, as per Canada Food Guide. My nursing education and experience really helped in coping with this challenge. I was amazed at how quickly Ajay learned to test and give himself insulin injections. Learning to eat a healthy diet was an ongoing process. We also had to learn how to pack everything Ajay needed, when he went on a road trip to play hockey out of town. What shocked us most was not knowing where this type 1 diabetes came from. As far as we knew, no one in my family or Ranjit's family had been diagnosed with type 1 diabetes. Then how could Ajay, an athlete, at the age of 16, develop type 1 diabetes?

I remember going through the grieving process of shock, denial, anger, and trying to accept the reality that my son has type 1 diabetes. Why the grieving process? You grieve when there is a loss. What was the loss here? I tried to understand the loss. The loss of Ajay's pancreas producing insulin; the loss of a life without insulin injections every day; the loss of having the freedom to eat what Ajay liked? I began to comprehend my new role, mother of a hockey-player son with type I diabetes. This role was in addition to my existing roles of, a hockey mom, a wife, a nurse, an educator, an administrator, and a regular mom of two sons. My life was getting more complex each day.

Even though I had trouble accepting the diagnosis of Type 1 diabetes, Ajay was more positive from the beginning. Ranjit was upset about Ajay having to deal with diabetes and taking injections. Ajay told his dad, having diabetes would make him a better person. One day he pointed out to Ranjit, a boy with cerebral palsy in a wheelchair and told him, how fortunate he was compared to that boy. Ajay taught us how to focus on the positive aspects of having diabetes. You learn humility and appreciate the good things you have in life. An important lesson we learned was, never to use type 1 diabetes as an excuse. Do not play the victim role because, if you do, you are using diabetes as an excuse. As a family we learned to live with Type 1 diabetes, no excuses.

Living with diabetes had its ups and downs. The most challenging experience with Ajay and his type one diabetes was in dealing with hypoglycemia (low blood sugar). Ajay's response to blood sugar varied, from being confused and disoriented to totally unresponsive to what was happening to him. It depended on how low the blood sugar was and how fast the blood sugar was getting low. Both Ajay and I learned that his blood sugar dropped quickly from taking too much insulin. Then he could not manage himself. He would need help in taking fast acting glucose tablet, juice, or coke to bring his blood glucose level up. Ajay detested when his blood glucose level was high. This made him to take more insulin to bring it glucose level down quickly, leading to hypoglycemia. Although, I am a nurse, I still get nervous when I see Ajay with low blood sugar. Now we learn that there is a technology available to alert us when blood sugar level is low. But it is costly, and Ajay did not have the medical coverage for it.

Back to hockey and Ajay, the final year of the Bantam was when players were scouted for playing in a Major Junior Team, for example, Western Hockey League (WHL). By this time the players were 16 years old. Two boys were drafted from Ajay's team, but Ajay was not one of them. This was a surprise to many of the parents including Ranjit and I. We believed Ajay and Brent should have been drafted.

Later in the year Ajay got listed by the Blazers, the WHL team in Kamloops. As a 16-year-old, Ajay played one year in the Midget Team. It was an exciting year as Ajay's team went on a trip to Eastern Europe to play hockey. Many parents went with the team. Ranjit, Anil and I also went with Ajay and saw him play in Austria, Hungary, and Slovenia. We toured some significant places in these countries. We also visited Trieste, Italy by the Adriatic Sea. It was a memorable trip and I am glad I had a chance to be part of the group. Ajay and I learned to manage diabetes while on an international trip.

Ajay loved playing hockey so much that he dreamed of choosing hockey as a career. Thus, as a family we explored his options for him.

Ajay in American Hockey League

Pursuing Pro-Hockey: We had to decide whether Ajay should try to pursue hockey as a career. The options were, play pro-hockey or go to university and play hockey in Canada or in USA. Ajay had done his homework and knew that if he played one regular game in a major junior team, he would lose his eligibility to attend an American university and play hockey. In the end, Ajay's dream of playing in the NHL, made him to choose the option of playing for the Major Junior. He believed he would have a better chance of making it to an NHL team if he chose the route of playing in a major junior hockey team. Thus, he decided to try to make the Blazers team in Kamloops.

Minor Hockey to Major Junior: Playing in a major junior team such as the Blazers was huge in Kamloops. The Blazers were treated as local celebrities. Most players came from out of town, and seldom a local player was selected to play in a home team. It seemed, there was more pressure on the player to play in front of the home crowd. I was also aware of the unique hockey culture, where Ajay had to hit, fight, slash, swear and did other things to show the coach, he was tough enough to play pro-hockey. As a mother I had to get used to it and I was told "it is part of the game".

Ajay: A Kamloops Blazer: The Blazer organization was one of the top teams in the Western Hockey League. Playing for the Blazers would be a dream come true for Ajay. In the past the organization had won three Memorial Cup trophies. In 1996 Ajay made the cut after their training camp and now became one of the Blazers.

I remember Ranjit and I meeting with the General Manager of the Blazer organization, Stu McGregor, and making a case for Ajay. The conditions we wanted were, that he would not be traded, and that he would be allowed to stay at home during his time with the Blazers. Another condition was that Ajay be allowed to finish his grade 12 at South Kamloops High School. Blazer players are expected to enrol at North Kamloops High School to complete grade 12. To our pleasant surprise, Mr. McGregor, agreed to all the conditions. Ajay played for the Blazers for four years.

Blazer Captain: During the second year Ajay was made Captain of the team and stayed as Captain for the remaining three years. He was the youngest and the longest- reigning captain in Blazer history. I would say, those four years were very significant years in Ajay's life. He finished grade 11 and 12 during his first two years with the team.

To our delight, Ajay became a local celebrity and a well-liked player. He was not the best player on the team, he was not the fastest player on the ice, and he was not the biggest player, yet he was regarded as a big part of the team. What made him to be the kind of player he was? Ajay was a natural leader, he was truly a team player, he gave his best at every game he played, he was one of the top players in taking the face offs, was gritty and would fight when needed, and was good in penalty killing. He was also good at scoring goals and passing the puck. His best quality was being a true team player. He got along well with his teammates, coaches, and others in the organization. He was also a fan and a media favorite.

It was a new experience for Ranjit and I watching our son Ajay on television on a weekly basis after the games. He represented his team well in his role as captain, in his hometown. He played for Ed Dempsey, the head coach in his first two years and then Mark Habscheid for the remaining two years. Under Mark Habscheid, the team had the longest winning streak, 26 games in a row. Each year Ajay played; they made the playoffs. The arena was packed with standing room only for each game they played. The Kamloops community was excited about their hockey team.

In fact, as a family, Ranjit, Anil and I watched most games he played in Kamloops. We also watched out of town games in Seattle, Tri-city, Spokane, and Calgary when possible. Ajay won many trophies, for example, Team MVP, best face off man, best defensive forward, and sportsmanship.

As a mother, it was no fun watching him fight and getting injured during a hockey game. I was told it was part of playing hockey. At one time I saw him on the ice, and he was bleeding from his face. I felt helpless as a mother and a nurse. Eventually, he got up still bleeding and went to the dressing room to get stitched up. I was surprised to see him play, during his next shift. Ajay explained to me later, you continue to play even when you are hurt, and play until you are injured and unable to play anymore.

The four years went by quickly. In his final year with the Blazers, the team almost made it to the Memorial Cup but lost to the Calgary Hitman during WHL Finals. I was sitting with Anil and Ranjit to watch this important game. To win the series, Ajay's team had to win this game. When Calgary scored during the third over-time period, my heart sank knowing that Ajay's team was down 3-1 in the series. It was a tough loss to take. I realized then, that was hockey: some great wins and some heart-breaking losses. Their dream for playing for the Memorial Cup was denied.

Sports Achievement Award: In 1997 Ajay was nominated by Dr. Gur Singh, a Neurosurgeon in Kamloops, for a Sports Achievement Award provided by India Club in Vancouver. Ajay did win the Award. The Award ceremony was held in Vancouver. The keynote speaker was the Indian Consulate official. Dr. Singh presented Ajay as a, "talented athlete, an honour roll student, a leader and a caring person, who participates in community services". Ajay was unable to attend the ceremony to receive the award. I was so proud to accept the award on my son's behalf. As an Indo-Canadian, Ajay was one of the very few who made it to hockey at a Major Junior Level.

Our son Ajay was depicted as a hard-working player with perseverance and dedication. He had also learned that life is not fair, but one must overcome the barriers to be successful. What a blessing he was. However, some barriers were hard to overcome, for example, your ethnicity, your size, and living with type 1 diabetes. Ajay realized that there was only one player (Robin Bawa) from Indo-Canadian ethnicity who had made it to the NHL during his time.

Size was an important consideration when scouts were drafting players in the1990s. If you were over six feet tall and weighed over 200 pounds you had a better chance over someone like Ajay who was five feet ten inches tall and weighed only 175 pounds. Ajay knew only two players who played in NHL, who were living with type 1 diabetes (Bobby Clark and

Kurt Fraser). Ajay knew that he would have to work much harder if he ever had a chance to make it to NHL. However, he was determined, and as parents, our role was to support him.

The Quest for NHL: Until Ajay was 20 years old, he played with the Blazers. Since he was not drafted by any NHL team, his options were limited. His dream however for playing professional hockey was still strong. Anil's friend Davis Payne was a player/coach in the East Coast Hockey League in Greenville. Davis called Ajay for a tryout. He made the team and played one year in Greenville. He fought many times, during the season. He told me he had to fight to earn a spot on the team. He made an impression. We as a family went to watch him play and loved the place and the people. Ranjit also had a chance to take his dad to watch Ajay play. They both enjoyed their stay in Greenville. It was a great year for Ajay learning to live away from home, managing his diabetes, learning to cook, and taking care of his own finances. He roomed with two other players from Czech Republic. One of them, Martin Massa became good friends with Ajay.

In American Hockey League (AHL); When Ajay got a call from the AHL for a tryout, his dream of playing in the NHL came closer. Trent Yawney, the coach for Norfolk Admirals in Norfolk Virginia was a good friend of Mark Habscheid. Mark contacted Trent and told him about Ajay. As a result, Ajay got a call from Al MacIsaac, GM of the Norfolk Admirals, Chicago Blackhawk's farm team. Ajay was thrilled about the call and made the team after the camp. He played with the team for six years, hoping each year at the end of camp, he would be called up to Chicago to play in the NHL. He was called up to play exhibition games and then sent back down to Norfolk. He stayed with the Norfolk Admirals Team because of Trent Yawney. After six years it was time for him to leave the team. His career took him to play with the Hamilton Bulldogs, Montreal Canadians' Farm team. He played two years (2006-2008) with the team and won the Calder Cup.

Ajay Baines with The Calder Cup 2007

Winning the Calder cup for Ajay was a perfect script. The third placed Hamilton Bulldogs were not expected to move past the third round in play-off. Under the leadership of four veteran players: Ajay Baines, Eric Manlow, Dan Janceski and Jonathan Ferland, the team kept improving with each play-off game. They also had the best goalie in the league: Carey Price. So, it was great that they beat Rochester Americans, the second-placed team in the North Division. Then they beat the first-place team, the Manitoba Moose in six games. In semi-finals, they faced the high scoring team, the Chicago Wolves. Bulldogs won the series in five games.

Now the Bulldogs were in the finals, and they had to play the defending champions, The Hershey Bears, who were the #1 team in the AHL. Ajay's best friend, Quinton Lang, who played with him in Norfolk Admiral for five years was playing for the Hershey Bears. The first two games were in Hershey and each team won one game. The next three games were in Hamilton. The town of Hershey was already preparing for a cup parade for the defending champions. No one expected the Bears to lose to the Bulldogs. But the Bulldogs won games three and four at home with the series: 3:1 for the Bulldogs. The fifth game, if The Bulldogs win, they would be the champions, if not they would go back to Hershey to play games six and seven.

Ajay scored the winning goal: The city of Hamilton prepared for the final game. The arena was packed. Ranjit, myself and Anil flew to Hamilton to watch the final game. Darshan and Ranjan flew in from Edmonton. Andrew Chaco flew in from Vancouver. Ron, Jessy, and family also came from Burlington to watch the game. We all were nervous, yet excited. The game was tied with one goal each, when Hamilton Bulldogs took a penalty. Ajay was killing the penalty with teammate, Maxim Lapierre. Maxim passed the puck to Ajay and he scored the winning goal to win the championship. This was a perfect ending. The cheers in the arena and the celebrations continued for a long time. I would say winning the Calder Cup would be the highlight of Ajay's hockey career. He played two more years in AHL. Ajay's dream of making the NHL was slowly fading.

Ajay retired from his hockey career in 2009 after playing nine years in American Hockey League (AHL), one year in East Coast Hockey League, and four years with the Blazers in Western Hockey League (WHL). He never played a regular game in the NHL. People have asked him, why he did not play in NHL. He summed up his answer like this:

*"There are many players who play in the NHL who are not as good a player as I am, and many players who are better players than I am, did not get a chance to play in the NHL. I was good enough to play in the NHL, but I did not get that opportunity to play".*

Looking back, although I was disappointed in that Ajay's dream to play in NHL did not happen, I am glad that he retired from hockey with no major injuries, especially concussion. He is well settled now as a husband of a beautiful and loving wife and father of two precious children, a daughter, and a son. I believe that, God has a plan for his life. I have also learned that parents who aspire their sons to play in NHL put a lot of pressure on them from a very young age, not realizing that only a very select few make it to the NHL.

Who would be your all-time favorite Blazer? To sum up, Ajay as a hockey player, the following example portrays him. On February 27th, 2017, a friend of mine wanted me to pass on a message to Ajay. She told me that she attended a function held for the Blazer fans and season ticket holders at which Earl Seitz was the guest speaker. Earl is a retired sports journalist in Kamloops and had worked as a sports reporter for over three decades. At the end of his speech one of the fans asked him, who would be his all-time favourite Blazer? He replied, "Ajay Baines".

I was rather surprised to hear this. As a mother I am humbled by this complement as there are many Blazers who went on to play in the NHL and have become famous hockey players, for example, to name a few: Marc Recchi, Darryl Sydor, Shane Doan, and Jerome Iginla. I thought that they were superior hockey players to Ajay. Then I questioned, why would Ajay be Earl's all-time favourite Blazer? It could be because of who Ajay is, as a person. He gave his best as a hockey player at each game he played, was respectful and loyal to Blazer management and coaches, provided leadership to the team and got along well with his teammates. He also gave his time generously to the Blazer community. Ajay is a good person. This sums up Ajay as a hockey player.

To finish my talk on hockey, I feel compelled to include a touch of hockey culture.

A Touch of Hockey Culture: Since both Ranjit and I were new to the hockey game in Canada we were naïve of the prevalent hockey culture. It was something I gradually learned by observation. Looking back at the Kamloops Minor Hockey games and its inherent culture, which I accepted as part of the game at that time, was really a unique culture.

I learned in a hurry that hockey was Canada's # 1 game and Kamloops being a hockey town, hockey was big in Kamloops. I was told that if we had a son it was important that we give him the opportunity to play hockey and that was what we did. We put both our sons in Kamloops Minor Hockey. I did not realize that because our sons were playing hockey, I became a "hockey mom" and part of the hockey culture.

In playing a hockey game, winning the game was the goal. Each of us had our part to play in winning the game. The players and coaches were the key players in winning, however, the parents played their part in cheering, giving encouragement and participating in Minor Hockey Association activities. I noticed that when our team played a hockey game, the opposite team we played was our enemy and no matter what, beating them was our goal. Some of the things I saw were players hitting, fighting, slashing, elbowing, tripping, and blocking the puck by risking injuries. Swearing was an ongoing strategy. It seemed to me that these strategies were promoted by the coaches. I also noticed that parents of the two teams got into arguments over what the players were doing on the ice. Occasionally it would escalate into physical altercation. I was glad this rarely happened when Ajay's team played.

In addition, players say and do things on the ice to distract players from opposing team from their game. This would include "calling names", for example, Ajay was called a "Paki". Ajay was not bothered by it. I often wondered if his brown colour and ethnicity was a barrier in Ajay not making it to the NHL. There was only player belonging to East Indian ethnicity (Robin Bawa) during Ajay's time made the NHL.

How we handled winning and losing hockey games was also part of the culture. If we won the game we celebrate and when we lost the game, we would find someone else to blame, usually the referee, by saying that the referee made a bad call. Some wins became exceptionally memorable, for example, winning the KIBIHT, and the Calder Cup. Some losses became heart-breaking events, for example losing the Western Hockey League Final to Calgary Hitmen in triple overtime. We lost the chance to go to Memorial Cup Event.

As parents, we tried to get along with the coaches as they hold the power over our son's hockey future. Parents tend to keep silent even if we notice some players were favoured over others. Parents of Rep hockey team players had a mindset that their sons were playing hockey to make it to the NHL. Thus, they took the game seriously and might miss the joy of watching the game. Parents were willing to spend large sum of money to make their wish come true. Many became disappointed in the end. It was

110

time we became realistic about the chances of a player making it to the NHL. If not, we could become disappointed and bitter. Both Anil and Ajay learned a great deal in playing the great game of hockey and as a family we had so much fun watching them play.

Having two amazing and loving sons is truly a blessing. Moreover, as a family we are truly blessed and personally I am so grateful for all the blessings I have in my life. Following is a brief account of my blessings for which I am genuinely grateful.

## Blessings and Gratitude

What do I consider as blessings, having good health, love, peace and joy in family life? Family is important to me. I want the best for my two sons, having proper education to get a decent job and of course, finding good girls, getting married and having their own families. In Indian culture, parents' wish for their children is to see them having a successful career and a family of their own. Mothers look forward to attending the wedding of her son or daughter and then to hold a grandchild.

In India, when I was growing up, I watched how parents became restless and anxious, if they had a son or daughter in their 20's. They kept searching for a suitable match for their son or daughter until they get married. The marriage was usually arranged by parents. It was so different in Canada as the responsibility of finding a partner was entrusted to the children. Searching for a partner was not an easy task. Some might get lucky and find the right partner and get married. Some might never find a partner.

Our sons, born and raised in Canada, valued the freedom to choose their partner themselves. I eagerly waited for the day when our sons would find their partners and get married. Since I did not have a traditional Indian arranged marriage, I was open to our sons choosing their own partners.

Joyti with Ajay, September 2014

Janice with Anil, December 2014

We were concerned when Anil was still single at the age of forty. Ranjit and I tried to introduce girls to Anil without success. As a mother, I was hoping he would find a partner and get married. Anil had girlfriends, but none a suitable match. Ajay was more open to being introduced to girls.

The year 2013 was a blessed year for our family. Ajay met Joyti while he was working in Vancouver. He told us later, they loved each other and were planning to get married. I was thrilled. We met Joyti's family: her dad, Baldev Kang and mom, Raghbir and found them to be loving and genuine people. Joyti's brother (Robbie) became Ajay's best buddy. Robbie's wife, Sukh and two sons (Emmet and Rylan) were very close to Joyti. We established a close and loving relationship with Joyti's family.

And thanks be to God, it all worked out well. We were so pleased to find out Joyti was born and raised in Kamloops, but they had never seen each other in Kamloops. It was a joyous occasion when they got married in September 2014. We were blessed again when they decided to move to Kamloops to live. They both were happy with their move to Kamloops. It bought great joy to us when they decided to live in the middle floor of our home and continued to live with daughter Mila and son Loic. Such a blessing could not be taken for granted.

That same year, to our pleasant surprise, we were blessed again, when Anil told us about Janice. He met Janice through mutual friends. Janice was originally from Hong Kong. She came to study in the US (Washington State). She had worked in New York for a while and then came to Vancouver to work. We had an opportunity to meet her mom (Helen), sister (Jennifer) niece (Rachel) and nephew (Jonathan). It was great to have dinner with them in a Chinese restaurant in Richmond.

Anil and Janice decided to get married and their wedding took place in South Surrey on December 27, 2014. What a blessing to have Anil married. God blessed us with two beautiful daughters-in-law. My message to parents who are waiting for their children to get married, be patient, support them and encourage them in their search and introduce a partner where possible.

Our Family, 2014: Ranjit, Chinnama, Anil, Janice, Ajay & Joyti

Our Grandchildren: Our blessings exemplified when our grandchildren were born. A family with little ones bring joy and wonder. It also gave us responsibility. We were blessed with three beautiful grandchildren. Our first granddaughter, Mila, was born to Ajay and Joyti in December 2016. A precious and beautiful child. Five months later, in June 2017, Anil and Janice were blessed with their precious daughter, Alea. Her birth was a miracle and a gift from God. In 2020 February our grandson, Loic was born to Ajay and Joyti. Our hearts were filled with gratitude and did not take such blessings for granted. Our son Ajay was sensitive to the feelings of those couples who were unable to have children, thus he was cautious about posting photos of his children on face book.

Having grandchildren not only made me grateful but also humble as I realized the stages in life, now a grandmother. Each day became very precious. I also came to the realization that I will not be there to witness major events in their lives. As I was getting older, it was time for me to fulfil another bucket list item, making a trip to the Holy Land.

Trip to Holy Land: It was a trip of a lifetime to visit the Holy Land. In March 2014, a trip was organized for us a small family group by Riya Travels with direction from my nephew, Thampy (President & CEO of Riya Travels). Thampy and wife Gracey also came with us on this tour. Molly and Jose (my sister and husband) also were part of this trip. We were a small group of eleven family members which made the trip joyful.

I will only mention what fascinated me the most during this trip. It was surreal to see where Jesus was born (Bethlehem), walk where Jesus walked (Nazareth, Bethany, Mount Zion, Mount of Olives), to see where Jesus was baptized (River of Jordan), to see the place where he performed his first miracle turning water into wine (Cana of Galilee) and where he was crucified and resurrected (within the walls of Jerusalem).

The wailing wall in Jerusalem is a place that I will not forget as I saw the Jews standing and praying by the Wall and leaving notes in the cracks of the Wall with the hope of going to the other side of the Wall where they are hoping to have the temple built again. Currently, Muslims have their mosque in Jerusalem. For Muslims, it is a Holy place as this was where Prophet Mohammed made the night journey into heaven. For Jews, it was where their ancient temple was built by King Solomon and the second temple was built by Herod the Great. For Christians, within these walls where Jesus was crucified.

Having a dip in the Dead Sea felt strange with the slimy mud touching your feet. However, this mud is medicinal for skin disorders. It is called dead Sea as it is the lowest section of the earth's crust and no living organism can survive in the Dead Sea.

The trip also included a tour of Egyptian pyramids and its surrounding areas. I was amazed how sheep would survive in the desert with very little green grass and vegetation. There is so much more to talk about this trip, but I will cut short by saying a big thanks for Thampy (my nephew) for making this happen. It was great travelling with the group under the leadership of Thampy. I consider this a blessing in my life for which I am truly grateful.

The next bucket list was to make one more trip to India.

A Special Trip to India: I made a trip to India with Ranjit in February 2018. I had a feeling that this might be our final trip to India. Ranjit made the trip after 27 long years. I had visited India eight years ago. Although I had made many trips to India since I first arrived in 1964, this final trip was special. There was a new direct flight from Vancouver to Delhi and it was special. We also got our tickets upgraded to business class (thanks to Thampy and Riya Travels). In addition, our travel within India was made easy and comfortable by having Riya employees who helped us in every airport we embarked. Thampy also made arrangement for his own driver and car for us to use in Kerala. In addition, he made arrangement for us for us to visit with an overnight stay in a popular resort (Adarapally) in Kerala. Molly and Jose also joined us with Thampy and Gracey.

Thampy and Gracey in Adarapally, Kerala (2018)

Wedding of Lawson and Zeba: This trip was also made to attend the wedding of Lawson and Zeba, my nephew's (Babu and Lily) son. It was truly a special wedding, an amazing occasion where relatives from far and wide gathered at a luxurious hotel in Cochin to attend this beautiful wedding. The wedding was beautifully and generously organized. Ranjit and I really enjoyed meeting everyone, the delicious food, and the stay at Crown Plaza hotel. I was able to reconnect with a lot of my relatives after a very long time. The reception hall was decorated with fresh flowers. A wide variety of freshly cooked Kerala food was available at a buffet style. The wedding was attended by many celebrities as the bride's father was a movie director in Kerala. Since the celebrities had only few minutes to spare for the wedding, when each one arrived, the wedding reception program was temporarily stopped to accommodate the celebrity. This was a new experience for me. All in all, the memory of such a wedding I would surely cherish.

We also visited Ranjit's hometown Dholpur and Delhi and Agra. It was great having the company of Andrew and Jamie, our friends from Canada, who joined us on this trip. I was glad that Ranjit and I made this trip together.

As I conclude Part One, my Personal Journey, I am reminded of how naïve I was, when I left Kerala for Canada, and how much I have changed during my 56 years in Canada. These changes involved every aspect of my life. I still have my brown skin, but my outlook is different. I realized this when I met one of my classmates from college during a visit to Kerala. We both had very little in common anymore. I guess I have become a "Canadian" in my thinking. Yet, I pray in humility for wisdom on a daily basis as each day brings new challenges.

[I have included a list of my family members (both immediate and extended). This list can be used as a reference to find out the children, grandchildren, great grandchildren, and great-great grandchildren (five generations) of my parents. It is updated to the year 2020]

# FAMILY TREE: 2020

My parents: (Late Pastor. M.J. John & (Late Mariyama) and their eight children, their grandchildren & great grandchildren & great, great grandchildren (five generations).

**Eldest Son - (Late) George (Kunjunju) &**First Wife (Late) Pennama: 2 children:  Leelamma & Thampy

    Leelamma's husband, Samkutty (Samuel): 3 children

        Benson, Bobina & Bivin

        Benson's, wife, Ani

        Bobina's husband, Sunil: 2 children: Richie & Davie

        Bivin's wife, Joy Mercy: 2 children: Aradhana & Arkyn

    Thampy's wife, Gracey: 2 children: Nitin & Riya

        Nitin' wife Shuchitha: 2: Aden & Kian

        Riya's husband, Anemon: 1child: Amaya

Second Wife Susamma: 6 children: Aniyan, Samkutty, Valsamma, (Late) Saji, Jessy & Suja

    Aniyan's wife Ruby: 2 children: Sherin & Merin

        Sherrin's husband Bency: 2 children (twins): Anna & Ann

        Merrin's husband Abel

    Samkutty's wife, Somini: 2 children: Levin & Shon

    Valsama"s husband, Sam: 3 children: Lizza, Lance & Leslie

        Lizza' husband, Jijo: 2 children: Ashly & Emily

        Lance's wife, Sneha: 1 child: Ethan

        Leslie

    (Late) Saji's wife, Jaya: one child: Sajin

Jessy's husband, Ponnachen: 2 children: Princy & Jensen

Princy's husband, Bijo: 2 children: Asher & Ashwin

Jensen's wife, Christina

Suja's husband, Thomas: 2 children: Jerrin & Joshua

**Second Son (Late) Samuel & First Wife (Late) Thankama**

2 children: Gracey & Mohan (San)

Grecy's husband, Thankachen: 2 children: Stanley & Stacey

San's wife, 2 children: Ninu (Emily) & Nebu (Benjamin)

Second Wife (Late) Kunjumole (Mary): 1 child: Babu (Sam)

Babu's wife Juji: 3 children: Amanda & (husband, Manu), Alvin & Alan

**Third Son Pappachen (Thomas) & Susama: 4 children:**

Mercy, Liz, Daisy & James (Saji)

Mercy's husband, Rusty Foerger: 3 children: Kara, Nathan & Joel

Kara's husband James: 2 children: Peter & Hope

Nathan's wife, Katie

Liz's husband, Geoff West: 3 children: Rachel, Katrina, Erica

Daisy" husband, Vinod Varghese: 3 children: Vijay, Isaiah & Maya

James's wife, Tina: 2children: Naliya & Anika

**First Daughter Annama & (Late) Kunjachen (Thomas): 6 children:**

Rosie, Shanti, Babu (John), Susan, Sherly & Biju

Rosie's husband, Aby George: 2 children: Crystal & Spencer

Crystal's husband, Jamie Pillai: 1child: Preston

Spencer's wife, Asha: 2 children: Sidney & Sierra

Shanty's husband, Varghese (Achankunju): 2 children: Gerry & Jesna

Gerry's wife, Rubal: 2 children: William & Arthur

Jesna's husband, Ashok: 2 children: Naomi & Grace

Babu's wife, Lilly: 3 children: Libby, Litty & Lawson

Libby's husband, Mannu: 2 children: Kaitlyn & Nathaniel
Litty's husband, Titus: 1 child: Lucca (Josiah)
Lawson's wife, Zeba

Susan's husband, Babykutty: 2 chidren: Sobin & Shawn

Sobin's wife, Deepa: 1child:----

Shawn

Sherly's husband, Victor Abraham: 3 children: Aaron, Alwin & Priscilla

Aaron

Alvin's wife, Rachel
Priscilla

Biju's Rani:3 children: Abigail (Ponnu), Adeline (Thenu), Anna-bell (Manna)

## Second Daughter (Late) Ammini & (Late) George: 5 children

Sheila (Kunjumole), Joemon (Joy), Laly, Jolly & Santhosh (Annie)

Sheila's husband, James Moozhayil: 2 children: Rahul & Jasmine

Joemon's wife, Suja (Annie): 2 children: Sara & Sheeba

Laly's husband, Benny: 3 children: Shelly, Sheethal & Sherin

Shelly's husband, Robbie Thomas: 1 child: Hanna

Sheethal's husband, Arun Joseph: 2 children: Itty (Rohan) & Ann

Sherrin's husband, Kevin

Jolly's husband, Kochumon (Mathew Thomas): 2 children: Noel (Chris) & Kyle

Santhosh's husband Gagan Walia: 2 children: Sahil & Manisha

## Third Daughter (Late) Rachel (Podiyama) & (Late) Mathew Thomas (Ponnachen):

1 child: Jaison

## Fourth Daughter Chinnama & Ranjit Baines:2 children: Anil & Ajay

Anil's wife, Janice: 1 child: Alea

Ajay's wife, Joyti:1 child: Mila

## Fifth Daughter Molly & Jose Kadavil: 3 children: Lenci, Shanti (Sheena) & Justin

Lenci's wife, Bilky: 1 child: Elraya

Shanti's husband, Aaron Grant: 2 children: Caleb & Sophie

Justin's wife Kiran

## PART TWO: THE HOSPITAL to UNIVERSITY

*"A thankless heart will wander through life deluded" (Author Unknown)*

Part Two describes my professional journey in a nursing career. Included in this part is my nursing education in the 60's, my first nursing job in Hazelton, my move from hospital nursing to nursing education, my transition from hospital nursing to an academic setting, and finally, my move from nursing education to nursing administration. It has been a long journey with many challenges and rewards along the way. All in all, it was a fulfilling journey, and I am extremely thankful for a successful and rewarding career.

# Nursing Career: Foundation

We all have had our own dreams of what we wanted to be in our lives. My dream was to be a teacher and to teach in an African country. When I was in high school, my friend and I talked about going to Africa to teach. We had not explored what it would be like for two girls from Kerala to go and teach in Africa. Girls had limited career options in the 60's. Most women in Kerala got married at a young age and became housewives and mothers. Those who completed high school and some college education chose to become teachers or nurses. Many girls from Christian families chose nursing as a career and went away to work in different parts of India. Some went to the Middle East (Kuwait, Bahrain, Persia (now Iran), Muscat, or UAE).

In the 60's, the majority of girls who chose to pursue a nursing career were from Christian families. Kerala had a higher percentage of Christians in its population, and the majority of nurses in India were from Kerala State. For example, I was in a class of 15 girls at CMCH in Vellore. There was only one girl from the Hindu religion, and there were no girls from the Islamic religion. The rest of us were from Christian families. Girls from Christian families saw nursing as a service and an opportunity to earn money to help their families. I must say, this trend has changed significantly. Today, women from all religious backgrounds choose nursing as a career.

I had never planned to be a nurse. Then, how did I end up as one? Was there a higher plan in my life to be a nurse? A door was opened for me to get an admission to a degree program in nursing at a prestigious School of Nursing in India.

To Be a Nurse? Why did I choose nursing as a career? Was it a calling? Certainly, when Florence Nightingale started modern nursing with the opening of her first school in 1860, it was meant to be a calling and a service. Nursing's traditional and historical roots were deeply anchored in military and religious heritages. Since then, nursing has gone through many drastic changes. These changes included: how nurses were educated, how the role of nurses evolved into health team members, and how the settings in which nurses worked became varied. Once prepared to a diploma level to practice as RN's, nurses were now prepared to a degree level. Nurses also have embraced collaborative practices to be members of health care teams. The context of practice has extended from institutions to community settings.

At the turn of the century, nurses and doctors were the two categories of workers in the health care system. The health care system was limited to acute care hospitals. Doctors prescribed medications and treatments and performed surgeries. Nurses performed the remaining tasks in a hospital in caring for the sick. There were no pharmacists, physiotherapists, respiratory therapists, dietitians, diagnostic technicians, laboratory technicians, etc. With the addition of a variety of heath care workers, tasks nurses once performed were now performed by these various health care workers. So, nurses explored other ways to expand their roles.

Correspondingly, as demands in health care changed, the role of nursing shifted. Nurses were needed in specialty areas, and this required advanced education, for example, in ICU, emergency, cardiac care, the renal dialysis unit, the neonatal intensive care unit, etc. While the demands for nurses in these specialty units were on the increase, the demands for nurses with advanced education also increased. Today, Nurse Practitioners are prepared with graduate degrees to provide leadership in clinical practice, especially in specialty areas, in care of the older adults and in primary care.

I had been encouraged by the increasing number of opportunities available for those who entered the nursing profession. Nurses could choose to work in acute care settings or in community settings or choose to become nurse educators or nurse administrators. These opportunities also came with the need for additional knowledge and skills. For example, to teach nursing in a college or university, a minimum of a Masters' degree was required. A PhD was required for a tenure track position in a university school of nursing. Thus, I recognized the need for additional education in nursing to fulfil my aspiration to teach nursing. However, it was important for me to obtain hospital nursing practice prior to going into teaching.

I was aware of the risks in nursing practice. I had heard of nurses being abused by some patients, especially those who worked in mental health settings. In addition, shift work was daunting. However, the rewards were the main reason many go into nursing. Traditionally, nursing was seen as a service. The reward was really when a patient told you, "Thank you".

A nurse is there when a baby is born, and a nurse is there during the times of illness and death. The nurse is the only health care worker who is there 24 hours of the day with the patients providing continuous care. Thus, the nurse is the pillar of the healthcare system and an essential member of the health care team.

Nursing, A Family Tradition? Although, I was the first to choose as a career in my extended family, nursing has now become a good career option for our young people. For example, my elder sister Rachel followed me to become a nurse. Similarly, my younger sister Molly also chose nursing as her career. Thus, three of the five sisters chose nursing as a career.

This trend has also been followed by my nieces. My eldest sister's two daughters Rosie and Shanti became nurses. Then, my sister Ammini's three daughters Sheila, Jolly, and Santhosh chose nursing as their careers. Ammini's son, Joemon, married a nurse (Suja) and both their daughters

Sara and Sheeba chose nursing as their careers. This tradition continued into the next generation in their family. My niece Laly's three daughters Shelly, Sheethal, and Sherin chose nursing as their careers. In addition, my nephew Mohan's daughter Emily also chose nursing as a career. I also learned that my eldest brother's grandson Lance married a nurse Sneha. Although the tradition of choosing nursing as a career started with me, it has been growing in my family. It took me by surprise when Santhosh's son (Sahil) entered a nursing program to be a nurse, the first male nurse in our family.

We are truly a family of nurses. I am proud of each of these family members who chose nursing as their careers, as I believe nursing is an honourable profession in which to serve society. Whether it is a calling or a career, I know we make a difference. I am proud to be a nurse. My message to all the nurses in my family and to those who are contemplating becoming nurses is this: nursing is a profession with vast opportunities. With more education in nursing, a person can become a nurse educator, a nurse administrator, a nurse researcher, a nurse practitioner, or a specialist in a practice area.

Now, a post-graduate education in nursing is readily available with flexibility. One can work and take courses online. A person also has the option to travel to other countries and practice nursing. So, I would say, consider nursing as a career choice and maximize the opportunity to get ahead in a career. Back to my story of starting my nursing career.

Admission to BScN at CMCH: I graduated from high school in 1958 and then completed one year in college (pre-university) at Catholicate College in Pathanamthitta, my home city. I was fortunate to pass high school with a "First-Class" and pre-university with a "Second-class". My uncle, C.M. George, who was a Malayalam Pandit and a high school teacher, suggested that I pursue a degree in nursing. By the way, in those days, most nurses pursued a nursing diploma, as a degree in nursing was offered only in few places in India. One such place was the Christian Medical College Hospital (CMCH), Vellore, in Madras State (now Tamil Nadu).

My uncle looked out for opportunities to help students with potential in his extended family. He encouraged and supported those who did well in school. By sponsoring me through a charitable organization, he paved the way for me to get an admission to the CMCH Nursing School. Because no one in my family was a nurse, I did not know what nursing entailed. However, once I began the nursing program, I was passionate and committed to becoming the best nurse I could be.

Getting an admission to the BSc Nursing at Vellore was difficult. Academic excellence was the main criterion for admission. My dad took me to Vellore by train for the admission interview and testing that lasted for three days. Out of many applications, 30 candidates were called for a three-day interview and testing. I was tested for my communication skills, observational skills, First Aid, and caring attributes. I had my final interview with the Director of the School of Nursing, Miss Taylor.

Miss Taylor, Director of CMCH School of Nursing with India's president
Dr. Rajendra Prasad 1960

Miss Taylor wore a white-dress uniform and a cap and spoke English with a British accent. I was nervous. She looked through my credentials and asked me a few questions. I had no idea how well I answered her questions and whether I was selected or not. The next day the names of those selected were posted on a wall in the School of Nursing. Thank God, my name was on the list. Of the 30 candidates who were interviewed, 15 candidates were selected and 15 were rejected. There were tears and expressions of joy and relief. The candidates who were rejected had the option to enroll in the nursing diploma program offered at CMCH, and most chose that option. I could only say that God had a plan for me, and I was admitted to the CMCH, BScN Program at Vellore.

CMCH had a hospital-based Nursing School, and it was one of the largest and most reputable hospitals in India. It was founded by an American missionary doctor, Ida Scudder. There were many aspects of this vast organization and its contributions that were worth mentioning. I will focus on Dr. Ida Scudder and Dr. Paul Brand. I considered it a great privilege to have met both Dr. Scudder and Dr. Brand.

Dr. Ida Scudder (Founder of CMCH) in 1959

Dr. Ida Scudder was the daughter of an American missionary doctor, John Scudder, and his wife Sophie. John's parents were also medical missionaries in India. They belonged to the Reformed Church in America. Ida was born in 1870 and was raised in Southern India. As a child, she witnessed bubonic plague, cholera, famine, and poverty in India. She went back to America to finish her schooling. Her goal was to complete her education, get married, and live in the US and not continue the family tradition of becoming a medical missionary. However, it seemed God had a different plan for her life.

When her mom in India became ill, her dad requested Ida's help. So, she returned to India to care for her mom. During her stay in India, she witnessed the husbands of three women in labour, one after the other, who came to Ida's house seeking help to deliver their babies. Due to culture and tradition, husbands did not want a male doctor to attend to their wives. So, they requested the help of Ida who did not have her medical training. Ida could not help these women. She found out later that all three women and the babies died during childbirth.

The death of three women and babies convinced Ida that God wanted her to become a doctor and help the women in India. She decided to go back to America to become a medical doctor and return to India as a medical missionary for the women of India. In 1899, she graduated from Cornell Medical College in New York City. Most notable was the fact that she was the first woman admitted to the medical school, thus the first graduate woman physician. She returned to South India as a medical missionary doctor.

Dr. Scudder received a small grant of $10,000. She started a tiny medical dispensary and clinic for women in Vellore. In 1918, she started a teaching hospital which became the CMCH. She dedicated her life to helping people in India. She stayed single, lived, and died in India. At first, she opened a medical school for women only, and then, she expanded it to admit men, also. She started receiving grants from missions in America. In 1928, she started the medical school campus on a 200-acre piece of land. She also started a training school for nurses.

In 1909, she started training nurses, and, in 1946, a college of nursing was established. The hospital expanded to provide services to people in both rural and urban areas. It also provided primary, secondary, and tertiary care services. At CMCH, the following advances in medical care were performed: a successful open- heart surgery in 1961, a kidney transplant in 1971, and a bone barrow transplant in 1986. CMCH was well-known for its advanced treatments, not only in India, but around the world.

In 1938, the Indian Government declared that only universities could grant degrees. So, Dr. Scudder upgraded the medical college to be affiliated with Madras University, and later, the nursing college also became affiliated with Madras University. CMCH also offered other healthcare programs, for example, a medical laboratory program, physiotherapy and rehabilitation programs, and a radiology technician program. CMCH admitted students not only from different states of India, but also from other parts of the world. For example, during my time, nursing students came from Singapore, Sri Lanka, Iran, and the Maldives. In India, it was a dream of many to be a graduate of CMCH program. I am grateful that I had the opportunity to be one.

A degree in nursing from CMCH was the key to my success in my nursing career as it lay the foundation. In the 60's, obtaining a degree in nursing was invaluable and rare; whereas now, a nursing degree is the requirement to practice nursing.

During my time at CMCH, I was able to meet Dr. Ida Scudder in person. She was in a wheelchair, and she visited our residence; thus, I had a chance to greet her. This was a dream come true for me as I was able to meet her face to face. She was mentally sharp, and she had a big smile. Dr. Scudder died the following year. CMCH had become a world-famous hospital with prestigious programs in Medicine, Nursing, and many Allied Health fields. Dorothy Wilson wrote the book, "Dr. Ida Passing the Torch of Life". It gave a detailed account of Dr. Scudder's life (Wilson, 1985).

Dr. Paul Brand, Surgeon for Lepers: Leprosy has been eradicated in North America. However, it is still prevalent in India. A cure has found to kill the bacteria causing leprosy. Yet, India still has the largest number of people with leprosy in the world.

Leprosy is a deforming disease caused by bacteria which can stay in the body for five to twenty years without causing any symptoms. The bacteria causing leprosy affects the peripheral nerves in the body, resulting in a loss of sensation. Gradually, symptoms appear affecting the skin, eyes, face, hands, fingers, and toes, with the main feature being the loss of any pain sensation. Absence of pain is the greatest enemy of a leper. As a result, the leper is not able to protect the body from injury. This leads to disfigurement of limbs, fingers, toes, nose, ears, eyes, and various other parts of the body. Ulcers develop in the limbs and body. The skin becomes abnormal-looking, and the lepers become a ghastly sight. Nobody even wants to look at or go near a leper. Lepers are treated as outcasts and are welcomed only in a leper colony.

In India, we observed that lepers lost their fingers and toes overnight. This was caused by rats nibbling at their fingers and toes at night. There was no pain for the afflicted to know to chase the rats away. Repeated injuries resulted in deformities. Another aspect of the disease was that lepers were unable to blink. Absence of blinking eventually resulted in blindness.

Leprosy is spread from one person to another by close contact for a long period of time. A mother can transmit the disease to her children. Because of the deformity and the fear of the spread of the disease, leprosy patients are kept isolated from the mainstream society.

The transmission of leprosy reminded me of a story that I heard when I was young. The story was about Father Damien, a Catholic priest from Belgium, who went to work among the lepers in Molokai Island in late 1800's. All those with leprosy in the Hawaiian Islands were sent to Molokai Island to keep them isolated. The lepers were quarantined with minimal medical care and help. Father Damien worked with these lepers and lived with them for years. He treated these lepers as his family members.

One day, Father Damien noticed, that when he accidently spilt hot water on his leg, he did not feel any pain. He realized then that he had also contracted leprosy. The next day, during morning devotion, he addressed the lepers as, "my fellow lepers" rather than "my fellow believers" as he had done in the past. The lepers came to know that Father Damien also had contracted leprosy. Father Damien died in 1889 in Molokai. The Belgian Government wanted his body to be buried in Belgium. The lepers wanted him buried in Molokai for what he had done for them. In the end, the people of Molokai requested his right hand, the hand that touched the lepers. The Belgian government agreed, and his hand was buried in Molokai. The rest of his body was sent to be buried in Belgium. I was moved by Father Damien's love for the lepers and his ultimate sacrifice of his life for them.

Back to Dr. Brand and his contributions, at CMCH, lepers were admitted and treated for reconstructive surgery by Dr. Paul Brand. He became a world-renowned plastic surgeon. His surgical interventions    corrected deformities of hands, fingers, faces and toes. In 1948 at CMCH, Dr. Brand performed the world's first reconstructive surgery. Since then, he performed countless reconstructive surgeries, many of them, medical miracles, enabling these patients to live fairly healthy lives. Dr. Brand corrected the absence of blinking by transplanting a piece of chewing muscle to a patient's eyelid. He dedicated his life to helping the lepers in India.

I was fortunate to have a practicum experience in the operating room where Dr. Brand did reconstructive surgeries. The love and care he displayed for the leprosy patients were palpable, and he expected the nurses and other health care professionals to show love and respect for leprosy patients. I was also fortunate to hear Dr. Brand speak at the morning chapel service at CMCH. He related his service to lepers as a symbol of his love for Jesus. Dorothy Wilson wrote the book, "The Life and Work of Dr. Paul Brand" which gave a detailed account of Dr. Brand's contributions to CMCH and leprosy patients (Wilson, 1989).

I also had opportunity to care for leprosy patients in the hospital and in community clinics.

My Leprosy Patients: So, as a nursing student, I had to take care of leprosy patients. At CMCH, there was a separate ward to care for leprosy patients. During clinical practice, nursing students were assigned to these  patients. I was posted in the leprosy ward during my second year of the nursing program. I do recall being afraid of caring for leprosy patients. I was afraid of being infected with the leprosy bacteria. I soon learned that normally, leprosy was not contagious and would take years of close contact to contract the disease.

Once I got to know my patients, I realized they were like me, except that they had leprosy. I was heart-broken to find young patients in the leprosy ward with such terrible deformities. I was able to communicate with them and hear their painful stories of having to leave home to live in the leper colony. Rejected by their own families was a devastating experience for these patients.

During my community posting, I also had the opportunity to care for lepers. There were roadside clinics held to change the dressings of lepers with open wounds. They were so appreciative of what we did for them. Although the Government of India had tried to eradicate leprosy in India, it was identified that in 2005, India was still home to 57 per cent of the world's leprosy patients. To this day, the plight of leprosy patients in India haunts me. Yet, I witnessed the love of Christ in Dr. Brand as he cared for the lepers of India.

CMCH: Its Christian Mission: Working as a student, I learned that Dr. Ida Scudder's motto for CMCH was "Not to be ministered unto, but to minister". As a Christian organization, Christian faith was practised in many ways. For example, there was a chapel inside the compound, and daily morning service was held for all staff and students. Before we went to classes or clinical practice, I remember attending the chapel service each morning. I noticed that the service was also attended by those who belonged to other religions. In the hospital ward, each morning we prayed before we started our day shifts. CMCH was funded by Christian missions abroad, mainly those in the United States. Many of the doctors, nurses, and other health care professionals who worked at CMCH practised the Christian faith.

Looking back, I recall a few incidents that occurred attesting to the Christian practices of CMCH. When I was a second-year nursing student, I was posted to a surgical unit and was assigned to care for a middle-aged man with a gastric ulcer waiting to have surgery. The surgeon was a missionary doctor from Australia. He came to examine the patient before surgery. It was customary that when a doctor came to see a patient, the assigned nurse be present at the patient's side. The surgeon did not speak the patient's mother-tongue, Tamil. After he examined the patient, he told me to translate to the patient that he could fix the ulcer in his stomach, but he needed a spiritual healing for the ulcer in his heart. I understood what the doctor was saying, but I could not be literal in my translation from English to Tamil and to my patient. The surgeon was using a metaphor here when he talked about the ulcer in his heart. The surgeon prayed with the patient showing his love for him. The patient was a Hindu by religion.

Another incident I recall was when I had to say good-bye to a 25-year-old young man who was diagnosed with renal failure. Both of his kidneys had failed, and he needed dialysis. Renal dialysis was not available at CMCH in the 1960's. So, he was sent home to die. This was hard on all of us who took care of this educated young man. The only thing we could do was to pray for him. Although, he was a Hindu by religion, he requested us to pray for him. I did not know what happened to him after he left the hospital. I felt very sad.

As a student, I had the opportunity to become part of the Student Christian Movement (SCM) at CMCH. A few of us joined the organization and attended meetings where we learned new Christian songs, listened to speakers, and studied the Bible. In short, life at CMCH was spiritually enriching.

CMCH Residence Life: The Christian way of living was also reflected in the residence life. There was a separate residence for nursing students and one for unmarried staff nurses. Life in the residence was a brand-new experience for me.

All nursing students were required to stay in the students' residence. Sharing the room with a stranger from another State who had a different mother-tongue, different culture, different interests, and different personality with not much in common was my experience when I started my residence life at CMCH.

The residence was only for women, and no male students were admitted to the nursing program. It was a four-story building with common bathrooms and showers on each floor. My roommate in first year was a girl from Madras State. My mother tongue was Malayalam and hers, Tamil. This pairing was intentionally done by our warden so that we would communicate to each other in English. In the residence, we had students from different parts of India and some from abroad. English was our common language.

We had a warden for the residence who made sure we followed the residence rules and curfews. If we went off campus, we had to sign out, indicating the date and time we left, and we were expected to sign back in before 9 PM. No male visitors were allowed in our rooms. We had to meet them in the visitors' lounge. Students were called to the warden's office for breaking rules and curfew. One of my classmates had to meet with the warden a few times during our first year in the program. During my residence life, I became friends with students from other countries as well as from the different States of India.

There were no cooking facilities in our rooms, so we ate in the common dining room at a time specified for each meal. Since my family lived in another State, I seldom had any visitors. Once my sister Rachel came to see me, and she stayed with me in my room. At the end of my first year, my mom and my niece Gracey (three years old) came to Vellore, and I went with them to visit my brother in Asansol, near Calcutta (now Kolkata). I did not like the place where I stayed with my brother, as there were mostly single men and very few families there. Calcutta was an extremely crowded city with beggars and people from all walks of life. I was happy to return to Vellore, two weeks later and continue my nursing education.

## My Nursing Education at CMCH

The BScN Program was four years in length, and included both hospital and community experiences, as well as rural and urban nursing practice. In contrast, the diploma nursing program was three years in length and focussed mainly on hospital nursing practice. The BScN program was a broader based education, including courses in Physics, Sociology, and English. The two novels I read as part of an English course were: "Far from the Madding Crowd" by Thomas Hardy and "Jane Eyre" by Charlotte Bronte. It was a treat for me to read these novels, as in the past, I had not read many English novels. Looking back, I regret not having the opportunity to read more books in English, both fiction and non-fiction.

The Anatomy and Physiology courses were offered in the Medical College, a few miles from the hospital. These courses were taught by physicians. We dissected human cadavers in the Anatomy lab. The dead bodies were kept in formaldehyde, and they had a pungent smell when we dissected them. The lab session was from 11 to 12 in the morning, and we got back to the residence just in time for our lunch. Some of us could not eat lunch on the day that we dissected cadavers. We took the hospital's private bus every week to go to the Medical College for attending classes. It was a fun trip as we sang songs during our bus trip. I remember Miriam Florence, my classmate with a beautiful voice, who knew many English songs.

Nursing courses were taught by nursing instructors. Most of them had completed a Masters' Degree in Nursing from North America or from Great Britain. They were well-prepared and were committed to the teaching service at CMCH. We had instructors from Canada, the US, England, and India. Practicum was integrated with theory from the beginning of the program. There was a lesser expectation from students in the BScN program to provide service to the hospital compared to students in the Diploma Nursing Program. We did not receive a monthly stipend, and we had to pay a monthly tuition fee. In the fourth year of the program, we had a course in Nursing Research, taught by a nursing professor from England, who had completed a doctorate in nursing. One of my favorite Nursing instructors was Violet. She had completed her MScN from abroad. She was born and raised in Madras State. She placed the learning needs of her students first. I wanted to be an instructor like her. It was one of my career goals.

Public Health in Nursing was a major component of the BScN program. In addition to the community nursing practicum in urban settings, we went to a rural place quite far from our residence for a three-month practicum. We lived in a small house with a cook who cooked our meals. We travelled by hospital van to villages and roadside clinics to see patients who had no other access to healthcare.

This Practicum focussed on how to care for those who were sick at home. We had an experienced nurse with us as our mentor. This experience provided us with the opportunity for practising assessment skills and quick decision-making in nursing. The common conditions we encountered were children with high fever, diarrhoea, and vomiting, older people with chronic productive cough, and women with pregnancy-related problems.

Most of the homes that we visited were built with mud walls without proper ventilation. This experience gave us the opportunity to talk about basic hygiene, nutrition, and prevention of infection. Sometimes, we did not have enough light in the room to do a proper assessment. Many houses did not have electricity or proper lighting. We would use our nursing skills to treat the various conditions that we encountered, for example, a sponge bath with cool water for high fever.

In addition to basic hygiene and nutrition, we also talked about family planning. The Indian government was trying to control the fast-growing population with a "Five Year Family Plan". With the village women, we discussed abstinence. Most of these women were illiterate. I was skeptical about the women being able to follow abstinence as the men had the upper hand, and they called the shots. Birth control pills were not yet available, and condoms were not popular among the villagers. In villages, a large family was considered a blessing as they needed more people to work on the farm. Even today, India is trying to control its overpopulation. I questioned how effective India's Five-Year Plan was?

So, our practicum in the community was varied, and so was our hospital clinical practice. It included the medical, surgical, orthopedic, neurology, gynecology, obstetrics, pediatrics, urology, and leprosy wards. We had a clinical instructor supervising us and evaluating us simultaneously. I recall a traumatic experience during my second year. I was posted to a medical floor, and one day I made a medication error. I had to fill up a medication error report with my clinical instructor. That was a stressful process. After I was reprimanded by my instructor, I had to meet with the Director of

Nursing of the hospital. I was so nervous while I was walking with the medication error report to the Director's office. I was afraid of being dismissed from the program. I met with the Director, and she gave me a warning. I was careful not to make another medication error for the remainder of the program.

One area I did not feel qualified to care for was with patients with psychiatric disorders. The hospital for mentally ill was in a different location a few miles away from the main hospital. We just had a tour of this building, and I saw patients were locked up in their rooms. In the 60's, treating the mentally ill with medications and modern treatment measures were not available. People in India were superstitious about mental illness. These superstitions influenced the care for the mentally ill patients. I saw a young woman with a psychiatric disorder immobilized with a chain around her ankle. This was a disturbing sight, and I did not know her specific diagnosis or the reason for the chain around her ankle.

After completing four years of study, we had to write provincial examination offered by Madras University which conferred our degree. I completed the program with a "Second Class". Out of the 15 students who started the program, twelve of us successfully completed the program. I do recall hearing that one student was expelled for an ethical violation. We were not told what really happened. I was fortunate and truly grateful to successfully complete the program.

Midwifery Program: After a nurse successfully completed the BScN program, the six-month Midwifery program was a requirement. We learned the theory component, and we had a practicum in delivering babies with a normal pregnancy. We had to deliver around thirty babies to complete the program. In a complicated childbirth, we only assisted the obstetricians.

In India, midwives delivered babies at home. Practising midwives would make house calls. However, in many villages, midwives were not available, and untrained women delivered babies. In the 60's, the infant mortality was high. Once trained midwives became available, the death rate of infants decreased. Again, I was grateful that I completed the

Midwifery Program with distinction. Although I never had a chance to practice as a midwife in India, I had the opportunity to practice my midwifery skills in Hazelton and in Kitimat hospitals.

At CMCH, we had to learn to speak and write Tamil, the official language of Madras State (Tamil Nadu). Also, I became more fluent in speaking English. I learned social skills in relating to people from different parts of India and abroad and generally gained more confidence. Yet, I was not sure if I was ready to travel abroad and practice nursing in a different country without work experience. However, when I got a job offer from Canada soon after my graduation, I had to be ready, and I prayed for God's guidance.

## Staff Nurse to Nurse Educator

I was thrilled to assume my first job in my life; yet, I had no idea what lay ahead. Kerala-girls did not have the opportunity to work and make money while going to school or college. So, I had never had a job until I came to Canada. The thought of earning my own money was truly liberating. I no longer had to be dependent. Moreover, it would be an opportunity for me to give back and help my family who put me through school, college, and the nursing program.

Staff Nurse in Hazelton, Canada: I worked as a staff nurse at Wrinch Memorial Hospital, a United Church Hospital, in Hazelton in Northern BC. When I began my job in Hazelton, I soon realized how different the two settings were at CMCH, where I studied nursing and the Hazelton hospital. CMCH was a 2000+ bed teaching hospital with many specialty units and up-to-date treatments, surgical interventions, and technology. Wrinch Memorial Hospital was a 35-bed rural hospital providing general care. The two settings were drastically different.

Hazelton Hospital had three floors: the first floor was the emergency room and OR for minor surgical procedures; the second floor contained medical / surgical units; and the third floor was for obstetrics and pediatrics. There was only one RN and one LPN on duty during the night shift. The LPN mainly looked after the medical / surgical patients, and the RN cared for patients on the third floor and attended to emergency patients. The RN was ultimately responsible for all the patients in the hospital during the night shift.

During the night shift, I had to care for sick children and to attend to the women in labour. Most patients in the hospital were Native Indians (now called Indigenous). The pregnant Indigenous women usually waited until the labour was well-advanced to come to the hospital. This meant that delivery of the baby happened quickly after admission before I had the time to call the doctor. Thus, I had to deliver the babies on my own. My midwifery training helped me to handle this challenge.

At CMCH, we had aides to clean up the linen and the room after each childbirth. At the hospital in Hazelton, I had to rinse the bloody linen and clean the room. Moreover, the linen had to be rinsed in cold water. It was a difficult task, and I questioned why an RN had had to do this task. It was the wrong question to ask, and the answer was in a church hospital, one must be willing to do menial tasks also. CMCH was also a mission hospital, but with a different culture.

As a new graduate, assuming responsibility for an entire hospital, albeit small, during the night shift was overwhelming! In each night shift, I was giving nursing care, delivering babies, doing administrative work, as well as janitorial duty. The experience was both challenging and scary at times. I remember once while I was on duty on night shift, a person came to emergency and rang the bell. I went down to attend the call. I noticed a Native man, quite drunk, and I was scared. I ran upstairs to get the LPN to come with me. I was not used to caring for intoxicated patients. I had to get used to these situations in a hurry.

The reward for the challenging work paid off with a salary of $323.00 per month including the Northern allowance. I had to pay back money each month towards my airfare and pay for room and board. I sent a portion of my salary every month to my parents (my family obligation). I hardly spent any money for personal needs. I had very little money in those days. My closet was bare compared to what I own now. We lived in the nurses' residence and had meals at the hospital. During the night shift, we could order a steak dinner if we wanted. The food was great once I got used to its taste. I do not recall going to any restaurants in Hazelton.

My social life in Hazelton involved going to the cabin at Sealy Lake owned by Dr. Whiting. When Ranjit came to visit me in the residence, he would also come to the lake with me. There were young and beautiful nurses who came from different parts of Canada to Hazelton to experience nursing and life in the North. Dr. Whiting's daughter Betty was a nurse educated in Eastern Canada. There were two other young nurses that came from the East. They enjoyed going out on dates, but suitable boys were hard to find in the rural fishing village of Hazelton.

My experience in Hazelton provided me with the opportunity to learn about the Native culture. I also did voluntary work in the Native community. I was surprised to see young girls coming to have babies in the hospital. The youngest girl I came across was thirteen years old. It seemed to me they had had little parental guidance. In addition, the lack of education in birth control was a major factor. Birth control pills were not yet available. I was also sad to see that a lot of young Native teens had lost many front teeth. Scabies and pediculosis were common conditions in the pediatric unit. I realized how important health education was to prevent these conditions. I also learned that issues related to Native health were much more complicated. Poverty, unemployment, and abuse of drugs and alcohol were some of the issues.

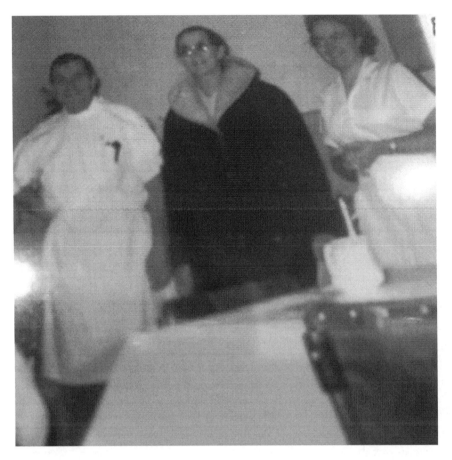

Doctor Whiting, wife Marjorie and Nursing Director Rena in Hazelton

As the WM hospital was a United Church Hospital, practising the Christian faith was expected of us as employees. So, I attended church services on Sundays. The church was located closer to the hospital and the nurses' residence. Most nurses and doctors were Christians. Our work was considered to be a service to those who came to the hospital. Since I was educated in a Christian hospital (CMCH), I was comfortable with incorporating the Christian faith into my work. I worked in Hazelton for one year. After being in a car accident and breaking my elbow, I had to have long-term rehabilitation in Kitimat General Hospital. Thus, I decided to move to Kitimat. I resigned from the Hazelton Hospital and was hired at the Kitimat General Hospital. Leaving the Hazelton Hospital after a year was unusual as I was expected to work there for at least two to three years. In hindsight, I consider the move a blessing as my goal of getting ahead in my nursing career would have been more difficult if I had stayed for a longer period.

I left Hazelton with lot of gratitude. I was grateful to Dr. Watt for giving me my first job, and Dr. Whiting for welcoming me with love to Wrinch Memorial Hospital. During this time in Hazelton, I had the opportunity to attend a church camp for girls as one of the camp leaders, my first experience in camping. One thing I really enjoyed was spending time with the Whitings at their cabin where I learned to sing country songs and hymns. To everyone's surprise, I contracted chickenpox while in Hazelton. I saw snow for the first time. Most importantly, I met Ranjit in Hazelton. My experience in Hazelton laid the foundation for my life in Canada.

Kitimat General Hospital: The Kitimat community was quite different from Hazelton as the Alcan Company employed many immigrants. They came from countries such as, Germany, Greece, Portugal, and Italy. In Kitimat, during the evenings, people belonging to the same ethnic groups stood around talking in their own language in the small shopping center; this was a common sight. Many new immigrants did not speak English. I do recall a German man who worked at the hospital saying that he wanted to learn English, and someone told him that the best way to learn English was to get into a group and start speaking the language. He did that and realized after a while, what he learned to speak was Portuguese, not English!!

In the Kitimat hospital, I was assigned to work in the obstetric unit as I had midwifery training. Once again, I was living in the nurses' residence, which was the top floor of the hospital. Here I learned to cook my own meals. There was a nurse from Thailand living in the residence. The remaining nurses came from different parts of Canada. I made friends with two amazing nurses from Saskatchewan, Susan, and Hertha. They were practising Christians, and I joined them in going to a Mennonite church in Kitimat.

I noticed some nurses would go out on "blind dates". This was a new word for me. Men who worked in the Alcan Company would call the residence

144

looking for a date. Some nurses would accept the date. I learned that when a person went on a date with someone she had never met before, it was called a blind date. The next day, we would wait in the lounge to hear about the experience of the blind date. I was gradually learning the Canadian culture.

After working one year at the Kitimat hospital, I realized it was time for me to move to a big city where I would be able to pursue my goal of higher education and to teach nursing. Ranjit encouraged me to move to Kamloops as the hospital in Kamloops offered a nursing program. Ranjit was a visionary; he was confident that I would get a teaching job in Kamloops. When I was leaving Kitimat for Kamloops, Susan and Hertha told me to attend the Alliance Church in Kamloops. Was it a coincidence that the place where I found accommodation in Kamloops was on the 700 block of Columbia Street, right across from the old Kamloops Alliance Church? Of course, I started attending that church. The Alliance Church has been our church since then (54 years).

Back to my nursing career, in the 1970's, nursing education was offered in hospitals in BC except that the University of British Columbia (UBC) offered a degree program in nursing. This was the trend in Canada and around the world.

Hospital School of Nursing: I moved to Kamloops in 1966 as there was a School of Nursing as part of the Royal Inland Hospital (RIH). I was hoping to get an opportunity to teach nursing at RIH School of Nursing. Ranjit believed in me in that, if given an opportunity, I would be able to teach nursing in Canada. Initially, I worked at the hospital as a staff nurse in pediatrics for six months.

Ranjit knew the Director of School of Nursing, "Miss Gerry LaPointe" and he mentioned to Gerry that I was interested in a teaching position. Gerry came to see me at the hospital where I was working. I did not have a formal application process or interview. She offered me a position to teach Anatomy and Physiology to first year nursing students. I was also assigned to take one group of students to a surgical unit for a practicum. I was s thankful to Ranjit for believing in me and paving the way for me to get my first teaching job.

Rookie Nursing Instructor

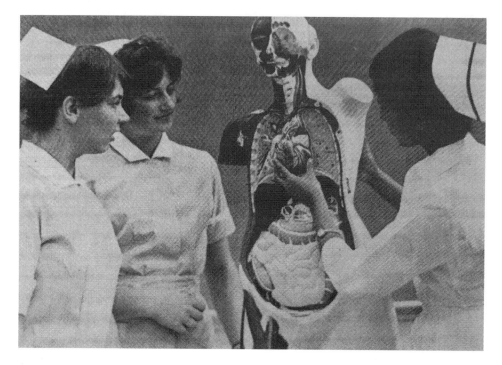

First Year Nursing Students, RIH and me as the Anatomy & Physiology Instructor

I was only 24 years old, and my students were mainly 19 and 20 years old. Nursing Students in the 60's joined the nursing program soon after completion of high school. There were no "mature students" seeking admission to nursing. They were mostly girls except for one male student in my first class of 60 students. Because I had an accent, I had to make sure that I pronounced terminologies the Canadian way. Before giving a class, I often checked with my office mate, Pam Pollard, on the Canadian way of pronouncing medical terms. I had to prepare a lot for each class. I used raw beef lungs, brains, and hearts, etc. to teach the anatomy of these organs. This was not new to me as I had to dissect human cadavers in Vellore when I learned Anatomy.

I worked with an amazing and experienced group of teachers (Dorothy Hales, Flo Backman, Marilyn White, Pam Pollard, Angela Collins, and Sheila Leonard). From this group, Marilyn and I are the only ones alive now. The rest have died. Marilyn and I are still friends and see each other whenever we are able. Our friendship spans over 54+ years. I am truly grateful to have Marilyn as a friend and a colleague.

Marilyn White, my friend, and colleague, & me

Gerry Lapointe was a single woman and a unique leader. She was involved in the provincial nursing organization (RNABC) and served as the president for one term. It gave me the incentive to become involved in nursing organizations, locally and provincially. I was also keen to learn about the changes occurring in nursing education. One major change was the transition of nursing education from hospitals to colleges.

Nursing Education Transition: In the 1960's, a major change in nursing education had been initiated, the transition of hospital nursing programs to colleges in BC. The RIH School of Nursing was also preparing for this

147

transition. RIH nursing was one of the most reputable diploma nursing programs in the province of BC; yet, it had held many traditional practices since its inception.

The RIH program during its 70-year existence held many traditions. In its inception, nursing students were expected to provide service to the hospital. Learning was considered a by-product of their service. Students worked mostly 12-hour shifts (days and nights) with one afternoon off each week. Practical work began on the first day of training with no prior classroom teaching. Students' work, while on duty, involved many non-nursing tasks, such as cooking supper for night shift nurses and scrubbing walls and windows. Students received a small amount of stipend per month (Scott, 1974).

Changes had been taking place in nursing education. When I joined the school of nursing in 1966, Nursing Educators were questioning the practice of using students for service. They demanded more control of the planning and implementation of the nursing curriculum. They wanted more time in the classroom and less time doing hospital chores. This change meant that hospitals had to hire more staff nurses, and it increased the hospital costs. Another change was replacing the uncomfortable bibs and aprons to a more comfortable dress uniform. Wearing a cap was made optional.

In the early years, nursing was taught by hospital supervisors and doctors. Classes were given in the hospital. This was changed when a separate building was allocated as a School of Nursing. Nursing instructors were hired to teach nursing. Doctors were used mainly as guest lecturers. The curriculum was now under the control of nurse educators.

Students came to classes on time and showed respect for nursing instructors. I was surprised to note that the students stood up when I entered the classroom to teach. Today, this practice would be ridiculed by students attending colleges and universities! Men rarely chose nursing as a career in the 60's. At RIH, the first male student graduated in 1964. Since that time, there has been a slow and steady increase in the number of male students admitted to the nursing program. However, this growth of men

148

entering nursing was still low (4-6 percent). The student population became more diverse with mature students, with a few more male students, and with the occasional Aboriginal students.

I taught for six years at the RIH School of Nursing. When I found out that the RIH nursing program was closing, and that Cariboo College was starting a nursing diploma program, I decided to take a break from teaching and go to university. Completing a Masters' degree in nursing was one of my goals when I left India. Since I had obtained my BScN degree in India, I believed obtaining a Masters' degree was important for me to advance in my nursing education career. So, in 1972, I resigned from RIH Nursing Program and began my education at the University of British Columbia (UBC). I completed the program in 1974 and joined Cariboo College as a Nursing Educator.

RIH to Cariboo College: Consistent with the trends in nursing education, the Royal Inland Hospital initiated a timely transition of the program from the hospital to Cariboo College. One of the reasons for the closure of the hospital program was the increasing cost of training nursing students in hospitals. As nursing instructors assumed more control of the curriculum, the focus shifted from providing service to learning. As a result, students were no longer available to staff the hospitals.

Hospital administrators soon came to the realization that hospital-based nursing programs were costly. Thus, RIH graduated its last class in 1974, and Cariboo College admitted its first class in 1973. One by one, other hospital programs in BC followed RIH, and colleges started offering diploma programs in nursing across BC. This trend was consistent with the trend across Canada.

However, the closure of the RIH program and the commencement of the Cariboo College Nursing program faced many challenges. Nurses, doctors, and hospital administrators identified that closing a well-established and reputable nursing program with credible graduates was an immense loss to the community. They had little or no faith that Cariboo College could replace the former reputable hospital program. Cariboo College was an educational institution, not a hospital, meaning that its nursing students and instructors were no longer considered part of the hospital. I was once a hospital employee and taught nursing at the RIH School of Nursing. Now, I was an outsider teaching nursing at Cariboo College. I lost my privilege of being an insider. Nurses and doctors at RIH also treated me as an outsider. This was a strange experience for me.

A major challenge was to achieve acceptance and credibility of the Cariboo College Nursing Program, its students, and faculty, by the doctors and nurses in Kamloops. This was difficult. I, along with the other Cariboo College nursing instructors, took on this challenge and worked hard to provide a quality nursing program. I am   proud to report that the TRU nursing graduates are now among the best in the province, and I was privileged to be part of that growth. (A Note: Cariboo College received a new name: Thompson Rivers University—TRU.)

Completing MScN in the 70's: The MScN program offered at UBC was a two-year, full-time, campus-based program. Thus, I had to resign my job at RIH and move to Vancouver for two years. This was the only institution that offered a graduate program in nursing in BC.

Because I had not been educated in Canada, the Graduate program was challenging for me. Writing papers, doing class presentations, and writing multiple choice examinations were a new way of learning for me. In addition, to complete each course, I had to get used to doing a vast amount of reading. Courses in philosophy and ethics were new content entirely. Since my long-term goal was to teach nursing, I took the education stream in the program with curriculum development as my focus. This really helped me when I started my teaching at Cariboo College as we had to develop a new curriculum in nursing which would meet the standards of the Registered Nurses Association of BC (RNABC). Only the Professional Association had the mandate to approve nursing programs in BC, and only graduates from an approved program were qualified to write the RN licensing examinations.

In 1973, I completed the first year of the program and had the summer off. During the summer, I worked as a staff nurse at RIH. The second year was a bit easier as I was familiar with the campus and had become better at completing assignments. The most difficult course for me was statistics. I remember my hands were shaking when I was writing the statistics examination. I was thrilled when I found out that I passed that course. I had to complete a research component as a requirement of the program. I chose to do my research at the Royal Columbian Hospital in New Westminster. I had to visit the hospital once a week to collect data. In the 70's, driving from UBC to New Westminster was a lot easier than now with much less traffic on the road.

Academic Settings: Contrasting Cultures: In reflecting on my education, I came to realize that the culture at CMCH was vastly different from UBC. Madras University had an affiliation with the CMCH Medical College and the College of Nursing. CMCH was a private Christian organization, founded and operated on Christian beliefs and values that influenced its academic culture. Love for God and love for others was portrayed through services provided by those who worked and studied there. Students who studied within such a culture were exposed to the Christian faith. UBC was a secular institution, thus God or religious beliefs were not acknowledged. The focus was on scientific naturalism and reason as its foundation of thought. God was not openly talked about on the UBC campus.

In the 70's, the academic culture at UBC was being molded by the emerging post-modern thought. I noticed that I was learning in a totally different culture. My colleagues, thirteen women and one man (from Taiwan), were unique individuals. I did not know how many of them practised the Christian faith. We openly discussed existential and post-modern philosophy that emphasized individual existence, freedom, and choice. This philosophy was in its inception in the 70's. I learned that humans define their own meanings in life, and there was no purpose at the core of human existence. I was told that there was no God or any other transcendent force in existence. People were free to make choices based on what made them happy. The pursuits of pleasure and happiness was the goal of life. This learning was rather shocking and foreign to me as it was challenging my beliefs.

This existential belief system was in a direct contradiction with my belief of the intrinsic worth of each individual and my belief that we were made in the image of God. I do recall an open discussion in the classroom about free sex as part of enjoying life. I was rather timid to openly criticize this belief system. Perhaps, I did not know enough about the post-modern philosophy, and I was mainly focussing on my course work in completing the program. However, it was a distressing introduction to Western academic culture.

Educator to Administrator: Looking back at my nursing career, I would have never imagined that when I began my nursing program at CMCH, it would be a steppingstone to becoming a future nursing leader in Canada. I believed it was truly a blessing from God. If anybody had told me when I left India as a 22-year old woman that I would be the Dean of Nursing one day in a Canadian university, I would have considered it an impossible dream. I was filled with gratitude.

In 1974, when I was completing my studies at UBC, I had a call from Cariboo College seeking to interview me for a teaching position in the nursing program. Don Couch, the Dean of Academic Instruction, and Sylvia Brough, the Chairperson of the Nursing Program at Cariboo College, came down to Vancouver to interview me. I was hired, and they wanted me to join Cariboo College as soon as possible. In May 1974, I started as a nursing instructor to teach in the summer practicum in the first year of the program.

When I joined the program, the Chairperson of the Nursing Program was Sylvia Brough and the four instructors were Judy Mogan, Maud O'Sullivan, Joan Redekop, and Sharon Simpson. I was the fifth Nursing Instructor hired at Cariboo College. (As I write my story in 2020, of that group of six, I am sad to note that I am the only one alive).

I completed my program at UBC in April and started teaching a clinical practice course in May at Cariboo College. I had no time for even an orientation to the program. However, my previous teaching experience at the RIH Nursing program made this transition easier. After the summer practicum, I started teaching in year two of the program, as the year two coordinator. I had to learn the Cariboo College Nursing Curriculum in a hurry.

## Cariboo College Nursing Program

In 1973, when the nursing program commenced at Cariboo College, the college was still in its infancy. Cariboo College had started in 1970 by offering university transfer courses at the Indian Residential School facility to teach the courses. A separate building for Cariboo College was being built in its current location, and it was called the Main Building. Portables were used to house the instructors and staff.

When I joined the nursing program in May 1974, I shared my office with another instructor. My office was next door to Jim Wright (Chair of the Social Science Department), who later became the President of the University College of the Cariboo. I do recall that Jim Wright had a typewriter in his office, and I could hear the noise of him hitting his keyboard. None of us had computers. The secretarial staff typed essential documents for us. When the program commenced in 1970, Mr. Jack Harrison was the first Principal.

Offering a nursing program at a college was a new initiative, and the college administration and non-nursing instructors were not familiar with what was entailed in a nursing program. The college offered only university transfer courses. In contrast, the nursing program included a theory component in the classroom, a laboratory component in a nursing lab, and a practice component in clinical settings. A lack of understanding by administrators of how to offer a nursing program at a college was a major challenge.

Program Challenges: The lack of resources like adequate classroom and laboratory space and an adequate number of qualified instructors were also major challenges. Initially, there was no nursing laboratory at the college for students to learn and practice their nursing skills. We borrowed space from the hospital to use as a nursing lab. There was no biology course developed for the nursing program or a qualified instructor to teach it. Added to this was the lack of acceptance of the college nursing program and the nursing instructors by doctors and nurses at RIH. There was a mindset that nursing must be taught in a hospital setting, even though the hospital administrators and government officials wanted the nursing programs out of the hospitals. It wasn't until we started to graduate credible nurses that this mindset changed.

In September 1974, we started the second year of the program. Soon after I had completed the summer practice course, I assumed the responsibility for coordinating the second year of the program. The initial nursing program offered at the college was a six-semester program over two calendar years. Students had a one-month vacation (August) at the end of each year. Instructors used this month of vacation time to develop courses for the second year. Thus, instructors hardly had any time for vacations.

The instructors who taught in the second year were: Jeanette Murray (maternal child nursing), Joan Redekop (mental health nursing), Bernice Muir (Anatomy, Physiology and Pathophysiology), and Helen Etsy and me (medical surgical nursing). Bernice taught until 1976 when RNABC, as part of the program approval requirement, mandated that a masters' preparation in biology was required to teach Anatomy and Physiology. Thus, Bernice was no longer qualified to teach Anatomy and Physiology.

In 1974, three more nursing instructors, (Claudette Kelly, Pam Stewart, and June Goldberg) were hired to teach the first-year nursing students. Since then, in each subsequent year, new instructors were hired to teach based on student numbers. Marion Greenwood, Sheila Leonard, Marian MacKinnon, and Dawn Patterson were new additions to the existing nursing faculty. After a courageous and quick battle with cancer, Sheila Leonard died. We were saddened with the sudden loss of an experienced and credible instructor.

The first three years were hectic as I started teaching immediately after the completion of MScN program. Thus, had no time for vacation as my responsibilities included teaching nursing practice course in the summer, theory course development, coordinating year two of the program, and participating in curriculum development. Since there was no time to prepare for classroom teaching during work hours, it was done at home in late evenings and early morning hours. Where did I find time to raise my four-year old son (Anil)? Did I deprive him of my love and care? I hope not. I was grateful, Ranjit took care of him when I was busy.

I also had to get used to nursing students who were quite different from what I was used to in the hospital-based nursing program. Students were quite diverse who came to study nursing at Cariboo College.

Diverse Nursing Students: Fifty-four students were admitted to the first year of the nursing program at the college. The following year, 75 students were admitted in order to meet the increasing demand for graduate nurses. Not all of these students were new graduates from high school. Many students admitted to nursing were mature students, students with post-secondary education, married students, students who became pregnant during their program of study, students with children, and single parents. (I recalled that in the RIH nursing program, a student that became pregnant during her studies was asked to leave the program).

There was a female student who was admitted to the nursing program who was 59 years old. She had been a schoolteacher for many years. She told me that she was planning to go to one of the African countries for mission work, and a nursing diploma would be valuable in her work. She also told me that carrying the heavy nursing textbooks across the campus was physically exhausting for her.

In addition, students had to find their own accommodations. Since students had to pay a tuition fee for their education, many of them worked part-time to earn money during the semester. Men who entered the program were also from diverse backgrounds. At first, the number of male students who sought admission to nursing were very few. However, this number gradually increased. I do recall a male student in my clinical group who had difficulty feeling a radial pulse in his patient. He told me he was a truck driver prior to starting the nursing program, and he had lost sensations in his fingertips. He believed it was the result of the callus formation from holding the big steering wheel for many years. For me, it was a challenging, yet a rewarding experience to deal with such diverse groups of students.

Nursing Leadership in Crisis: The Nursing Program Leader was faced with many challenges. As stated previously, a lack of a clear understanding of the needs of the college nursing program by college administrators weighed heavily on the Nursing Leader. The Nursing Program Chair was in a unique role as a result of the expectations placed by RNABC, the program approval body. This requirement was new to the college administrators as nursing was the only program at the College in the 70s, that required approval from an external agency. There was also pressure from the RNABC to develop a curriculum with a theoretical framework. This was stated as a requirement for the RNABC approval of the program.

In addition, there was a difference in what was expected of a Nurse Leader by RNABC and by college administrators. RNABC expected the Nurse Leader to have more decision-making power compared to existing chairs of other programs in the college. In addition, there was a lack of support from doctors and nurses at RIH, for the newly established nursing program at Cariboo College. This was also a burden for the nursing program leader. These challenges were complex, and Nurse Leaders paid a big price.

Nurse Leaders became ill or they quit. The first Nursing Leader was Sylvia Brough. She was hired as Chair of the program, which was not an administrative position. Sylvia became ill. June Goldberg was hired to replace Sylvia. June assumed her role as Chair during a difficult time in the program. A year later, June resigned from the program.

In 1976, a consultant Dorothy Barker was hired to deal with the issues facing the program, and I was released from my teaching responsibilities to work with the consultant. The consultancy time frame was six months. Dorothy Barker compiled a report (The Barker Report) with 26 recommendations. One of the recommendations was that the vacant nursing program chair position be replaced with an administrative position. This recommendation was in direct conflict with the existing college structure. To further complicate the issue, the RNABC had indicated that the nursing department head should be entrusted with the authority to make decisions for the program beyond a faculty position.

Initially, there was resistance from the college administration to act on the recommendations as it came from an external source. Eventually, most of the recommendations were implemented as they were requirements for the RNABC approval of the program. Working with Dorothy Barker was a great experience for me as it gave me the opportunity to have more interactions with college administrators.

Based on the Barker Report recommendations, in 1978 Phyllis Johnson was hired as a Director (an administrative position) of the nursing program. Judy Mogan assumed the role of Chairperson (This position was mandated by the Collective Agreement.). Nursing was the only department in the college with a Director and a Chairperson for a single program. The Faculty Association grieved the position of the Director. It was a difficult time for both the Director and the Chairperson. Judy Mogan resigned from her role of Chairperson. Phyllis Johnson became ill and left on a sick leave. The Nursing Department had four leaders within a period of six years. There was no continuity of leadership.

In 1980, Phyllis returned to her role as the Director after her illness. During her absence, no one replaced the vacant Chairperson position. I was year two coordinator, and Jeanette Furber, who was hired in 1979, was the year one coordinator. Since the faculty was grieving the Director position, the communication between the faculty and the Director was difficult. To ease this situation, Phyllis Johnson created a new position, Program Coordinator, and I was appointed to that position. I assumed that role for one year (1980-1981). "Jeanette Furber recalled that at that time Chinnama carried the Program" (Simpson & Abbott, 2010, p.42). Phyllis became ill again and resigned from her position. The Nursing Department was experiencing a very difficult time.

Together, Jeanette Furber and I organized a retreat for the faculty. Bob Crosby, a consultant from Spokane, Washington, was hired as the facilitator to lead the retreat. The retreat was held at Lac Le Jeune. Crosby interviewed each faculty member individually before meeting them in a large group. Crosby asked each faculty member to describe her "paranoid fantasy" and the "kernel of truth" about what was going on in the nursing department. When we met as a large group, people became quite emotional, and there were a lot of tears. The purpose of the retreat was for faculty to talk about the issues and begin to heal and build relationships.

Phyllis Johnson had resigned before the retreat. James Wright, Educational Vice-principal for the college, acted in her position. The Director's position was advertised and offered to an external candidate. The Faculty had an opportunity to meet the candidate and really liked her. After the retreat, the nursing faculty found out that the administration had cancelled the Director's position in the nursing department and had reverted to the Chairperson model. Jeanette Furber assumed the role of Chairperson. She continued in that role until she resigned from Cariboo College in 1985 (Simpson & Abbott, 2010).

In 1985, I was elected to assume the role of Chairperson, Nursing. I reported to David Cane, the Director of the Sciences and Health Sciences Division. David Cane reported to Jim Wright. The RNABC expressed congratulations to Chinnama Baines who had been appointed Department Chairperson for her "commitment to an administrative style that has proven to be effective. The committee also strongly supported the College's decision to provide a full-time release for a Chairperson" (Simpson & Abbott, 2010, p 84).

In 1986, Jim Wright became the President of Cariboo College, and David Cane assumed the position of Vice-president. Paul Egan, the Chair of the Animal Health Program, assumed the role of the Director of Sciences and Health Sciences Division. Nursing was part of the Health Sciences Division, and I reported to Paul Egan in my role as Chairperson, Nursing.

Leadership in the Nursing Department had been in crisis from the inception of the program. Although I had been a Nursing Leader in my role as a year coordinator and a program coordinator, my leadership role was affirmed by being named the Chairperson of the Nursing Department. My leadership style was based on my belief that, in an educational institution, students are the most important people, and we, the faculty, staff, and administrators were there to serve the students. To this end, I worked collaboratively with the faculty, staff, and administrators in preparing competent graduates.

One of my strengths as a leader was my ability to work collaboratively with others. I used a consultative management style in decision-making where input from faculty was obtained in making departmental decisions. I also believed that the vision for the department should be a shared vision. This meant that I worked with a group of committed nursing faculty in sharing the vision and making sure that the faculty were part of the vision. I also had the courage to share the vision for the department with the college administrators.

I was known as a caring leader as I was able to pay attention to the interests of the group over my own interests. I called this servant leadership. I tried to foster a culture of trust and mutual respect within the Department as I believe that these values were essential in helping others grow professionally. We maintained a nurturing and relationship-oriented culture. My success as a leader was a result of having an amazing group of caring and competent nursing faculty with whom to work. We worked together as a committed and passionate group to prepare competent nursing graduates.

Quest for a Nursing Degree: During my leadership period, there was a national movement in nursing education called "Entry to Practice" (ETP). It meant that a degree in nursing was required to practice as a registered nurse in BC. At this time there was only one four-year degree program in nursing offered in BC. It was through the University of BC (UBC). The University of Victoria (UVIC) had a post basic degree in nursing for diploma prepared RN's.

In 1982, the RNABC, at its annual convention, passed a resolution supporting the Canadian Nursing Association's (CNA) position that by the year 2000, the minimum education requirement for entry into the practice of nursing would be a baccalaureate degree in nursing. In January 1983, the RNABC formed a steering committee to study how RNABC should proceed with its position. I was chosen to Chair this provincial committee as a RNABC Board member. Discussions were taking place across Canada for a baccalaureate degree in nursing as entry to practice. In my role as the Chair of the ETP Committee, my biggest challenge was helping the existing diploma prepared nurses to understand the rationale of the proposed entry level requirements.

Although the position statement was only for the nurses who would enter the profession in the year 2000 and beyond, the diploma-prepared nurses felt threatened that they would be devalued as nurses by not having a degree in nursing, I travelled around the province and met with diploma-prepared nurses. Many of the nurses whom I met expressed their desire to complete a degree in nursing. They also requested that access to degree completion in nursing be made flexible in their community. In 1986, the University of Victoria made it possible for RN's with at least two years of work experience to complete a degree by distance education. A few nurses, who chose to enroll in the UVIC nursing degree by distance education, found it difficult and requested a campus-based program.

In May 1980, the Cariboo College Nursing Department received an inquiry from UBC requesting a "show of interest from community colleges in the BC interior regarding implementation of an external degree program in nursing" (Simpson & Abbott, 2010, p. 57). Based on a survey conducted by Nursing Department, fifty-five nurses in the community expressed interest in pursuing a nursing degree.

"In September 1980, a proposal for a Bachelor of Science in Nursing external degree program for Kamloops was submitted to UBC. It was written by Chinnama Baines, Sharon Frissell, and Dawn Patterson. It responded to the questions posed by UBC: (a) Why should we consider a BSN degree program, and (b) Why should Kamloops be chosen as the site for such a program?" (Simpson & Abbott, 2010, p. 58). In the proposal, several arguments were also presented as to why Kamloops should be a site for the program. I also received a letter of support from the Nursing Program Advisory Committee, signed by the Chair, Dr, H. Murray. However, UBC did not proceed with this endeavour. The Nursing Department continued their efforts toward achieving a nursing degree program in Kamloops.

Access to a Nursing Degree in the Interior of BC: In my role as the Associate Dean, Nursing, I was responsible for leading the access to a nursing degree education initiative in 1989. On July 13, 1988, a meeting was held with Dr. Howard Petch, President of UVIC and the senior administration at Cariboo College. Following this meeting, David Cane, Vice-president; Colin James, Dean of Sciences and Health Sciences and I, in my role as Chairperson of Nursing, visited UVIC and met with Dr. Howard Petch. I do recall during this visit that we were served tea in the President's office using Royal China teacups.

We also met Dr. Carolyn Attridge, Director of Nursing, and Dr. Brian Wharf, Dean at UVIC, to discuss the possibility of offering UVIC's post RN/BSN program at Cariboo College. Following this meeting, a letter of agreement was written between the two institutions, and a proposal with input from the Nursing Department was prepared by David Cane. This was the beginning of the collaboration between Cariboo College and UVIC. As a result, we began to offer UVIC's post RN/BSN program at Cariboo College. We were the first program in BC to initiate such an arrangement with a university. The other colleges "followed suit".

In the Fall of 1989, in support of the initiative of the access to a degree program in BC, the Minister of Advanced Education and Job Training announced that 90 new spaces had been designated for the education of nurses at the baccalaureate level. These spaces were allocated to Cariboo, Malaspina, and Okanagan colleges (Simpson & Abbott, 2010). Accordingly, in 1989, we admitted the first class of Post-RN BSN students at Cariboo College. This was the beginning of the degree program offering at Cariboo College.

The next major initiative was the offering of a four-year generic BSN program. This initiative was also in collaboration with UVIC. The existing diploma program in nursing was phased out. In the fall of 1989, UVIC, Camosun College, Okanagan College, Malaspina College, and Cariboo College formalized a commitment to develop a collaborative, generic, baccalaureate nursing degree. I represented the Cariboo College Nursing Department as a participant in this collaborative group. The partnership was officially named, "The Collaborative Nursing Program in BC". This collaboration grew from the original five partners to 10 partners by 1995.

Most of the colleges offering nursing diploma programs in BC joined this collaborative partnership group.

A Steering Committee, consisting of Program Heads from participating institutions, was formed. I was the Steering Committee Member representing Cariboo College. To develop a generic nursing degree curriculum collaboratively, a curriculum committee was also formed, with two faculty members as representatives from each program. Developing a collaborative curriculum was a major undertaking. Dr. Marcia Hills from UVIC was the Collaborative Curriculum Project Director to move the project forward. Throughout the development period, the Steering Committee and Curriculum Committee met both separately and jointly on a regular basis.

The Collaborative Nursing Curriculum: The new curriculum was innovative and revolutionary. Its philosophy had humanistic, existential, phenomenological, and socially critical influences. Foundational constructs were ways of knowing, personal meaning, time/transitions, and context. The conceptual model for the curriculum had caring as the meta-concept; including people's experiences with health, healing, self, and others, and professional growth as themes (Collaborative Nursing Program in BC, 1992). This whole project was costly, time-consuming, and extremely challenging. Curriculum experts from the USA, Dr. Em Bevis, and Dr. Jan Storch, were brought to UVIC to conduct workshops in curriculum development. Nursing program representatives from colleges in BC were invited to participate in these workshops. A group of nursing faculty and I represented Cariboo College.

As the Nursing faculty and I were busy with the development of the Collaborative Nursing Program at the department level, at the institutional level, Cariboo College was being changed to the University College of the Cariboo (UCC).

## Cariboo College to University College of the Cariboo (UCC)

In 1989, the Minister of Advanced Education announced that Cariboo College would become a university college and would grant its own degrees. In 1991, the name "University College of the Cariboo" (UCC) replaced the existing name of Cariboo College. The concept and the name of "University College" was new in Canada. I was appointed as the Associate Dean, Nursing. This was an administrative position, and I left the Collective Agreement to accept the administrative position. I reported to the Dean of Sciences and Health Sciences Division. I also worked closely with Chairperson of Nursing. Val Mackay-Greer was the first Chairperson with whom I worked. Diane Wells followed Val as the Chair of Nursing when Val's term was completed.

My main responsibility included implementing the four-year BSN program and promoting the BSN program to external agencies, as well as to within UCC and its community. A major strength of my leadership had been my ability to work well with others, the faculty, administrators, and staff at UCC. I had an excellent working relationship with other administrators, Leo Perra, David Cane, Colin James. I worked well with the President and Vice-president, Registrar, and other administrators at Cariboo College and UCC. However, I faced conflicts in my working relationship with the Dean of Health Sciences when I began my role as Associate Dean.

I had reported to the RNABC as part of the approval report in 1987 that the management style most effective for the Nursing Department was one of a consultative management style. Such a management style required full-time faculty to be involved in several committees and meetings. I do recall my Dean questioning me on this management style in the Nursing Department, stating that the "nursing faculty spends far too much time in meetings". It seemed to be that the Dean did not value a consultative management style of leadership, nor did he understand the complexity of leading a Nursing Department with many new initiatives being implemented simultaneously. For example, the diploma program was being phased out, curriculum was being collaboratively developed with many partner institutions in the province, and our department was implementing a post/RN BDN program for RN's. I tried to have a meaningful working relationship with the Dean, but I was faced with ongoing conflicts in my interactions with him.

The Darkest Time in My Career: One main area of conflict between the Dean and I was in offering a BSN degree in nursing. I had been working with the University of Victoria in bringing its post/RN/BSN program to Cariboo College. This initiative was undertaken based on requests from local RN's prepared at the diploma level. There was also a provincial initiative to offer a four-year nursing degree program in the Interior of BC. RNABC was also developing a position statement on, the BSN degree as the requirement for the entry-level practice of nursing.

The Dean had indicated to me that "the access to a degree education initiative" would be a great opportunity to work towards developing a joint degree in Health Sciences rather than a nursing degree. He stated that such a degree would include nursing, respiratory therapy, and medical laboratory programs. This would be a new degree that was not offered in BC or in Canada. I was not in support of a joint health science degree with Nursing as one component.

My vision for the nursing program at Cariboo College was a BSN degree. I believed that a joint health science degree would not be acceptable to RNABC provincially; it would not be acceptable to the CNA nationally; and it would be different from nursing degrees offered by universities across the country. Moreover, only those graduates from an approved nursing program would be qualified to write the RN Examinations. A graduate must pass the RN examination to be licensed to practice nursing.

Based on this dispute and other issues between the Dean and the Nursing Department, the relationship between the Dean and me  deteriorated. He gave me an unsatisfactory evaluation and recommended to the President a non-renewal of my contract if I did not show improvement in my performance. This was a shock to me as I had always received excellent performance evaluations in the past. I had never received an unsatisfactory evaluation in my entire nursing career. I must say that this was the darkest time in my nursing career because, I found it impossible to work with my supervisor. I decided to resign from my position of Associate Dean, Nursing, and I informed the Nursing faculty of my decision.

As I stated before, because I left the Collective Agreement when I accepted the role of Associate Dean, I had no union to protect my rights as an employee at UCC. I was at the mercy of my superiors: The Dean, the Vice-President, and the President. During this time (1992), Val MacKay-Greer was the Chairperson of Nursing, Neil Russel was the Vice-president and Jim Wright was the President. Val and I had worked well together in addressing various issues facing the nursing department and moving the department forward. Val also had difficulty in relating to the Dean in her role as the Chairperson. However, she was protected by the collective agreement. The Dean had only a minimal role in evaluating her.

I had written a letter to the President with a copy to the Vice-president outlining my objection to the Dean's evaluation and recommendation. I believed that I had the support of almost all of the nursing faculty, both full time and part-time.

Nursing Faculty: Caring & Competent: Sharon Simpson, who was one of the original four nursing faculty members, was a competent and a well-respected colleague and a true friend. She was extremely concerned about the future of the nursing program and was quite upset with what had happened. She took a risk in meeting with the President to explain the situation from her perspective. Sharon was well-respected by the college community including the President. She was recognized as an advocate for nursing education. I did not know the details of her conversation with the President, but I believed the President had a better understanding of how difficult it was for me and the department to move forward under the existing arrangement. I was extremely thankful to Sharon and the faculty for their support and belief in me during this difficult time.

In addition, the nursing lab demonstrator and the secretarial staff also supported me in my role. Amy Doi, the lab demonstrator, had written a letter to the President in support of me. A paragraph from Amy's letter stated:

"Chinnama's concern of unresolvable conflict with the Dean and powerlessness in her position has been a concern of our department and I hope there is some measure within our collective power to resolve this situation without her resignation. Chinnama is very highly respected in Nursing circles of administration and education. Without Chinnama, our department and UCC will lose her high profile and esteem among the higher levels of Nursing within BC and nationally".

I was touched by reading such a letter by Amy to the President. .

Vote of Non-confidence: On March 29, 1993, the Dean proposed to restructure the Nursing faculty release time, decrease release time for the Chairperson, and limit funds for the development of a generic BSN program. He also proposed to create a BSN Coordinator. This proposal by the Dean was discussed at a Nursing faculty meeting. The faculty met as a group. I was not part of the group as I was an administrator. The next day, I noticed that a large group of nursing faculty were walking from the Science building to the Clock Tower, the administrative building, to the President's office. I found out later that they had a letter typed with a "motion of non-confidence in the Dean". The letter was signed by most of the nursing faculty. They presented the letter to the President, Jim Wright. One paragraph from the letter read,

"Chinnama has contributed 20 years of service to UCC. Under her guidance the nursing department has become a leader in nursing education both provincially and nationally. In our opinion, her receiving less than a satisfactory evaluation is unjust since our input was not considered. In recent weeks we have become increasingly concerned about Chinnama's well-being in this position and we have watched her struggle to maintain her integrity, and enthusiasm for the job. This department needs stability and strong leadership as we implement our new curriculum. At a time when we are all energized, it is frustrating that Chinnama, who has worked tenaciously to get us to this point, should feel so devalued and de-energized. We feel that given a supportive, collegial work environment Chinnama would continue to provide strong leadership in assuring the realization of department goals".

166

Based on the information received, the President appointed Colin James, Associate Dean of Sciences, to replace the Dean from his administrative role for the nursing department. As a result, all personnel in the Nursing Department would report directly to Colin James. The President also arranged for a mediator to resolve the conflict between the Nursing Department and the Dean. Eventually, the Dean resigned from UCC and went to work elsewhere.

The Nursing Department flourished and moved forward in realizing its vision and goals. I continued in my role as Associate Dean until 1998 when I assumed the role of Dean of the School of Nursing until I retired. I am truly grateful to the nursing faculty and the President Jim Wright for their supportive action. A special thanks to Sharon Simpson for meeting with the President and to Amy Doi for writing a letter to the President on my behalf. Above all, I thank God for His mercy.

Was I discriminated by the Dean? I had pondered this question while I was dealing with the conflict between myself and the Dean. I called this period, "the darkest time in my professional life". I wish to revisit this question. However, it is not my intent to discuss racism or discrimination (it is currently a serious topic of discussion in the US and Canada) but to share my experience in relation to discrimination.

The conflict between myself and the Dean, I believed, was mainly a professional issue. I was seen as someone who was loyal to "Nursing Education" and did not support the Dean's vision for a Health Science degree with nursing as one component, rather my vision of BSN degree. I also believed that the Dean had the "positional power" to give me an unsatisfactory evaluation. I am not sure it was racism or discrimination.

As I understand racism is when one race claims superiority over another race. For example, the White race claims that the White race is superior to the Black race. Whereas discrimination is acting on the racist thought of White superiority.

In my professional life, working in hospitals and in college and university settings, I had the opportunities to advance in my career. Thus, I do not believe I was discriminated against. I had observed that in many contexts I was the only "Brown woman" when I first began my career in Canada. In my passion for advancing in my career, I had not paid attention to racism or discrimination issues. I was just grateful for every opportunity I had and cherished the loving relationships with my friends and colleagues.

However, I was aware of the fact that I had to work harder and prove myself that I am just as competent and worthy as my White colleagues. Many a times I had experienced that in a new setting where nursing colleagues who did not know me tend to ignore me until they found out my credentials and my positional status. I had wondered if it was a result of a stereotype or an unconscious bias that a Brown woman with an accent, might not be as competent as a White person. For me, these incidents were minor compared to all the opportunities I had had in my career and for that I am for ever grateful.

## Nursing Program Initiatives

After all of the drama and conflict was dealt with, I was re-energized to work hard and resumed my work on nursing program initiatives.

As a Nurse Leader in an educational institution, I believed that I was responsible for responding to the needs of the college community. Although I had devoted a large amount of my time in the pursuit of a nursing degree program, I also had the opportunity to offer other programs, based on the needs within the college community. In my roles as Associate Dean and later, as Dean of Nursing, I was passionate and committed in working with the college community and external agencies in initiating and offering relevant programs.

My success was a result of the cooperation and contribution of the Chairperson and the nursing faculty. The three chairpersons that I had worked with were Val MacKay-Greer, Diane Wells, and Penny Heaslip. They were also committed and supportive through good times and tough times. We worked well as a committed group in achieving departmental goals. Based on community needs, the major initiatives implemented were as follows: (Those programs which had a significant impact in the community are presented here.).

168

The RPN/RN Access Program: This program was developed and offered in response to the identified need for re-training RPN's who were laid off in 1983 when the Tranquille School for the Mentally Handicapped was closed. The Tranquille facility was formerly called the Tranquille Sanatorium which was opened in 1907 for people suffering from tuberculosis. A cure for tuberculosis was found in 1943 and in 1958 the Sanatorium was closed. In 1958, the facility was re-opened as the Tranquille School for the Mentally Disabled.

The closure of the Tranquille facility resulted in 60 unemployed psychiatric registered nurses in the Kamloops area. David Cane and I met with these nurses. They were older nurses who had worked in the Tranquille facility for many years. They were educated as "Psychiatric Nurses", a program that was offered in Alberta. They had no experience with working in an acute care hospital, which was the main practice setting for a Registered Nurse. Thus, preparing them to become RN's was a real challenge.

When we met with the psychiatric nurses, I noticed that they were visibly nervous in facing the challenge of being a student again and learning to practice in an acute care setting. Many of them were doubtful if they could do it. They had lots of questions for Dr. David Cane and me. We had to develop a curriculum to prepare them to practice in acute care settings and to pass the RN Licensing examination. It was a unique program in the Province of BC.

With Dean David Cane's support, we developed and offered a 44-week access program for the RPN's to become RN's. Star Mahara coordinated the program. The program was made available to the RPN's who lost their jobs. The RPN's were extremely grateful for the retraining opportunity and continued employment. I must say that it was great working with Dr. David Cane. There was a mutual respect between us for each other's expertise. We graduated a total of 25 RPN's to RN status. They passed the RN examinations and were employed as RN's.

Aboriginal Initiatives: My experience with the Native population in Hazelton gave me the incentive to be involved in offering programs that would benefit the Native people in the Kamloops community. In the 1980's, I participated in the Native Health Careers Access Program. The intent of the program was to increase the number of Indigenous students accessing health related programs including nursing. I do recall how grateful the two Indigenous students were, who took this access program and then successfully completed the RN program at Cariboo College.

Dr. Neil Russell, Vice-President, and I had meetings with the representatives of the Secwepemc Cultural Education Society (SCES) to initiate an agreement between UCC and SCES. In 1997, an agreement was signed. In addition, after the negotiations with the relevant stakeholders, we had formalized a process by which four seats in the BSN program at UCC were designated for Indigenous students. This came into effect in 2002.

LPN Program: This program was developed in response to an identified need by a group of care aides from the UCC community. Some of them approached me individually and informed me about the need for an LPN program. A session was organized and held in the science building for those interested in an LPN program. To my surprise, the Science Auditorium was packed. I heard loudly and clearly the need for an LPN program. Since there was no government funding available for the program, I worked with Norquest College (Alberta) in offering its LPN program by distance education through UCC in 2002. The program was a success story as it is still being offered at TRU in 2020.

Mental Health Specialty Program: In July 1995, one of the city councillors, Sandy Mallory, wrote a letter to the UCC President, A.J Wright, indicating the need for nurses with a mental health specialty to staff the proposed psychiatric care facilities for the Interior of BC. I organized and chaired a meeting in September 1995, with key stakeholders to begin discussion and share information. A task force was formed with nursing faculty representation to begin work on this project. In 1997, an Educational Planning Committee was established under the auspices of Thompson Regional Health Board (TRHB) comprised of representation from both nursing practice and nursing education. The main features of this project were collaboration between nursing practice and

170

nursing education and inter-disciplinary courses for multi-disciplinary practice.

The plan was to develop and implement a post basic specialty program, targeted at nurses, social workers, and other health care workers. This would prepare them to work in the new mental health tertiary care facility in Kamloops. The TRHB and UCC jointly undertook course development in mental health nursing. Funding was granted by the Ministry of Advanced Education Training and Technology (Simpson & Abbott, 2010). Marilyn School and Helena Paivinen assumed the responsibility for developing the courses in the program. We also had input from Dr. Mohammed, a Psychiatrist at RIH. The interdisciplinary courses were developed and offered starting in 2001. These courses were essential in preparing nurses to care for the mentally ill in psychiatric facilities (Hillside Psychiatric Unit).

Nursing Programs in Williams Lake: Williams Lake was located about 285 kilometers north of Kamloops with a population of 12,000 people in the 1990's. Cariboo Memorial Hospital was the main health facility in Williams Lake. Because of a RN shortage in Cariboo Memorial Hospital, the Williams Lake civic politicians and the community lobbied the UCC administration to offer a nursing program in Williams Lake. The nursing department suggested that we offer an LPN/RN Access Program for LPN's to become RN's.

This program was comprised of 48 weeks of full-time study and clinical experience. The LPN's had to complete prerequisite courses in Biology, English, Sociology or Psychology, and Pharmacology with a minimum of a C+ average prior to being admitted to the program. After completion of the pre-requisite courses, they enrolled in a four-month access program and then, the eight-month Cariboo College diploma nursing program. Fifteen students completed the program in 1991. Shona Johansen was the coordinator of the program with Molly Sangster and Debra Palin as instructors (Simson & Abbott, 2010).

The Chairperson at that time became more involved with the Williams Lake program as I took on the responsibility for the nursing degree program. I do recall driving many times from Kamloops to Williams Lake to meet with faculty and students. The Chairperson and faculty of the Nursing Program in Kamloops were also committed to supporting the Williams Lake faculty. I commend the Williams Lake faculty for their enthusiasm and commitment in offering a nursing program in Williams Lake. It was lots of fun and rewarding to work with Shona and the rest of the faculty in Williams Lake.

First Call and Primary Care Projects: This was another unique project to prepare nurses to provide "First Call" service when there were no physicians available in emergency departments. I was fortunate to have a qualified and experienced nurse (Shona Johansen) to teach this program. I worked with Pauline David from the Medical Services Branch of Health Canada who funded the program. The program included advanced nursing skills and knowledge. We needed the cooperation of the emergency physicians in offering the program, and we experienced some resistance from the RIH emergency doctors. However, we were able to graduate a total of 54 nurses in three offerings. These nurses were needed in rural settings and in outpost nursing.

In addition to offering programs based on identified community needs, the nursing faculty and I took part in International Initiatives.

The Nepal Project: The Nepal Project inspired the nursing faculty and students to become involved in international nursing. International education is now a big part of the School of Nursing at TRU.

The Nepal Nursing Initiative was the Rural Health Worker Development Project in Dhulikhel, Nepal. Ivan Somlai from the UCC International department obtained CIDA funding for the project. In the School of Nursing, we established an International Nursing committee to plan and implement the project. The initial committee consisted of Donna Petri, Penny Heaslip, Sharon Simpson, Cheryl Lyall, Karen Abbott, Sue Holmes, and me.

To learn about Nepal and its culture, the committee met with Ivan and his wife Sabita, who was a nurse from Nepal. The main goal of the Nepal project was to provide continuing education to Nepalese nurses on leadership and management. To facilitate this, Penny and I developed a course in Introduction to Leadership and Management in Nursing. In December 1999, Penny and I went to Nepal to interview nurses and introduce the course. This course was later revised and was offered as a three-credit course by distance delivery to nurses in BC. Until 2007, I assumed responsibility for teaching the course.

During our visit, we met with the administrators of the Dhulikhel Hospital, Dr. Ram Shrestha and Dr. Sharma, and the Director of Nursing, Lina, who was a nurse from the Philippines. We visited a government hospital in Kathmandu, and the conditions in the hospital were deplorable. It reminded me of the government hospitals I had seen in India. The hospital was dirty, and the patients who required care seemed to be left alone with the family. Dhulikhel Hospital was a private hospital, and it was clean compared to the government hospital. Patients were much better cared for. In Dhulikhel, we were treated with love and respect by the Nepalese nurses.

A highlight of my visit to Nepal was witnessing the marvel of Mount Everest as the early morning sun shone on it. I wondered how people could climb to the top of such a tall and rugged peak, beautiful and scary at the same time. In Nepal, I could not keep myself warm in bed as there was no central heating, not even a heater in our hotel. It was a four-star hotel. I was given a hot water bottle to keep my feet warm. Nepal was really cold at night.

One day Penny and I walked along a narrow street to see the town of Dhulikhel. We saw two women cutting fresh vegetables from the farm. Penny took a carrot and placed in her mouth. It was not washed, and, sure enough, she had diarrhoea for the next couple of days. A lesson learned was that one should not eat anything raw from the streets of Nepal without washing it.

As part of the project, 12 nurses from the Dhulikhel Hospital came to Kamloops between 2000 and 2003. Two nurses came at a time for a period of four months. They attended classes at UCC and did a practicum at Royal Inland Hospital. The nursing faculty took a special interest in helping these nurses, making sure they had a great experience here. Some nursing faculty went out of their way to help them. I do recall Cheryl Lyall and her husband Rob became very fond of the Nepal nurses and helped them in many ways. For example, they helped the nurses in packing their luggage with gifts from Canada for their return trip to Nepal. Once back in Nepal, these nurses assumed leadership positions in the hospital. They kept in touch with many of the UCC nursing faculty.

Not only did nurses from Nepal come to Kamloops, but also, we sent UCC nursing students to Nepal for a six-week practicum experience. We sent a total of 16 students (four groups consisting of four students per group). An instructor went with each group. Students reported that it was a life-changing experience. The students who went had to raise their own funds. Upon their return from Nepal, the students gave video presentations of their experiences to the UCC community. Many of the faculty and students made lasting friendship with Nepal nurses at Dhulikhel. Dr. Sharma from the Dhulikhel Hospital was able to visit UCC, and the nursing faculty offered a warm welcome to him. We even had a celebration where we hailed Dr. Sharma as an honorary nursing faculty member by decorating him with a nursing cap. Sharon Simpson took on a lead role in hosting Dr. Sharma.

The Nepal exchange was rewarding. Ivan Somlai's expertise in proposal writing helped in obtaining the CIDA funding for the project, and his years of experience working and living in Nepal contributed to the success of the project. His expertise certainly facilitated our travels to Nepal and accommodation in Nepal. I am indeed grateful to Ivan for his commitment to the Nepal project.

The Malaysia Project: Another International project I participated in was the Malaysia project. The plan was to offer the post-RN/BSN program in Malaysia. Cheryl Zawaduk and I were invited to go to Malaysia with Dr. Neil Russell, his wife Ellen, and Cyndi McLeod (Director of International Education at UCC). Hoping the project would become a reality, the agent in Malaysia facilitated the meeting between UCC and the University in Malaysia. We met with nurses at the hospital and administrators at the university. The agent organized meals for us in high-end restaurants.

I do recall that I was not familiar with the Islamic culture in Malaysia, and mistakenly, I tried to shake hands with a male administrator at the University. He told me he would not shake hands with women, instead he just bowed his head. Women wore their hijabs; however, it was acceptable for us to wear our western outfits. Although the project did not become a reality, the visit to Malaysia was educational and enjoyable.

MSN Program: The last program I initiated at UCC before I retired was the MSN program. In the Spring of 2002, an ad hoc committee was formed within the School of Nursing. Joanne Jones chaired this committee. Joanne conducted a survey of nurses in the community and identified 38 nurses interested in starting graduate level study. Dr. Neil Russell had indicated that UCC was ready to offer graduate level programs.

The Nursing Council decided that initially, the graduate program would be offered in collaboration with an established university. So, the committee decided to approach the UBC School of Nursing. I had initial discussions with Dr. Sally Thorne, the Director, about the offering of UBC's MSN program at UCC. The UBC School of Nursing expressed its interest. Sharon Simpson assumed the responsibility for coordinating this initiative at UCC. Although a collaborative MSN program was offered initially, today Thompson Rivers University (TRU) offers its own MSN program. The first graduate program offered at TRU was in Nursing.

On reflection, I was able to lead these major initiatives, because I had the support of a group of committed nursing faculty and UCC administrators who believed in me and valued these nursing initiatives. I would say this with lot of humility realizing that I almost lost my job at one point at UCC.

It is with great joy, humility, and gratitude that I celebrate my successful nursing career. What I valued the most was a group of incredible nursing faculty with whom I had the pleasure of working. They were not only competent but hard-working and highly professional. They also worked collaboratively with nurses in practice settings. They always put the needs of the students first. I was so fortunate to be a part of this great team of nursing faculty. We had fun working together, and we gave our best as a team. I broke the barriers between the administration and faculty in our collaborative efforts, and it worked for us. At times, it was a fine line.

Nursing Faculty, A Fun-Loving Group: Telling the story of my nursing career at Cariboo College / UCC would not be complete without including the fun times we had as a group in the School of Nursing. The nursing faculty, as a group, really knew how to organize and celebrate social events and have fun. I was privileged to be a part of these social events. We, in the School of Nursing, valued social gatherings, with food served, as we strengthened relationships with each other. There were numerous social events. The Nursing faculty also organized social events with nursing students where appropriate. I will select a few as examples.

We, as a group, were exceptional in organizing potluck luncheons and dinners. One such lunch became a signature event during the first Nursing Council meeting in the Fall session of each year. Everyone contributed generously to the lunch. The Faculty had mentioned how much they had enjoyed the baked salmon, my contribution to the lunch each year. We invited the President and / or Vice-President and our secretaries to these special occasions. It was truly a great way to begin the academic year as it provided a forum for everyone to gather over lunch to share and catch-up before the hectic work schedule began.

The group also organized mystery bus tours. I could not keep up with some of the fun activities, for example, having a skinny dip with a plastic bag over you in a cold lake as part the mystery bus tour. The Faculty were good at telling jokes as we travelled in the bus. Some dirty jokes I did not fully understand, but I laughed with everyone else. I was feeling badly for the bus driver, but I guess that he was also having fun.

The Christmas party was a special event celebrated each year at the Accolade. Although, we all contributed, Sharon Simpson and Maria MacIntosh took on the responsibility for organizing it. They dressed up with their fancy aprons and joined the Accolade staff in serving the rest of us a fine meal cooked by the culinary staff. We exchanged gifts by playing a game in which your gift could be taken away by the next in line. We had lots of fun.

The Nursing faculty was generous in opening their homes to host special events in School of Nursing. One event of significance was when Dr. Sharma came from Nepal to visit us at UCC. Sharon Simpson hosted him at her home, and we had a social gathering at her place to honour Dr. Sharma. Those students who visited Nepal were also invited to this event.

We celebrated the special birthdays of colleagues by gathering at Chapters. It was informal and voluntary. Farewell parties were never missed. A core group of nursing faculty made sure that they represented the School of Nursing at events organized by the students. I really appreciated that although I had not been able to attend many of the student events.

I had heard from others in the various departments that the nursing faculty really knew how to have fun at the workplace. These social events helped us to cope with the tension and stress of the workplace. Celebrating special events was a hallmark of us in the School of Nursing.

## Celebration: Awards & Accolades

I have included here the awards and accolades that are worthy of celebration. While my nursing career was filled with opportunities and challenges, there were moments of celebrations with rewards and accolades. These moments were not just handed out to me, but I had to earn them.

 It is with humility and gratitude that I include awards and accolades as causes for celebration. I considered them more as blessings. During my career at Cariboo College / UCC and now TRU, I had the opportunity to participate in several activities which gave me the opportunity to advance professionally and to become a leader. I was involved in nursing professional organizations, both provincially and nationally. A brief outline of my career-related achievements, awards, and accolades follow.

PhD Program Completion: Completing the PhD Program in the latter part of my career, I count as a blessing and an achievement. In 1993-1994, I was able to obtain a one-year educational leave from my work, and I completed my course work through the University of Victoria (UVIC) and the University of British Columbia (UBC). I found these courses provided me with the foundational knowledge to do my research in Nursing Leadership in Rural Hospitals. These courses included: "Quantitative Research Methodology" and "Professional and Business Ethics" from UBC, and "Organizational Change and Leadership", "Collaborative Decision Making and Gender Perspectives", "Qualitative Research Methodology" and "Caring Theory in Action" from UVIC.

After completing my course work, I resumed my fulltime position at UCC which turned out to be the "darkest period in my career" as I have previously indicated. Thus, I was not able to continue my doctoral studies until the year 2000. During this period, I was drawn to the concept of Servant Leadership, a phrase first coined by Robert Greenleaf in 1970.

In Servant Leadership, an individual was a servant first and then a leader. By serving first, one made sure that people's needs were met first. Greenleaf claimed that great leaders were servants first, and leadership was bestowed upon a person who was by nature a servant. He described strong leaders as those who served the needs of their followers by empowering or enabling them to do their work for themselves. This concept was complementary to the concept of "Caring Leadership" that I had been studying. Thus, I chose to pursue the study of Servant Leadership from Greenleaf University in Missouri where I completed my doctoral dissertation.

I completed my doctoral studies in 2003, the year I retired from the university. The doctoral degree was an asset when I worked for the University of Northern BC from 2003 - 2004 and then, during my consultancy work for the professional nursing organization, RNABC (now CRNBC).

RNABC Board Member: Being elected as a member of the RNABC Board was certainly a milestone in my career. I considered the opportunity to serve on the RNABC Board for four years (two terms) as a real honour and a highlight in my career. It was an elected position, and I was a representative of the district where I lived. I had to run a campaign and convince the voters that I was the worthiest candidate from my district.

Being a woman of colour and speaking English with an accent might have been barriers, so I felt I had to work harder as a candidate. I learned a lot during the four years while I was on the Board. I was the spokesperson for the association in my district. In this regard, I had to be available for radio interviews and meet with local MLA's.

As a board member in 1987, I was appointed to the Entry to Practice Committee (ETP) with a mandate to make the baccalaureate degree in nursing a requirement to practice as a RN by the year 2000. I chaired this committee during my term on the board. This was a challenging role for me. Practising diploma nurses, the BC Nurses Union (BCNU), and government officials were all against this initiative. I had to meet with politicians to explain the rationale of this position statement. I also went around and met with practising nurses in the province to clarify their questions. It was important for the nurses to know that registered nurses with a diploma were able to continue their practice as RN's, and there was no requirement for them to obtain a degree. The degree requirement was for those nurses entering the profession in the year 2000 and beyond.

I also promoted this initiative within the Cariboo College community, both with college administrators and nursing faculty. When this initiative became a reality, I was elated. Moreover, at UCC, we were able to offer the degree program in nursing. Diploma nursing programs were replaced with degree programs across Canada. Chairing the ETP committee was rewarding for me. I was passionate about this initiative because I believed in educating nurses at a baccalaureate level for RN practice.

Winning an RNABC Award of Excellence for Nursing Education

RNABC Award of Excellence in Nursing Education (1992): In 1992, I received the RNABC Award of Excellence in Nursing Education. The award was presented to me at the Annual General Meeting at the Hyatt Regency Hotel in Vancouver. Ranjit came to see me receive the award, along with our friends, Brij Sharan and wife Pushpa. I wore a sari for the occasion, and, of course, I was the only woman in a sari. I was truly humbled as some of my colleagues from the Nursing Faculty nominated me for this award. Sharon Simpson and Val MacKay-Greer took the initiative to collect letters of support from people at different levels in the college community. I was grateful for their actions, their professional commitment, and their belief in me.

YMCA/YWCA Woman of Distinction Award: Not only did I receive an Award of Excellence from the RNABC, my nursing students nominated me for the YMCA/YWCA Women of Distinction Award in 1999. One student, Sabrina Gill, took the initiative for the nomination. It was a grand event that was well-organized by the YMCA/YWCA, a non-profit organization. It was stated in the script that I was "a role model for all young Indo-Canadian women". This was humbling to me, and I have tried in my career and in my retirement life to continue to be an example for other young women. I was pleased that a group of Nursing Faculty, and the nursing secretarial staff joined me at the Award ceremony. Below is part of the script printed and distributed by my nominator, Sabrina Gill, nursing student:

"Chinnama Baines' passion has been, as the Associate Dean of School of Nursing, to promote quality and standards in nursing education. As the Associate Dean of School of Nursing at the University College of the Cariboo, Chinnama has influenced many young people by providing a model of caring leadership and quiet yet firm strength. Chinnama is not afraid to voice her opinion, even if it is controversial".

*You are cordially invited to celebrate the retirement of*

**Chinnama Baines**

*Dean, School of Nursing*
*University College of the Cariboo*

Bachelor of Nursing Degree in India (This photo was used for the Retirement Party.)

The last professional celebration was my retirement. I wanted to retire when I was still in good health as I had observed that many people retire and become ill, and before long, they die. I retired in August 31, 2003, at an early age of 61 years. I had worked at Cariboo College/ UCC/ TRU for 29 years. The nursing faculty organized a dinner and a tribute celebration on May 9, 2003. The cafeteria was decorated beautifully with colorful tablecloths and multi-colored fresh tulips. Most of the faculty members wore saris or Indian suits for the occasion. They came and got dressed at my home. I had enough saris and suits for all those who wanted to wear Indian outfits. Molly (my sister) helped dress those who needed help. Thanks to Molly for coming all the way from St. Louis to attend my retirement party.

Although a core group of faculty members organized the event, most faculty members helped with the event. Sharon Simpson was the Master of Ceremonies for the evening. They had sent invitation cards out to most departments at UCC, and I had received best wishes from so many people from throughout the university. I was so humbled by the tributes, the slide presentation, the photo album created by the Nursing Faculty, and a beautifully framed group photo of myself with the Nursing Faculty. A song about me narrated by Cheryl Lyall and sung by the Nursing Faculty to the tune of "It's a Small World After All".

A video clip was played from Ajay, my son, in Norfolk who was unable to attend the party. Everything was a complete surprise to me. I was honoured by the speeches given and gifts presented by many. Anil, my son, gave an amazing speech, and the Nursing Faculty was impressed. Molly, my sister, spoke and told everyone how much I loved nursing. Sheila, Rahul Jasmine, Jolly, and Mathew came from Vancouver to attend the party. John Parks in the Chemistry department took beautiful photographs of the evening activities. Ranjit was by my side all along to celebrate the occasion with me. All in all, it was an unforgettable event. I could not thank the Nursing Faculty enough for such a grand celebration.

While the Nursing Faculty honoured me, so did the administration. A reception was held in the Horticultural Gardens organized by the UCC administration. There were many faculty, staff and administrators who attended this event. Ajay was also able to attend this event with Ranjit. I was touched by the words spoken by Ajay at this event. As part of my legacy, I had the "Chinnama Baines Scholarship for Nursing" established at TRU. This bursary would be awarded every year to a student who demonstrated exemplary leadership qualities.

As I look back at the beginning of the Nursing Program at Cariboo College in 1973 and take a look at how far we have come to 2020, it has been an incredible achievement. When I started at Cariboo College in May 1974, there were 54 students in the program (year 1), a Chairperson, and five instructors. The entire campus consisted of the main building to house the administrative staff, the library, and the classrooms for teaching students. There were two portables to house the instructors who taught at Cariboo College. The College mainly offered university transfer courses. Nursing was the first program to be offered. There were no computers. Two instructors shared one office room. The top administrator was called the Principal. That was Cariboo College.

Today, in 2020, Cariboo College has become the Thompson Rivers University (TRU). The School of Nursing will have a separate building (Nursing and Population Health) scheduled to open in the Fall of 2020. It will have updated nursing lab with new technologies, artificial intelligence, and advanced simulation learning. The School of Nursing has expanded from one diploma nursing program to offering the BSN program, the MSN program, the LPN program, and the Care Aid program. Nursing -related programs are also offered through Open Learning. Tenure track faculty in the School of Nursing are prepared at the PhD level. The Leadership team includes the Dean, the Associate Dean, the Chairperson, and coordinators. We have come a long way.

And so, I must say that I am forever grateful for my successful and rewarding career at TRU. I have so many precious memories and I had so many enriching experiences. I started my career as a nursing instructor and finished as the Dean of the School of Nursing. Who could have predicted that would happen? I am extremely grateful and thank God for all my blessings.

**<u>Life After Retirement</u>**

Once I had retired, I was determined to do what was important to me. I wanted to live a balanced life, so Ranjit and I bought memberships at the Kamloops Y Fitness Center. We began exercising on a regular basis. I also joined two book club groups: one was with women affiliated with our church, and the other one was founded by Sharon Simpson; it was with a group of women from TRU sciences and the Nursing Faculty.

I was able to spend more time at home cooking and gardening. I really enjoyed gardening. I continued my volunteer work with Diabetes Canada, the work I started in 1994 when Ajay was diagnosed with Type 1 diabetes.

After retirement, I did work as a Nursing Education Consultant for five years; one year at the University of Northern BC and four years with the Professional Nursing Organization in BC (CRNBC). As a consultant, I worked on the approval of the RN programs in BC. At UNBC, I was called to provide leadership in the nursing department. I assumed the vacant position of chair on a temporary basis. My role was to some extent

184

to re-build a working relationship within the Nursing Faculty. I visited UNBC every other week and worked closely with the Dean and the Nursing Faculty. I was able to provide collaborative leadership for one year.

The UNBC President nominated me to be member of the newly established provincial committee on the Degree Quality Assessment Board (DQAB). I was pleased to be selected as a committee member. It was a meaningful role as I was involved in assessing new degrees in BC.

Building Our New Home

Laying the Foundation of our new home, 2011

In 2011, I took on the initiative of building a new home. We wanted a house with living space for us at the road level as we did not want to climb stairs. Ranjit had built houses before, so as the main contractor, he assumed the overall responsibility. This was a new experience for me, but

I became passionate about the project and assumed responsibility as a coordinator. My main responsibilities included keeping track of all the necessary paperwork, including bills, invoices, and receipts. Under Ranjit's guidance, I hired subcontractors to build the house. The project was challenging as our lot was very steep.

Initially, we had to build a 13-foot-high retaining wall. By default, the building had to be three stories tall as we wanted our living space to be at the street level. We had the services of a structural engineer and a geo-technical engineer to supervise the construction of the house. We started the project in January 2011. The house was completed a year later in September 2012. We were able to establish and maintain respectful relationships with all those who provided services for us in building our house. The project was a real success in that we now have a comfortable and spacious home with a beautiful view of the Thompson Rivers and the Mount Paul.

A significant challenge I am feeling in my retired life is the awareness that I am getting older. However. I am not the only one getting older; my family and friends are also getting older, and some are suffering with illnesses. I attend more funeral services than ever before. It made me realize that it will be my turn one day, but I do not know when. Thus, I have become more realistic in accepting death as a natural and inevitable process. Yet, I was shaken when three of my close friends died quickly, one after another. Thus, I have become more convinced that our life on this earth is temporary, and we need to be ready to say good-bye at any time. This awareness has become more real during my retired life.

The Loss of Three Great Friends & Colleagues: Although, I was in an administrative position during the latter part of my career, many Nursing Faculty members were my friends and colleagues. Sharon Simpson, Marion Greenwood, and Sai Choo, who were my dear friends, died quickly in a short span of time. How could this happen? How could I lose three of my great friends shortly after they retired? These deaths were tragic events, and they were such a great loss for me personally. I felt compelled to include their deaths as part of my story.

Sharon Simpson was not only a colleague who worked with me for almost 30 years, but also, a genuine friend. We were also close family friends and neighbours. Sharon's son Phillip and my son Ajay were school buddies and best friends. All of us were extremely fond of Sharon and her family. I do not think I have ever found a friend with such a generous heart who would go out of her way to help a friend. She would find time to celebrate with us on our special occasions. Sharon did so much for me in my life and in my nursing career that I am forever grateful to her. During the darkest period in my career, Sharon took a risk and met with the President in support of me. Sharon would take such risks in standing up for justice. She was also the epitome of a person who lived a healthy lifestyle. She had often opened her home for both faculty and students from our workplace.

Sharon had just retired from work after almost 40 years. She was diagnosed with pancreatic cancer, and she was given six months to live. It was hard for me to imagine my friend Sharon would die in six months' time. I struggled to find words to talk to her when I went to see her. Sharon died on Christmas Day in 2013. Our whole family was shaken by her untimely death. I had come to know how frail our life was in this world.

Sharon had completed writing her doctoral dissertation after she was diagnosed with pancreatic cancer. She planned her own funeral service with her family. I was still trying to grasp what it would be like knowing that one had only two months left in life to live. As each day passed by, that individual would be closer to the time of death. The person dying had to say good-bye to all the loved ones left behind.

Whenever I walked by Sharon's house, I had the strange feeling that Sharon was lying in her bed unable to get up and waiting to die. How could this be? The person I knew who was always full of energy and passion for life was dying. Her life was celebrated by hundreds of loved ones at the Calvary Community Church. Cheryl Lyall and Cheryl Zawaduk gave the eulogy. Her husband Terry, and her children Phillip and Sarah spoke briefly. The celebration was fitting for Sharon with beautiful music.

Joyti had never met Sharon but came from Surrey to attend her celebration of life. At that time, she was dating Ajay. I was impressed with Joyti for taking the time to come to Kamloops to attend Sharon's celebration. Joyti is now a good friend of Phillip's partner, Jamie, and Mila is a play mate for Phillip's daughter Adelyn. Thus, goes the circle of life.

Sharon Simpson, (Friend & Colleague) and me

Marion Greenwood also was a colleague and a close family friend. I cherished my friendship with Marion. I really appreciated when Marion came and spent a few days with me when I was distraught as a result of the suicidal death of Jim Bungerz. Marion took care of her health, ate healthy food, exercised, and travelled with her husband Len to many places. It seemed to me that she had been enjoying her retired life.

In the spring of 2016, to my surprise, I received a phone call from Len. (It was Marion who always called me and not Len.). I asked Len why he was calling me, and he said Marion had died. We both started crying as Len explained that they were visiting their daughter Jennifer in Ontario and during dinner, Marion choked on a piece of steak and collapsed. Len and Jennifer tried CPR until the paramedics arrived. None of them were able to revive Marion.

Marion's death made me realize again how fragile life on this earth was!! A healthy woman suddenly collapsed and died. Marion's family held a celebration of her life with her family and close friends. I was thankful that Ajay and Joyti went with me to Vancouver to attend Marion's celebration of life. I was honoured to be asked to say a few words at the event. I had had an opportunity to discuss with Marion her beliefs, and she had told me she was raised believing in the Christian faith. However, she had lost her belief in God. I never had a chance to discuss her reason for losing her belief in God.

Sai Choo had been a colleague and a family friend for over 35 years. In fact, she had been like a family member. When she first came to Kamloops in 1981 as a single woman looking for her first teaching job, I was involved in hiring Sai as a nursing instructor. That was the start of our friendship. Although she left Kamloops to pursue a family life, we kept in touch and visited each other.

Sai and I also shared our faith in Jesus. I kept in touch with Sai, especially regarding her two daughters Sara and Rosie of whom she was extremely proud. When Sai retired from her full-time teaching position at Douglas College three years ago, she found the retired life a difficult transition. She

190

had worked hard all her life, held a full-time job, studied part-time, raised her two daughters, and supported her mom and siblings, which kept her extremely busy. After retiring, she told me she was depressed, getting help from a counsellor, and seeing a psychiatrist. We frequently talked on the phone.

On the evening of March 27, 2017, Sai phoned me to say that she was not doing well, and she was not able to sleep at night. The side effects of the medications that she was taking were seriously affecting her health. Both Ranjit and I talked with Sai. There was an urgency to her conversation. I told Sai to come to Kamloops if she could. She did not reply. The following evening, Brian her husband phoned me and gave me the unexpected and shocking news: "Sai has killed herself". I was in shock, I began to cry, and I asked myself, "What could I have done to prevent this tragic death?" I was broken-hearted with the sudden and unexpected death of Sai.

Sai had such a strong faith in Jesus, and I questioned why she was not able to find solace in her faith. I had no answers. I began to search for answers. Sai had done so much for her family. She brought them to Canada and supported them, but she did not feel appreciated for what she had done. I wondered if she had received more love and support from Brian, would she had killed herself? Still, how could she take her own life? The pain was too much for her to bear, and that broke my heart.

I felt some closure after I attended her memorial service. It was held at the Chinese Evangelical Bible Church in Burnaby. Sai's daughter Rosie was brave in giving the eulogy; she cried and laughed as she talked about her mom. I was also honoured to share my admiration for Sai at the service. I will miss Sai forever as she was a special friend.

I questioned why a Christian who had the assurance of eternity with Christ and believed in the sanctity of life would commit suicide. John Lennox, a Christian Mathematician from Oxford university, stated, a person's mind can be broken just like the body. When it is really broken, we do not how the mind would react. It is not for us to judge the person. This helped me and brought peace to my heart.

Another Death That Shook Me

Jim Bungerz, a veteran of Hitler's army, part of our family

And while I am on the subject of losing colleagues and friends, I would be remiss if I didn't mention Jim Bungerz who lived in the basement of our home on 708 Chaparral Place. He was an elderly gentleman of German origin. During the Second World War, he was a mechanic in Hitler's Army. He was a widower and never had any children. He had a sister in Montreal who came to see him once during the 15 years he lived with us. He had another sister in Vancouver with whom he did not get along and who did not want to see him. He considered us his family. He was very happy living in our house and told us many times how much he appreciated having a loving home in which to live. He loved and adored Ajay and considered himself Ajay's butler. He loved watching Ajay play hockey.

He owned a car and a motorcycle. He was a motorcycle racer in Europe and had won many awards for racing. He was known in Kamloops as the elderly man riding on a Yamaha motorcycle. When he turned 80 years old, he returned his valid driver's license to The Victoria Motor Vehicle Branch. A couple of years later, he registered the motorcycle in my name and gave me the motorcycle as a gift. It sat in our garage for many years and finally, we gave it to Ajay's hockey coach with the Blazers (Mark Habscheid) who lived on a farm in Swift Current. His son loved riding the motorcycle in and around their farm.

Jim was very devoted to me and addressed me as "Madam". He had a respectful friendship with Ranjit. He used to wait for me to come home from work, and he would open the car door for me. We also learned that he was very loyal to Hitler and justified his actions towards the Jews. He seldom talked about the atrocities he had observed and experienced during second world war.

One time our son Anil interviewed Jim and taped the conversation as part of his counselling program at UBC. Jim shared some of his inner secrets with Anil. Jim was not afraid of death; yet, he was afraid of moving into a care facility when he was no longer able to care for himself. He told me that he would like to stay in the basement until he died. I was working full-time, and I told him I would not have time to care for him when he grew older and needed care. He told me again not to send him to a facility for old people. We noticed he was depressed at times, and he felt lonely when we went away for a couple of days.

One Saturday, I was looking for Jim as he was missing from home for a while. I thought he went to the grocery store as he did on weekends. I phoned Save-On Foods to check if he was there. The store people knew who Jim was and told me nobody had seen him that day. I phoned Ranjit to check if Jim was with him and found out that Jim was not with him. I went to the basement again, and I found his bedroom door was open. I went into the back yard calling his name, "Jim" many times. I found him sitting under our cherry tree with his head down, and I noticed a rope around his neck. I cried out loudly, and then, ran upstairs and phoned the 911 line. I was alone in our house. In the meantime, Ranjit arrived. The

193

ambulance came in minutes, took him to the hospital, and Dr. Terry Simpson, his Doctor, certified his death.

An investigator came to our house and interviewed me. He asked me to describe what I knew about Jim's death. I was shaking with fear and grief. On further investigation, he found out that Jim committed suicide by hanging. Jim had left a suicide note on his desk in his bedroom. He had left whatever money he had in the bank to my name.

We, as a family, held a funeral service for him at the Kamloops Funeral Home. Jim was not affiliated with any churches. He told us earlier, that in the event of his death, he wanted his body to be cremated and his ashes to be deposited in the Thompson River. To this day, Ranjit and I wonder what else we could have done to prevent such a tragic event. From the money he left behind, we sent a portion as a money order to his sister in Montreal and to his disabled nephew. For the first time, we heard from his sister in Vancouver after Jim died asking for her share. We sent a money order to her as well. We also donated some funds to the Kamloops Alliance Church.

A year later, Ranjit, Anil, Ajay, and I took Jim's ashes from the funeral home and found a peaceful spot along the Thompson River, said a prayer, and deposited his ashes in the river, as Jim had told us to do. We all missed Jim very much. I have not yet fully recovered from the shock of finding Jim dead in our back yard.

In concluding Part Two, I have realized that my transition from a hectic career-oriented life to a retirement life was emotional. One can never fully prepare for it. Fortunately, I was able to keep myself occupied with family related activities, consulting work, and voluntary work. I have an obligation to help others and participate in taking responsibility for alleviating the suffering around us. I thank God for each day I have. I know that death is inevitable, but I have the hope of an eternal life. This takes me to my Spiritual Journey, Part Three.

# PART THREE: UPHOLDING MY BELIEFS IN A POSTMODERN CULTURE

> *"I would maintain that thanks are the highest form of thought, and that gratitude is happiness doubled by wonder"* – G.K. Chesterton

Part One is my personal journey, which is called, "Mylapra to Hazelton". In Part Two, my focus is on my nursing career, and it is titled "The Hospital to University". Part One and Two relate to my life experiences. Part Three is my spiritual journey, and it is titled "Upholding My Beliefs in a Postmodern Culture". Part Three has taken me on a long and challenging journey of learning. The reasons for my keen interest in understanding and upholding my beliefs in the current postmodern culture are as follows:

In my early years in life, I learned about my Christian faith from my parents and siblings, from reading the Bible, and from participating in church and Sunday School activities. I did not question my faith at the time. However, later in my life, I began to ask questions about what I believed. I had come to realize that I did not have a deeper knowledge or understanding in order to defend my faith and my belief system. For example, one day a very close friend told me: "Chinnama, I can believe that Jesus was crucified, but I cannot believe that He was resurrected". I did not know how to respond meaningfully to my friend's statement. She was seeking evidence for Christ's Resurrection. I could not give her the evidence she was seeking.

In addition, I was raised to believe in Creation and learned that "In the beginning God created the heavens and the earth" (Genesis 1:1). God also created Adam and Eve, the first created humans. I did not learn about evolution in school, nor was there any discussion about it at home. Thus, I could not defend my belief in Creation to someone who believed in evolution. At university, I learned that evolution was scientific (evidence-based) and Creation was a belief system with no scientific evidence. This motivated me to learn more about both Creation and evolution.

When I began my nursing career, I was busy with work and learning to advance myself in the field of nursing education and leadership. I spent little time learning about other fields of study including the foundations of my belief in God. My retired life has provided me time to explore the foundations of my belief in a deeper way than ever before. One thing I learned was that the "well of knowledge" would never run dry, and I hoped to continue learning until I was no longer able to do so.

My Motivation: I was introduced to Postmodern thought in the early 70's while at UBC completing my graduate studies. Some of my colleagues became enchanted by the new philosophical movement of Postmodernism. However, I sensed that this learning was at odds with my Christian beliefs. For example, I learned that in Postmodern thought, there was no absolute truth, but truth was subjective. There was no objective morality. Morality was relative. There was no certainty in life and no destiny.

During my nursing career at Cariboo College / UCC / TRU, I participated in developing the Collaborative Nursing Program (CNP) curriculum in BC. This curriculum was revolutionary in the 90's because of its philosophical foundation and teaching-learning processes. This curriculum originated from a culture of Postmodern thought and included the philosophical foundations of Phenomenology, Feminism, Critical Social Theory, and Humanism. These constructs, as defined in the Collaborative Curriculum Guide (2002), were as follows:

Phenomenology is the understanding of a person's lived experiences. That truth is constructed by a person from his/her lived experiences. Therefore, any objective truth is dismissed, and truth becomes relative to a person's lived experience.

Feminism is viewed as a dynamic and evolving ideology which focuses on equality for women. Feminists assert that women and men have equal rights. They also claim that patriarchal structures are organized to support male characteristics over female traits. Such structures have the potential for the oppression of women. Thus, feminists claim that women have been oppressed, and they call it "patriarchal tyranny". Feminists are committed to making the necessary changes to end patriarchy and the oppression of women.

Critical Social Theory: Critical theorists reject all forms of rationality and assert that knowledge should be used for the emancipation of oppressed people. An assumption in Critical Social Theory is that oppression and domination are embedded in the basic structures and the functions of society. Critical theorists call for a raising of the collective consciousness to liberate and emancipate oppressed people.

Humanism emphasizes the importance of human beings rather than the Divine or any form of religion. Moreover, a belief in an afterlife is rejected. Humanists believe that people are able and can discover their own resources and directions for growth. In addition, people will eventually evolve towards being more aware of their own inner experiences.

I was motivated by the new and innovative teaching-learning processes and strategies. They were presented in the curriculum as the interactions between and among students, clients, practitioners, and faculty. Emphasis was placed on the quality of the interactions between teachers and students. Teachers were seen as expert learners working with students in partnership. Faculty were no more information givers but facilitators and co-learners in the teaching-learning process (Collaborative Curriculum Guide, 2002).

However, the philosophical terms were new constructs to many of us and we probably had only a limited understanding of these constructs and the potential implications for a nursing curriculum. Because my understanding of the above constructs was limited, I unwittingly endorsed them. I have since learned that these constructs were based on a Postmodern ideology. So, I began my search to have a deeper understanding of Postmodernism in relation to my Christian beliefs.

Thus, in Part Three, my focus has been mainly to learn about the current Postmodern culture and to examine my beliefs within this culture and context. Learning my own worldview and the worldviews of those around me has been an integral part of examining belief systems. In exploring and learning worldviews, Murray (2014) has asserted that a worldview must be comprehensive and coherent in answering questions related to the fundamental areas of life. I have learned from Zacharias (2000) that life's big questions are related to the four fundamental areas of life. These fundamental areas are origin, meaning, morality and destiny.

Our worldviews are influenced by concurrent philosophical and intellectual movements. In the 21st century, Postmodernism is identified as the current philosophical and intellectual movement influencing our worldviews. The big questions related to origin, meaning, morality, and destiny have prepared me to defend my beliefs within postmodern culture. So, my focus in Part Three has been to learn about worldviews, postmodern culture, and my beliefs within this culture.

The Following is an outline of Part Three:

**Introducing Postmodernism**

- Neo-Marxist Postmodernism: Our Current Reality?

**Exploring Major Worldviews**

- Atheism and Secular Humanism
- Pantheism and the New Spirituality
- Islam: God Is Great
- Christianity: Gospel of Jesus

**Tenets of Postmodernism and its Impact on My Beliefs**

- Deconstruction of Objective truth
- Identity politics: Individual vs groups
- Critical Theory / Critical Social justice

**Conclusion**

- What Can I Say and What Can I Do?

Learning Sources: I was relieved to know that I could learn all that I needed to know without having to go back to school or take courses. Since the information available on the internet was vast, I had to select authors, books, presentations, and debates to make a manageable number.

I watched several presentations and debates on YouTube and then read relevant books written by Christian apologists, atheists, skeptics, and other scholars. I utilized the time I spent at the gym on a treadmill to listen to YouTube presentations. I found this an efficient and effective way of learning. It was efficient because I was learning while I was exercising. It was like listening to a lecture, then reading relevant books, and finally, writing down what I learned. To me, this learning was enjoyable. I learned from many Christian Apologists, New Atheists, and other scholars. (The Learning Resources are placed in Appendix A.)

A big part of my learning was through asking questions and seeking answers. Growing up in Kerala, although I was encouraged to ask questions at home, I seldom asked questions of my teachers. Students did not ask questions; instead, teachers asked questions and we students were expected to answer their questions. Answers were judged as either right or wrong. We were punished if the answer was wrong. The notion of "truthful answers" was not a familiar term during my school years.

Answering a question with another question was one way to learn the worldview of the questioner. Zacharias emphasised that one must answer the questioner rather than the question.

The following are two examples of how Jesus answered questions by focusing on the questioner:

One example was when Nicodemus asked Jesus: "You are good, what do I need to do to receive eternal life?' (John 3:2). Jesus responded by asking him a question: "Why do you say I am good?'. Why did Jesus answer Nicodemus' question with another question? Was it to find out about his worldview?

Another example was how Jesus answered the question posed by Pontius Pilate during what was considered as the most famous trial in the history of mankind:

"Pilate said to Him, 'Are you the King of Jews'? Jesus answered him, 'Are you speaking for yourself about this, or did others tell you concerning Me'?" (John 18: 33-34). Here again Jesus was focusing on the questioner. Did Jesus use this technique to find out more about the underlying assumptions of Pilate's question and his worldview?

Moreover, questions and answers reflected the worldview of the person asking the question and the one giving the answer. This took me on a path to learn what was a worldview and what were the major worldviews. Since our worldview was a mental model of our reality and there were different worldviews, my next step was to identify the major worldviews. This gave me an opportunity to learn my own worldview. I learned that in the 21st century, Postmodernism was the prevailing intellectual movement that had a significant impact on My worldview. So, I have begun this section with an introduction to Postmodernism.

## Introducing Postmodernism

People almost invariably arrive at their beliefs not on the basis of proof but on the basis of what they find attractive (Author unknown).

In exploring the roots of Postmodernism, I have learned that every few hundred years in Western History, there occurs a transformation that leads to changes in basic values, social and political structure, and changes in worldviews. Thus, we cannot imagine the world in which our grandparents lived, and the worldview held by them. Similarly, for our grandchildren, the world in which their grandparents have lived will be totally strange for them. I know very little about the world in which my grandparents lived in the 1800's. Their worldview would have been quite different from mine. I was born in the mid-20th century; our children were born in the late 20th century; and our grandchildren were born in the early 21st century. I have lived through part of Modernism, and I am currently living in a Postmodern culture in the 21st century.

Our worldviews have been influenced by social, political, economic, and philosophical trends. For example, during the modern era, there was the re-birth of great interest in ideas, arts, and literature, "the enlightenment period or Renaissance". Leonardo de Vinci was called the "Renaissance Man" because he was a great artist and a painter. Modernism was also influenced by the Industrial Revolution that brought progress to the way people lived. For example, the invention of the steam engine by James Watt made transportation more efficient, and various other inventions raised the standard of living for people. Knowledge became more accessible through universal schooling. In addition to technological advancements, there was progress in science and philosophy.

In science, the universal law of gravity and the laws of physics discovered by Isaac Newton laid the foundations for further advancements in the field of science. One example was the invention of nuclear bombs. Philosophical trends included the power of human reason developed by Immanuel Kant, who defined an enlightened human being as one who trusted in his or her own power of reasoning and thinking (Rationalism). Whereas philosopher David Hume held the view that knowledge was derived from sense experiences and is the source of all beliefs (Empiricism). He went onto assert that God's existence and origin of the universe that transcend our human experience were unverifiable and meaningless (Zacharias, 1994).

Another major change during Modernism was the belief in Naturalism and the development of Darwin's Theory of Evolution. In Naturalism, supernatural and spiritual explanations are excluded. Those who believed in Naturalism lost their belief in God.

In the 1900, existential philosophers; Jean-Paul Sartre, Soren Kierkegaard, and Friedrich Nietzsche shared the belief of the existence of the individual as a free and responsible agent. Freedom was considered its predominant value. They asserted that individuals created their own values and determined meaning to their lives. Yet, I have learned that we do not create values but discover them.

People that lived during Modernism also experienced the horrors of World War I (1914-1918), the Russian Revolution (1917) and the devastation of the World War II (1939-1945). The American youth detested the Vietnam War (1955-1975) as fifty thousand lives were lost without winning the war. The lingering Cold War (1947-1991) between Russia and the US was felt in the West without a solution with each super-power being afraid of one another. In addition, the post war depression, the thalidomide tragedy, the widespread environmental pollution, and the tragedies of the atomic bomb attacks on Hiroshima and Nagasaki led people to question the progress of Modernism.

With the advancement in technology, transportation, scientific inventions, philosophical reasoning, and progress, people also began to lose their belief in God. They also became skeptical about scientific advancement, growth in technology, and even logic and reason. Such skepticism and loss of belief in God paved the way for planting the roots of Postmodernism.

Postmodernism has had a huge influence on one's worldview in the 21st century. The impact of Postmodernism has become entrenched in the Western culture since the end of the 20th century, and it invaded every aspect of life with a devastating influence on us, our children, grandchildren, and society at large. Yet, as a philosophy, it is vague and complicated with a set of beliefs that oppose the foundational and traditional beliefs of Western society.

What concerns me the most is that we are living in a Postmodern culture and have been influenced by its ideology in our everyday living; yet we are not aware of its impact on us. For example, Postmodernists have redefined the institution of family and marriage, the constructs of sexuality, gender, and even the nature of the individual. On a broader level, arts, literature, music, and even architecture have been reconstructed. Thus, I began my search for answers.

In searching for answers from psychologists, philosophers, apologists, and scientists, I have learned that I am living in a Postmodern context plagued with unrest and uncertainty, in addition to fear and anxiety. Postmodernism is deeply entrenched in a Neo-Marxist culture. This culture seems to be the reality for us and our future generations. Therefore, I have tried to understand the Postmodern culture in some detail. Following is a brief account based on my understanding of Postmodernism and its impact on me, my family, and others.

# Neo-Marxist Postmodernism: Our Current Reality?

In exploring Postmodernism, I have noted that complex changes are happening so quickly at different levels within Postmodern culture. I have found the analysis of Postmodernism to be diverse and complex to follow. At a deeper level, in Postmodern ideology, there is no objective truth, but truth is relative, which means that each person constructs his or her own truth from subjective experiences.

Moreover, inherent in this ideology, I have been introduced to a set of new terminologies, for example, unconscious bias, identity politics, white privilege, white fragility, microaggression, diversity, inclusion, equity, intersectionality, critical race theory, and critical social justice. The definitions of these terminologies are continuously evolving while more terminologies are being added. To begin, I will explore: How Postmodernism has become rooted in North America?

As a philosophical movement, Postmodernism was initiated in North America mainly by French intellectuals, Jacques Derrida, Michelle Fuoco, and Jean-Francois Lyotard, who were Marxist sympathizers. They claimed that there was an accumulation of power and domination in Modernism. They accused the Modernists of using power and domination to control those without or with less power. This idea originated from Marxist philosophy. Karl Marx, a German philosopher, and an economist introduced the class division. He divided people mainly into two classes: the rich and the poor. This was a new way of thinking about people.

Since Postmodernism is described as an ideology originating from the Marxist philosophy, its tenets are rooted in Marxism with its underlying philosophy of Socialism and Communism. Thus, Socialism, Communism, and Marxism form the basis for the new version of neo-Marxist / postmodernism. The Marxist theory is contained in a political pamphlet written by Karl Marx and Friedrich Engels, called "The Communist Manifesto" (1848). It has been recognized as one of the world's most influential political manuscripts.

The "Communist Manifesto" explains the goals of Communism, Economic Socialism, and the underlying theory of Marxism. Its strongest claim is that "ideas have been used to dominate people". This ideological domination of a society is called Hegemony. I do recall that Hegemony as a construct was being included in the newly developed Collaborative Nursing Curriculum with the intent to critique the power differential among health care workers, for example, the power of doctors over nurses.

However, Marx's ultimate goal was to change Capitalism to Communism / Socialism. Marx posited that money and ownership should be available to everyone, and they should get what they needed to live and in turn, work as much as they could. All manufacturing products should be equally owned by members of the State. This sounded great in theory, but it was disastrous in practice because those who worked hard became resentful of those who did not work hard. Yet, they all received similar rewards. This would build up resentment in those who worked hard. Those who became resentful also became bitter in their lives.

Communism removed the incentive to work hard. In Communism, there was no private property ownership, and all property was communally owned. Each person received a portion based on need. The state decided and controlled all aspects of economic production and provided citizens with the basic necessities of life (food, housing, medical care, and education).

In Marxist theory, Communism dealt with the Political component, and Socialism dealt with the Economic aspect. In this Economic Socialism, people were divided into two groups; those who owned the land, (the bourgeoisie: the rich) and those who were the working-class peasants (the proletariat: the poor). At the core of Socialism was the philosophy of a socially owned economy and the State ownership of wealth. This meant replacing private ownership with collective ownership of the means of production. Social ownership happened at the expense of private ownership by using coercion in taking away the right to private ownership. In fact, it was stealing, as private owners did not have the right to keep what once belonged to them.

Marxists also accused the Capitalists that they exploited the poor in creating their wealth. Whereas Socialism presented a utopian vision of bringing about equality of resources. People were drawn to this utopian vision. This vision was based on the premise of achieving equality of wealth by taking it from the rich and distributing it to the poor. It sounded appealing in theory, but it was a disaster in practice. Marx was expecting a revolution to occur whereby the working class would revolt and overthrow Capitalism. However, that did not happen. As a result, the Postmodern French philosophers substituted the component of Economy in Socialism with Power.

Postmodernists asserted that in order to sustain power, structures of hierarchy should be maintained. They claimed that men held primary power in a hierarchy, and this was called patriarchy. They also claimed that power was manifested in hierarchical organizations when those on top of a hierarchy oppressed those below. Postmodernists also claimed that women were usually lower in a hierarchy. Thus, they were oppressed by men who were higher on the hierarchy. Postmodernists, including radical feminists, were extremely critical of white men, accused them as the oppressors, and called it "patriarchal tyranny". This ideology became entrenched in feminism and became popular among feminist nurse theorists as well.

Lenin's Russia was the world's first socialist state, founded in 1917. Stalin inherited it from Lenin. Socialism collapsed in Russia after Stalin's regime tortured and killed over 15 million of his own people, of which over four million died of starvation. A detailed account of the suffering and deaths in Russian concentration camps was narrated in the book, "Gulag Archipelago" by Aleksandr Solzhenitsyn (1973). In addition, George Orwell, in his book, "The Road to Wigan Pier" (2001), also outlined the failures of Socialism in the UK. It helped me to understand the worldview of Socialists and the hatred they had for those who owned private property or had enough food to eat as a result of their hard work. China retained Communism, the political component of Marxism, and got rid of Socialism, the economic component. Thus, China became a dictatorial and economic superpower.

It is hard to believe that a Communist party was born in 1939 in the State of Kerala in India where I was raised. In 1957, the party was elected to form a Communist government, the first elected Communist party in the world. The current ruling party in Kerala is also Communist. This meant that I grew up in the Communist State of Kerala. The Indian central government had imposed restrictions on what type of Communist ideologies were practised in Kerala, thus, it had a modified version of Communism. As a result, the core ideology of the equity policy in relation to the economy had not been a viable practice in Kerala. I was exposed to both Communism and Socialism in my growing-up years.

My Experience with Socialist /Communist Ideology:  Growing up in a modified version of Communism in Kerala and a milder version of Socialism in India, I remember the following experiences: (1) Our family was given a ration card to buy household commodities such as rice, sugar, and oil. Each family was allocated a certain amount each week, and the ration card qualified us to buy these everyday essentials. (2) We stood in long lines in front of government offices to get jobs done by government officials, for example, state banks and land title offices. People lined up, forming long queues, and then, suddenly, someone would jump the queue. We knew that he/she had bribed a government official to get ahead of the queue. In fact, bribery was the norm in India. (3) We waited long years to get household services, for example, telephone and electrical services. It was a seven-year wait to get a telephone hook-up in our house. I am glad this has changed in India. Since the early 1990's, Socialism has been gradually replaced by a market-based economy.

Canada (now my country) is a Capitalist country since its inception in1867, and its economy is driven by a free market and private enterprise. However, a Socialist movement began in 1898 in Vancouver, and the Communist party of Canada was created in Ontario in 1921 by a group of Marxist activists. Now, the New Democratic Party (NDP), a federal political party, adheres to social democracy. Although, the NDP has governed certain provinces and has become an official opposition, it has not formed a government federally. However, Canada has socialized health care and social assistance or welfare programs including Old Age Security and Employment Insurance.

More recently, Postmodernists in the West have introduced a new set of theories with unique terminologies. These theories are foundational and are integral components of Postmodern ideology. The underlying ideology of these theories have become entrenched in academic institutions, the media, in Hollywood and its productions, and more recently, in professional sports. So, I set out to understand these new sets of terminologies and tenets of Postmodernism. The more I have tried to keep up with the emerging theories and their terminologies, the more I have become disillusioned. Yet, I believe it is important for me to learn its impact on my belief system.

In my quest for understanding Postmodernism, I have explored the worldviews and the fundamental areas in life. It provided background knowledge for me to better understand the complicated and vague Postmodern philosophical movement. In learning about worldviews, my main source was Murray's book, "Grand Central Question: Answering the Critical Concerns of the Major Worldviews" (2014).

## Exploring Major Worldviews

What is a worldview? Growing up I was not familiar with the term worldview. Thus, I did not have a concept of my own worldview. Later in my life, when I was at university, I learned that a worldview was a broad category of ideas and beliefs. It was one's conception of the world or reality, a lens through which one viewed the world. It was a mental model of our reality. Our worldview has helped us to understand the world around us, and how we have made judgments about others. For example, a worldview of Atheism was a belief that God did not exist; whereas a worldview of Theism was the belief that God did exist. Thus, Atheists and Theists held opposing worldviews in relation to the existence of God.

Further, I learned that my worldview was not my physical reality (that was science). It was the metaphysical (beyond the realm of science), philosophical, and ideological reality of the world. I learned that my worldview governed me in how I lived, what I lived for, and what I appreciated and rejected. I found out my worldview was not explicit. I was not able to articulate it. I understood that my worldview might change as I grew, matured, increased my knowledge, and adapted to a new culture. Furthermore, in order to understand the culture of a society, I needed to understand the worldviews held by that culture.

Murray's (2014) assertion of worldviews shed more light into my analysis of worldviews. Murray stated that for a belief system to qualify as a worldview, it must be comprehensive and coherent in addressing the deep questions in life related to the four fundamental areas: origin, meaning, morality, and destiny. My worldview was foundational in how I would answer the deep questions in life. Thus, worldviews and answers to the four fundamental areas became the cornerstone for my understanding of Postmodernism and my belief system.

I will first explore my own worldview.

My Worldview: Growing up, I did not formulate a conception of my worldview. Once I grew up, I began to ask questions of the world around me. My spiritual reality was that there is a God, and Jesus is the Son of God. I believe that Jesus died for my sins on the Cross, and He rose from His death on the third day. I also believe that this universe was created by God.

I had figured that people around me, for example, many of my friends in school, had different realities than mine because they believed in different religions. As friends, we did not discuss our beliefs, but we accepted one another for whom we were. Although I had certain beliefs, I did not have a deeper understanding of my conception of the universe and God.

The Postmodern society in which we live today does not hold a specific worldview, but it is a pluralistic culture with a collision of multiple worldviews. In a context with many competing worldviews, how do we know which worldview is true?

What are the Major Worldviews? Murray (2014) has identified four major worldviews. They are: (1) Naturalistic Atheism and Secular Humanism; (2) Eastern Religions and Pantheism; (3) Islam; and (4) Christianity. Others have identified each major religion as a separate worldview, in addition to Atheism and Humanism. Abdu Murray has concluded in his book that the Gospel of Jesus does answer life's deep questions related to four fundamental areas, coherently. I have chosen to discuss the following four worldviews based on Abdu Murray's conclusions with minor modifications.

These Four Major Worldviews are:

- Atheism and Secular Humanism
- Pantheism and New Spirituality
- Islam: God Is Great
- Christianity: The Gospel of Jesus

Atheism, Pantheism, and Monotheism are the three broad categories of belief systems. Again, under each of these categories, I have taken the liberty to focus on the most significant worldviews that are relevant in the 21st century. For example, in Atheism, the Secular Humanists are an active group that is growing fast. Similarly, in Pantheism, the movement of New Spirituality is spreading in the Western World. Under Monotheism, Islam and Christianity are the two predominant worldviews as these two represent the majority of Monotheists.

Judaism is also a monotheistic worldview. The Old Testament in the Bible gives the foundational beliefs for Judaism. The difference between Judaism and Christianity is Jesus. The Jews are still waiting for the Messiah to come as the King of Jews. For Christians, The Messiah is Jesus.

Following is an overview of these four worldviews about which I have learned, mainly from the writings of the Apologists and the new Atheists. Since Apologists Zacharias and Murray have confirmed that the worldview of the Gospel of Jesus answers the big questions related to origin, meaning, morality, and destiny. Therefore, questions related to these four fundamental areas are discussed under the Gospel of Jesus.

# Worldview (1): Atheism and Secular Humanism

Is Secular Humanism the New Face of Atheism? In my growing up years, I had heard of Atheism, but not Secular Humanism. Secular Humanism has been gaining popularity in recent years. It places an emphasis on the human being over the divine while denying any religious or spiritual basis to one's belief system. The Atheistic worldview assumes that only natural laws and forces operate in the world as opposed to any divine or spiritual laws. Thus, Atheism is also called Naturalism. If a person is a Naturalist, all explanations must be from the bottom up. There is no top-down explanation as there is no divine. Similarly, in an Atheistic worldview, mass and energy are the ultimate realities. This is called Materialism, another way of describing Atheism.

I have learned that in Atheism, there is no objective truth, no absolutes, no morality, no meaning in life, no hope, and no justice, rather there is a world with no boundaries. The universe is everything, and only science can describe the world. Even the psychological and spiritual dimensions of experiences in life are rejected. Materialism has been a dominant view among Atheists, and they affirm that Materialism is the best way to explain the ultimate reality (Turek, 2014).

Secular Humanism is a softer version of Atheism in that it values human dignity without a belief in God. Deep down in its core beliefs, both Atheism and Secular Humanism deny the existence of God and condemn all religions. During the 20th century, Atheists in Western societies have become more active and have begun to form as an organized group. They are called the Secular Humanists. They assert that humanity is capable of practising morality without divine intervention. Its goal is self-fulfillment, and it rejects any religious dogma. They demand that all religious expressions must be conducted in private.

Although Secular Humanists believe in the inherent dignity and purpose of being human, they seem to struggle in justifying their beliefs without a transcendent being. I have observed that the Secular Humanists and the new Atheists differ somewhat from the Atheists of the past. So, I tried to find out more about how the New Atheistic Movement differ from Atheism of the past.

The Atheism of the Past? I knew very little about the history of Atheism and how it originated. I learned that although Atheism originated in the fifth century BC, it did not emerge as a belief system until the AD 16th century, when philosophers began to question the existence of God. For example, in Scotland, philosopher David Hume (1711-1776) wrote: "God's existence, the origin of the world, and other subjects that transcend our finite human experience are unverifiable and meaningless" (Zacharias, 1994, p 198). Hume's writings influenced many in Scotland to reject the existence of God. During the French revolution (1790's), Hume's writing played a significant role. For example, the secular symbols in France replaced the cross, France's Christian calendar was abolished, monasteries, churches and convents were seized, and monks and nuns were expelled.

I was concerned when I learned about the 19th century philosopher, Karl Marx (1818-1883), an Atheistic political economist, who condemned religion as the "opiate of the masses" and ridiculed those who turned to religion for the relief of suffering. Karl Marx wrote the "Communist Manifesto", a document that paved the way for establishing Communist regimes.

Similarly, the German genius, Friedrich Nietzsche (1848-1900), condemned Christianity for its weak value system and rejected it for that very reason. He went on to claim that "God is dead, and we have killed Him". Although Nietzsche condemned Christianity and coined the phrase of "God is dead", he said it with fear. He questioned if God was dead, who would replace Him? He went on to predict that because God was dead, millions would die in the 20th century. Nietzsche's prediction proved to be true in that more people died in the 20th century alone than in the previous 19 centuries put together.

The New Atheistic Movement: In the 20th century, Atheists began to organize themselves as a voice for the Atheistic group. I was dismayed to learn that the first proclaimed Atheist in the West was a woman named

Madalyn Murray O'Hair. She was the president of the American Atheists Organization which was founded in the 1960's. She was a militant Atheist, a radical feminist, and an activist. The goal of the American Atheists in the 60's was to fight for the separation of the church from the state and to argue for the cessation of prayers and the reading of the Bible in schools. Atheists asserted that praying and reading the Bible in schools was unconstitutional. The American Atheists succeeded in stopping the prayers and the reading of the Bible in schools.

In the 21st century, we are witnessing the emergence of a new breed of Atheists, and we call this a "New Atheists Movement". They are different from the Atheists of the past in that they ridicule Theists and treat them as intellectually inferior. The "four horsemen" among these atheists are Richard Dawkins, Sam Harris, Daniel Dennett, and the late Christopher Hitchens. These New Atheists consider Theists as not intelligent enough because of their belief in a supernatural God.

In recent years, in academic settings, those who believe in God and question Darwin's theory of evolution are faced with difficulties in getting tenure tract positions and promotions. Similarly, graduate students who are theists have also faced difficulties with their atheist professors. Dawkins has gone so far as to ridicule theists in public for believing in God.

An example of ridiculing those who believed in God was when Dawkins was at a conference. Dawkins told his devotees to mock Theists publicly during a "Reason Rally" gathering of approximately ten thousand Atheists and Agnostics in Washington, DC, held on March 24th, 2012. He told his followers to: "Mock them! Ridicule them in public! Don't fall for the convention that we're all too polite to talk about religion. Religion is not off the table. Religion is not off limits. Religion makes specific claims about the universe which need to be substantiated and need to be challenged and, if necessary, need to be ridiculed with contempt" (Murray, 2014, p 50-51).

Dawkins, who was known as the Guru of the New Atheists, stated that using ridicule was one way to treat those who were religious and those who believed in God. Dawkins wanted to deny admission to Oxford University for those who believed in a Creator. I am glad to note that the motto of the Oxford University is: "The Lord is my light". I have been disheartened by Dawkins' behaviour towards those who believe in God.

The agenda of the New Atheists is different from that of the Atheists in the 60's and 70's. New Atheists want to attack Christianity and other religions wherever they are practised. They condemn all religions and assert that religion is causing violence in the world. The late Christopher Hitchens wrote a book, "God is not Great, Religion Poisons Everything" (2008), blaming religions for the atrocities committed in this world. Dawkins has claimed that teaching children religion is "child abuse". Harris also has made an extraordinary claim that some beliefs are so dangerous that it might be ethical to kill people for believing them. He made this claim in the context that the "West is in a war of ideas with radical Muslims who carry out their beliefs in the form of violence" (Murray, 2014, p.51).

Richard Dawkins asserted that his view on people's belief in God was that faith and science were deeply opposed to each other, and faith suspended critical thinking. His stance on miracles was that it was a violation of the laws of physics and nature. He claimed that God was a delusion, and he defined delusion as a psychiatric disorder. Based on this belief, Dawkins published a book: "The God Delusion" (2006). Dawkins asserted that belief in a personal God qualifies as a delusion. Whereas the American Psychological Association defined delusion as an extreme deviation in thought content, fixed false beliefs, despite evidence.

Dawkins depicted God as evil and called Him a "moral monster". He also denied good and evil as absolute categories. I wondered if Dawkins realized that while he was denying evil and at the same time accusing God as evil, he was being contradictory. I had great concerns regarding Dawkins' assertions, as Dawkins was considered the Guru of the New Atheists and had a significant influence on young people in universities.

Another prominent member of the New Atheists, Sam Harris, contended that those who believed in God should not qualify for a job in a public office. Atheism appealed to the young people of today because, if they did not believe in God, they were free to do as they pleased. It was in keeping with the Russian philosopher, Dostoyevsky, who said that if there was no God, everything would be permissible.

In addition to the many false claims made by the New Atheists against those who believed in God, they also accused Theists as terrorists and murderers. For example, Atheists claimed that the attack on the World Trade Center was an attack by terrorists as a result of religious beliefs. Although the attacks on the Twin Towers were carried out by Islamic militants, Atheists suggested that Christian religion also had a history of violence and killing. They used the examples of the "Spanish Inquisition" and the "Salem Witch Trials".

I have learned that during the Spanish Inquisition that lasted for 200 years, a total number of people killed were 32,000. During the Salem Witch Trials that lasted for 400 years, the total number killed was just 25 people. If we compared these numbers to the killings that occurred under the Atheists' regimes in the 20th century alone, the numbers were in the millions in countries, such as, Russia, China, and Cambodia.

I have also noted that the denial of the existence of God and the contempt for any religious affiliation is growing steadily. Large numbers of young people in colleges and universities are giving up their beliefs in God. They claim that there is not enough scientific evidence to prove the existence of God. In addition, evolution is now taught in schools in a way that solves the problem of God's existence. Moreover, Secular Humanism, with its emphasis on human flourishing, is spreading. Most significantly, the New Atheist movement is spreading fast in the West.

I am extremely grateful that I have had an opportunity to learn the atheistic worldview and the New Atheistic Movement. It gives me some level of confidence in dialoguing about Creation and evolution with someone who does not believe in God. In the past I had avoided talking about both Creation and evolution.

## Worldview (2): Pantheism and New Spirituality

The next worldview that I explored was Pantheism and the New Spirituality. I was intrigued to learn that the core beliefs of the New Spirituality were borrowed mainly from Hinduism and Buddhism. Some Christian beliefs were also mimicked in the New Spirituality.

Being born and raised in India, I grew up with many Hindu friends who held beliefs in many gods (Pantheism); whereas a belief in one God is called Monotheism. The religions of Islam, Judaism, and Christianity are Monotheistic, and the Eastern religion of Hinduism is Pantheistic.

Although I was exposed to Pantheism, my knowledge was limited in relation to Pantheistic beliefs. Murray (2014) asserted that Pantheism was an umbrella worldview that covered a wide variety of religious or spiritual expressions. As the word "pan" meant "all" and the word "Theos" meant God, in its core belief, "All is one, and All is God". Because all is God, the distinction between God and human was an illusion. Although Pantheism was Eastern in its origin, and Hinduism was the major religion of India, its belief system spread widely in the West. For example, Scientology was a new version of the Pantheistic belief system, and the New Spirituality was the counterpart of Hinduism.

In learning about Eastern religions, I must say that I have not read the original sacred books of these religions. Hinduism has several scriptures. The Vedas and Upanishads are considered its sacred books. They are written in Sanskrit (the ancient and primary language of Hinduism). It is a very difficult language to learn. I attended a Sanskrit school from grades six to nine. The subject of Sanskrit was very hard for me to learn. So, I left the school after grade nine. However, my brother (Thomas) also attended the same school for the last two years of his high school. All the students in the final year who wrote the Provincial Examination (SSLC) failed. It made breaking news in Kerala: "Zero pass at Sanskrit High School in SSLC Examination in 1955".

Is the New Spirituality Spreading Fast in North America? I was surprised to learn that the New Spirituality was the Western counterpart of Eastern Pantheism and has become a popular belief system in North America.

Hinduism was the largest Pantheistic religion and has its roots in India. Buddhism, which originated from Hinduism, did not continue as a Pantheistic belief system. Similarly, Sikhism also originated from Hinduism, but it identified its belief as a Monotheistic religion.

My interest in the New Spirituality began when a friend of mine said to me one day during a conversation; "I am not into religion anymore. I am spiritual now". This came as a surprise to me as I was under the impression that she was a Christian. Moreover, it was not clear to me what she really meant by being spiritual. I was not informed about the doctrines of the New Spirituality.

I have learned that the New Spirituality subscribes to a Pantheistic philosophy. Murray (2014) asserts that the Pantheistic worldview seems to be quite large, consisting of over 60 million people in the world now with Hindus, Buddhists, and those who believe in the New Spirituality. The book by Ravi Zacharias, "Why Jesus: Rediscovering His Truth in an Age of Mass Marketed Spirituality" (2012) is my main source of information in discussing the New Spirituality.

The spread of Hinduism and the New Spirituality in the West began as early as the beginning of 1900 with the arrival of the three Gurus from India.

The arrival of the three Gurus from India opened the door for planting the seeds of the New Spirituality in America. The first Guru, Swamy Vivekananda, came to the West as early as 1893. He attended the Parliament of World Religions in Chicago. He was brilliant and, when he got an opportunity, he got up and addressed the audience, although he was not an invited guest speaker. The audience applauded and welcomed Swamy Vivekananda to the West. The universities opened their doors wide for Dr. Vivekananda. He was fluent in English. The West embraced his Eastern philosophy.

The second Guru, Yogananda, came to the West in 1920. He was charming and eloquent. He wore a cross around his neck. He taught a blend of religious teaching called Kriya Yoga, "the yoga of action". Yogananda appealed to the West with a plea for blending the philosophy

216

of the East with the West. He believed in the divinity within each person, the core belief of the Hindu religion.

Maharishi Mahesh Yogi was the third Guru, who came to the US in 1968, with his Transcendental Meditation (TM) technique. His meditation was embraced by celebrities, for example, the Beatles. He packaged his philosophy and the TM for the West. By the 1970's, more than five million people were said to be practising TM in the West. By the 80's, he had established schools across the world, built a multi-million-dollar business empire, and sold Ayurvedic medicine and cosmetics developed with the funds collected from donations. He charged a fee of $2,500 per person to learn TM. In 2002, Maharishi announced that with $1 billion, he could train forty thousand expert meditators and combat terrorism and war. He also had the plan that with $10 trillion he could end poverty by sponsoring organic farming in poor countries. He was ridiculed for these unrealistic ideas (Zacharias, 2012).

I was curious to learn that the well-known television personality in the US, Deepak Chopra, has become a household name in the New Spirituality and a leader in Maharishi Mahesh Yogi's TM and Ayurvedic medicine. Similarly, television celebrity Oprah Winfrey is also committed to the New Spirituality and has made it look glamorous in the West. I was also dismayed to learn about how generous the people in the West were in welcoming the Gurus from the East, following their beliefs, and making them rich and famous, as well as, helping them to spread their religious ideology in the West.

I was also reminded of how one of Christ's disciples, St. Thomas, who went to Southern India in 52 A.D. and preached the Gospel of Jesus, was killed in Chennai in 72 A.D. Since then, missionaries have gone to various parts of India to work among the poorest and the outcasts, barely having enough money for daily bread. Many of them were persecuted, and some were killed in India. What a contrast in how the West welcomed Eastern spiritualists and made them millionaires, while the missionaries, who went from the West to the East, lived in poverty and suffered persecution.

The three Gurus planted the seeds of the New Spirituality and it spread across North America. The West was ready for a change and ready to embrace something new, the New Spirituality. The mixing of beliefs from Hinduism, Buddhism, and Christianity made beliefs in the New Spirituality contradictory. For example, belief in God as the universe was contradicting the Christian belief of God as the Creator of the universe.

The New Spirituality included the Hindu beliefs of karma, moksha (nirvana) re-incarnation and ahimsa (non-violence). In addition, it included the Four Noble Truths from Buddhism. Gautama Buddha was born a Hindu, but he rejected Hinduism, and founded Buddhism. It confirmed to me that beliefs in these two religions were different.

An assumption of the New Spirituality is that "God is All, and All is God", meaning God is in everything. This is Pantheism. There is no distinctiveness in God, and no separation between God and His creation. God is also seen as a force, and the force can be good or bad. For example, in the "Star Wars" movies, God is depicted as both a good force and an evil force. The producer of "Star Wars" is a New Spiritualist.

Another assumption in the New Spirituality is that humanity is divine with unlimited potential. It is based on the premise that "God is all, and all is God," and "God is in man and man is a part of divinity". If humanity is divine, there is no sin, and then, there is no need for atonement and forgiveness. Man must develop cosmic consciousness and aim towards enlightenment. The goal of enlightenment is to abandon our ego so that we have a better chance to merge with the universal mind.

Zacharias compares the New Spirituality to a "spiritual supermarket", in that we can choose what we like or want and follow whatever path we want based on what is most appealing to us. The analogy of the spiritual supermarket includes beliefs in evolution, ecology, feminism, mysticism, channelling, the practice of yoga, meditation, and globalism etc.

Belief in evolution is based on the notion of life starting from the primitive and moving towards the complex. Ecology is placing emphasis on environmentalism. Thus, the Green Peace Movement, as well as the concept of Mother Earth and nature-centered practices, are emphasized in the New Spirituality. Globalism or Ecumenicism holds the assumption that all religions lead to God. Feminism in the New Spirituality is the notion of women being superior to men, and they are considered goddesses. Mysticism is defined as having an emotional and non-reasoning experience with God or a spiritual reality.

Those practicing a new form of yoga and meditation treat this as an experience with the divine by whispering the word "mantra" to get in touch with one's self. The practice of meditation is to become one with the universe, to empty one's mind and to be open to anything. Channelling is the practice of contacting and communicating with the spirits of the deceased for direction and guidance. Satanism is worshipping Satan and having a belief in witchcraft. These practices are also part of the New Spirituality. It identifies Lucifer as the New Age Master. Worshipping idols is also a common practice in the New Spirituality.

### Worldview (3) Islam: "God is Great"

Although, I had a Quran (English translation) at home, I must admit that I learned about Islam through Nabeel Qureshi, a devout Muslim by listening to him on YouTube and reading his book: "Seeking Allah, Finding Jesus" (2014). The book was a New York Times best seller, and it was my main source for understanding the religion of Islam from the perspective of a devout Muslim. Nabeel's ardent faith in Islam, his life as a devout Muslim, and his conversion to Christianity through a lengthy and painful process gave me an inside source for learning about Islam.

Growing up in Kerala, I had Muslim friends in school. I was familiar with Muslims attending mosques to worship Allah. I had questioned why only men and boys went to the mosques and not women. The only answer I was able to get was that women could not attend mosques during their menstrual periods as they were considered dirty during that period. I had heard about the pilgrimage to Mecca as a life-time trip to please Allah. Again, women seldom went on such a pilgrimage. Learning about Islam through Nabeel Qureshi was an inspiring experience and he gave me a meaningful education to understand Islam as a worldview.

Nabeel Qureshi was raised by his devout Muslim parents. His maternal grandfather was a Muslim missionary in Indonesia. Nabeel was a Muslim of Pakistani heritage, born and raised in the US, belonging to Ahmadi, one of the minority Muslim sects. Sunni and Shia were the two majority sects in Islam. For example, Iraq was a country with a Sunni majority while Iran was a country with a Shia majority. Kurds were also a minority sect of Islam. The Sunni Muslims made up eighty percent of the world's Muslims, while Shias made up only ten per cent. The remaining minority groups made up the rest. Qureshi asserted that the Ahmadis had been persecuted by the majority Muslims (Sunni and Shia) as the Ahmadi beliefs varied slightly from the beliefs of the majority of Muslims.

Nabeel's mother played a big role in Nabeel becoming a devout Muslim from a very young age. "Adhan", the Muslim call to prayers, were memorized and recited as daily rituals. When Nabeel was born, his father spoke softly "adhan" into his ears. "I had been taught to recite the Arabic phrase of prayer 132 times every single day from a time before I even knew my name" (Qureshi, 2014, p 21). Nabeel also learned to recite the entire Quran just before he turned six years old. When the Muslims prayed, they faced towards the Muslim holy shrine in Mecca and recited portions of the holy Quran. The language of the Quran and their prayers were in classical Arabic, which was learned in school. However, most Muslims spoke colloquial Arabic, thus, they did not understand the classical Arabic.

"Don't become Americanized" was the advice given to Nabeel by his parents and the Muslim leaders. Nabeel soon realized that the Muslim immigrants from the East were starkly different from their Muslim children born in the West. Muslim immigrants believed that the West was a Christian nation, its culture was promiscuous, and these Christians were the enemies of Islam. Thus, Muslim immigrants encouraged their children not to pollute their purity and to stay away from Western culture.

Nabeel followed the core beliefs of Islam and lived a life as a devout Muslim from a very young age. The words: "Allahu Akbar" (God is Great) were uttered during the attack on the World Trade Center in New York in 2001. Thus, for non-Muslims, these words were associated with terrorism. However, for Muslims, these words were an expression of praise and a short prayer. The core belief of Islam is that God is greater than anything we can conceive, the Greatest Possible Being (Murray 2014). "A man is Muslim if he exclusively declares that Allah is God, and Muhammad is Allah's messenger." (Qureshi, 2014, p 56).

Nabeel identified that the central proclamation of Islam was: "No God but Allah, and Muhammad as his messenger". The Quran was the Bible for Islam written by the prophet Muhammad and was considered the word of God. What was written in the Quran was revealed to Muhammad by Allah. "Muslims believed that every single word of the Quran was dictated by Allah, through the Archangel Gabriel to Muhammad" (Qureshi, 2014 p. 36).

Nabeel followed the five pillars of Islam, the fundamental practices required of all Muslims. They were the following: (1) Recite the Shahada, the central proclamation of Islam, "There is no God but Allah and Muhammad is his Messenger", (2) Pray the five daily prayers, (3) Fast during the month of Ramadan, (4) Give alms, and (5) Undertake a pilgrimage to Mecca. For the five daily prayers, all men, rich or poor, statesman or workmen lined-up, side by side, and prayed as one (Qureshi, 2014). Muslims claimed that dreams were the only means by which the average Muslim expected to hear directly from God. There was no personal relationship with God.

Ramadan is the Muslim holy month. For thirty days, Muslims fast from sunrise to sunset without food or water. This practice is obligatory for all able-bodied Muslims. Qureshi expressed concern about the prohibition of water as it was difficult for him to go without drinking water for 12-18 hours, part of it during school time. There would be a feast before one started the fast and then at the end of the fast on a given day.

I was surprised to learn of the paradise spoken about in Islam which was depicted as a place of carnal pleasure: wine, sex, perpetual virgins, and young boys who waited on men. According to Islam, the way to paradise was Sharia, a code of law to follow that would please Allah and earn his favour. Sharia was the Islamic law and dictated every aspect of a devout

Muslim's life. The word Sharia meant path, meaning, "In the correct path we must walk according to Allah's will". There was no book of Sharia, but an explanation of it was found in a source called "Ulema" (Qureshi, 2014). A Muslim must also outweigh the bad deeds that he has committed by good deeds in order to reach paradise.

Muslims claimed that Islam was close to Christianity in its beliefs; for example, Muslims believed that Jesus was born of a virgin, He performed miracles, and He was the Messiah. However, they did not believe that Jesus died on the cross and disagreed with the claim: "Jesus is God" (Qureshi, 2014). Nabeel grew up believing and practising all that was required of a devout Muslim.

Through reading about Nabeel's ardent faith in Islam as a devout Muslim, I gained a better understanding of Islam as a worldview. I am really grateful to learn this worldview through the writing of Qureshi. It portrayed the application of Islamic faith by a devout Muslim. Although I was exposed to the religion of Islam in India, I was not familiar with its doctrine. I am thankful that I had the opportunity to learn it during my retired life.

## Worldview (4) Christianity: Gospel of Jesus

This takes me to my fourth and final worldview Christianity and the Gospel of Jesus. In exploring Christianity as a worldview, Murray has confirmed that it is the Christian worldview (Gospel of Jesus) that answers the big questions related to the four fundamental areas in life. The four fundamental areas in life are origin, meaning, morality, and destiny. I will explore these four fundamental areas and seek answers to my big questions related to each area within the worldview of Christianity and the Gospel of Jesus.

Origin: Does God Exist?

Meaning:     Can One Find Meaning Through Suffering?

Morality:    Is There Objective Morality?

Destiny:     Is Jesus My destiny?

222

I have observed that the Christian worldview of people is changing as they are adopting other worldviews; for example, many are drawn to the New Spirituality or Buddhism and more recently, Marxist socialism. In addition, the new Atheism and Secular Humanism are becoming more popular amongst the younger population.

I knew that people in the East looked to the West (The US, Canada, and the UK) as Christian Nations. So, when I left India, a country where more than 80 percent of the population belonged to the Hindu religion, and where Christians were only a small minority group, I looked forward to coming to a Christian Nation. Soon, I realized that although Canada was founded upon principles that recognized the Supremacy of God and the rule of law according to the Canadian Charter of Rights and Freedoms, Canada had become a secular nation. In fact, Canada is one of the most secular countries in the world. Canada has no official religion now, and Christianity has been on the decline. Canada is officially committed to religious pluralism, a Postmodern characteristic.

I will begin with the origin of life, the origin of universe, and its related question, "Does God exist?"

Origin: My big question is: "Does God Exist?" I would have never asked such a question during my growing up years because most people believe in God in India. However, in Canada, "Does God exist" has been a widely debated topic. When I began to seek answers to the origin of life and the universe, two distinct worldviews began to emerge. One worldview was that life evolved over millions of years, and the universe was eternal and came into existence out of nothing. This worldview was naturalistic (evolution).

In the other worldview, there was intelligence and a mind behind the origin of life, the origin of universe, and the fine-tuning of the universe to sustain life. This worldview was called Theistic (creation by God). Inherent in these two worldviews was my Big Question: "Does God Exist?" Questions of the origin of life, the origin of the universe, and the fine-tuning of the universe have been widely debated by both Theists and Atheists.

"Does God exist?" is literally life's most important question (Turek, 2014). The two opposing worldviews are Atheistic (God does not exist) and Theistic (God does exist). Atheists differ from Agnostics who claim that they do not know if God exists. Similarly, a Skeptic is one who has a doubt about the existence of God.

Secular Humanism is a growing group among Atheists, and it includes Agnostics, Skeptics and even Theist Evolutionists (belief in both the existence of God and evolution). Theistic Evolution is not a scientific theory. Frances Collins, a Theistic Evolutionist, asserts that evolution is real, but it is set in motion by God; however, human beings came into existence as a result of the evolutionary process. Secular Humanists believe that humanity is unique with dignity, value, meaning, and purpose in life, and these can be achieved without reference to any transcendent being (Murray, 2014).

On the origin of life: "And God created man in His own image, in the image of God created him: male and female" (Genesis 1:27). In an Atheistic / Naturalistic worldview, origin of life and the origin of the universe remained unanswered, except for the explanation that life evolved over a long period of time through a process called evolution. This statement assumed that there was life already in existence. The process of evolution was theorized by Charles Darwin. The Theory of Evolution was a difficult area of learning for me as I believed only certain aspects of evolution.

Darwin's theory is explained in his book, "On the Origin of Species" (1859). I must confess that I have not read this book. So, what I have learned about this theory is from other sources. Darwin is better known as a Naturalist, who held the view that nothing exists beyond the natural world. There is no transcendence (God). Such a claim by Darwin is in direct opposition to my belief in God who is the creator of the universe. Darwin describes evolution as an unguided and undirected natural process in which life has evolved gradually and steadily. Evolution and scientific laws do not explain the origin of life, but they explain the processes of evolution.

Darwin explained that natural selection was the process by which organisms became better adapted to their environment. Thus, they survived and produced more off-springs. Darwin also observed individual variations in appearance and behaviour within populations, and he called this process random mutation. I believe natural selection and random mutation are evolutionary processes. This occurs at the level of Microevolution. However, natural selection and random mutation cannot explain the higher-level formation of body plans, which is at the level of Macroevolution. So, how are the body plans formed? I have not found answer to this question.

Darwinists asserted that we human beings shared a common ancestor with apes or birds evolving from reptiles. This meant that multiple species derived from a single ancestor. It was called a universal common ancestry, where all organisms shared a common genetic heritage. A universal common descent through an evolutionary process was proposed by Charles Darwin. However, for this unguided Macroevolution to be true, the first life must have originated spontaneously from non-living chemicals.

Common descent is a concept that postulates one species is the ancestor of two or more species or multiple species derived from a single ancestral population. Furthermore, all currently living organisms on Earth share a common genetic heritage, the single ancestry of life. Naturalistic biologists assert that life generated spontaneously from nonliving chemicals by natural laws without any intelligent intervention. They also assert that the one-celled amoeba came together by spontaneous generation, and all biological life has evolved from that first amoeba. This is the Theory of Macroevolution.

I learned that there is no clear evidence in evolution by which one type of species is evolving into a different type of species. There is agreement that evolution is a fact at the micro level (Microevolution) and not at the macro level (Geisler, 2004). There is no creative power in natural selection and random mutation.

Moreover, Darwin's theory could not account for the Cambrian explosion, when most of the major groups of animals appeared abruptly in the fossil record (Geisler, 2004). All animal groups appeared separately, fully formed, and at the same time. This was inconsistent with the gradual evolutionary process of Darwin. For me, Darwin's Theory of Evolution did not answer the questions of the origin of life and Macroevolution from one species from a different species.

In addition, the origin of the information code in DNA remain unanswered. How did life originate and where did the three billion bits of information in DNA come from?

DNA is called the instruction book of life, and its structure and functions are highly complex and miraculous. Stephen Meyer, the founder of the Intelligent Design (ID) Institute, has argued that the information code in DNA is designed by an intelligent mind, not an accident in the process of evolution. The most complex molecule in the cell is the DNA (deoxyribose-nucleic acid) with 3.7 billion codes arranged in an organized and meaningful fashion to carry out information. DNA, the instruction book of life, is made up of genes, the genetic code for life. The discovery of DNA has only strengthened my belief in Creation. I cannot help but believe that humans are created by God with meaning and purpose in life.

I have learned that belief in God (theism) is meta-physical and focuses on the "why" questions in life whereas science deals with the physical and natural world and focuses on the "how" questions in life. Thus, theism and science do coexist. However, since Darwin published his book, "On the Origin of Species", evolution became a popular belief based on the rationale that evolution is evidence-based; therefore, it is scientifically accepted. Thus, children are now taught evolution in schools.

Those who question the inadequacies of Darwin's theory have pointed out three of its deficiencies: the human being is merely another animal, there is no absolute standard of morality, and the human being has no purpose.

Scientists had not fully answered the question of the origin and the fine-tuning of universe. The claim that the universe was eternal with no

226

beginning was discredited when scientists agreed that the universe had a beginning; it started from a single point and then expanded.

On the Origin of the Universe: "In the beginning God created the heavens and the earth" (Genesis 1:1). "Heavens declare the glory of God; the skies proclaim the work of His hands" (Psalms 19:1). These Bible verses form the basis of my belief on the origin of the universe. For those who do not believe in a living God, the universe is eternal, uncaused, timeless, spaceless and nothingness. This has been the position of Atheists until the "Big Bang" happened.

At the Big-Bang event, matter, energy, space, and time came into existence in a single moment about 13.8 billion years ago. If the universe had a beginning, it had a cause. Thus, the notion of an eternal universe was no more a valid claim. Prominent scientists (including the late Stephen Hawking) agreed that universe, with space, time, and matter, had a beginning. Moreover, the universe was expanding.

This expansion of the universe was confirmed by Edwin Hubble, astronomer, and Albert Einstein, scientist. Hubble was able to observe the expansion through his telescope that the galaxies in the night sky were discovered, and they were moving away and expanding. Although initially denying his own findings in the general relativity formula, Einstein later was convinced by Hubble's discovery. This was upsetting to many scientists as it shook their belief that, "the universe is eternal". Atheist scientists agreed that the universe appeared to have a design but rejected the notion that there was a designer.

William Lane Craig, a Philosopher, and a Christian Apologist, has asserted that God is the best explanation for the origin of the Universe. Scientists are not certain about the actual age of the universe or cosmos. It is important to note that no specific time is given in the Bible for the origin of the universe. It just says, "In the beginning". Isaac Newton (1642-1727), the greatest scientist, marvelled at the design of our solar system; he wrote: "The most beautiful system of the sun, planets and comets, could only proceed from the counsel and dominion of an intelligent and powerful being" (Geisler, 2004, p.95).

The field of Cosmology is overwhelming to me. I admire the cosmologists who have done ground-breaking research and made discoveries in relation to the Cosmos. There may be many more stars and galaxies that are yet to be discovered and many more unanswered questions to be answered, for example, the black holes and clusters of stars.

It is rather humbling to me when I look up at the sky and see its vastness, complexity, and beauty. There is so much I do not understand about the Cosmos. I have learned that the Cosmos is everything that exists, including time, space, matter, and the laws that govern them. The universe and its existence are used as evidence for the existence of God. It is called the cosmological argument. I believe that God caused the origin of the universe. God created time and space along with universe. I also believe that God created the universe with a design for life to exist.

The Fine-Tuning of the Universe: There simply cannot be a design without a designer. The universe is designed and fine-tuned in such a way that life can exist. The fine-tuning is so precise that there is only one rational conclusion; someone designed the universe. Even Atheists admit that fine-tuning is the strongest argument in favour of a designer. The fine-tuning of the universe is beyond the human ability to design and maintain. Atheists have very little defense in arguing against a designer for the fine-tuning of the universe.

Atheists have claimed that with the advancement in science, the need for God had vanished. For example, Stephen Hawking, the late 21st century, prominent scientist, had claimed that because we had gravity, the universe could originate from nothing. He denied the existence of God. Whereas, the 17th century, prominent scientist, Sir Isaac Newton, did not deny his faith in God when he discovered gravity, rather he praised God. Newton was the brightest scientist that ever lived. His chair at Cambridge was occupied by Hawking until Hawking's death in 2018.

I have heard Atheists ask the question, "If God created the universe, who created God?" I learned from John Lennox that the God of the Bible is not a created God. Created gods are idols and delusions. The Bible tells us that the same God who created the universe also created the mind to do science. God has created the universe, and he has revealed himself in the Bible.

I have also learned that science cannot answer the "why" questions. For example, why is there a universe? Why are we here? Science deals with the "how" and "what" questions. Science cannot tell us why there is evil and suffering in the world. Thus, a belief in both God and science are compatible and essential to understanding the nature of God and the logic of science.

In summary, although, I cannot prove the existence of God, there is evidence that God exists. From what I have learned, I believe that God is the source for the origin of life on earth. Similarly, the universe has had a beginning, God is the creator of it, and the universe is finely tuned for life. This God is also a personal God. Thus, we can have relationship with God. I thank God for giving me the wisdom to believe in Him.

Meaning: Can One Find Meaning Through Suffering? The second fundamental area to explore is the meaning and the purpose of Life. My Big Question is: Can one find meaning through suffering?

"Life is not primarily a quest for pleasure, as Freud believed, or a quest for power, as Alfred Adler taught, but a quest for meaning" (Frankl, 2006, p. x).

If life is primarily a quest for meaning, what gives life meaning? Does having a purpose in life give a meaning to life? An even more difficult question is that during suffering and pain, does life have any positive meaning?

I will begin my exploration of this question with an incredible experience shared by the world-renowned apologist, Ravi Zacharias, who has been an inspiration to me in my spiritual journey.

As a young man growing up in Delhi, India, Ravi said he had no meaning or purpose in his life. He did not like the way life felt, so he decided to end his life by taking poison. He ended up in an intensive care unit of a hospital in Delhi. His family lost hope for his survival and, with his mother by his side, a man came to see him with a Bible in his hand. Ravi's mom told the man he was too sick to have visitors. The man requested that she read a few verses from the Book of John, Chapter Fourteen to Ravi and handed her the Bible.

As she read, Ravi heard the verse, "Because I live, you shall live also" (John 14:19). Ravi latched onto the word "live" and responded. If God gave him his life, he would live for Him with no stone unturned. Ravi walked out of that hospital as a changed man with meaning and purpose in his life. He lived his life as he promised to God and became one of the greatest apologists of the 21st century. The pursuit of meaning is the greatest pursuit in every person's life. New desires and new hungers will emerge with finding a meaning in life.

In my growing-up years in India, I had certain goals in life, but I did not ponder what was the meaning and the purpose in life. One of my goals was to do well in my studies at school and at college. I never had a job, and I did not make any money in India. Thus, I never had any "pocket money". I was dependent on my family for my financial needs. Children did not get a family allowance in my family. So, my goal in life was to get an education, get a job, make money, become financially independent, and help my family. Of course, I believed in God and the Gospel message. However, I did not make the connection that I would find meaning and purpose in life through my relationship with a personal God. If I had relationship with God, would I be free of suffering?

We tend to ask the question that if God is benevolent and almighty, why is there so much evil and suffering? Apologists have confessed that the question of suffering is a difficult one with which to deal. Even more difficult is when there is suffering of children involved. I also find suffering from malevolence and from natural disasters difficult to comprehend. How can we console a mother who just lost her child as a result of a drunken driver? I questioned God when my sister suffered and died, asking why it happened to her? I asked the question why when Nabeel Qureshi died at the age of 34 years leaving behind his young wife and a two-year old daughter.

Think of the children in Auschwitz, where suffering was the consequence of conscious malevolence. Can we find positive meaning amid the suffering from malevolence? We all have had to endure suffering; however, our suffering has been exacerbated by evil in our hearts and others' hearts. Evil was a separation from God, and it could lead to malevolent suffering. It was evil in people's hearts that led to malevolence. It was not a new phenomenon. It had been there from the beginning of times.

For example, Victor Frankl, in his book, "Man's Search for Meaning" (2006), described so vividly and with passion how he survived the concentration and death camps. Frankl quoted Nietzsche: "He who has a Why to live for, can bear almost any How" (2006, p. IX). Frankl had the love for his wife and the hope of seeing her again someday to give him meaning in life, a source of strength for which to live rather than die. His three sources of strengths were: doing something meaningful, caring for another person, and having courage during difficult times. Frankl made unimaginable sacrifices in the death camp to stay alive.

I have learned that there is malevolence in this world. We must confront this malevolence and accept responsibility for it at the individual level. Suffering from malevolence intensifies, the pain, and we become more bitter and resentful, leading us to a state of despair and Nihilism. Existential philosopher Nietzsche said he went looking for God and could not find Him; that led him to a state of Nihilism. Psalmist David said: "Where can I flee from Your presence, wherever I go, you are there" (Psalm 139: 8-9). This gave the Psalmist David hope. Stop running from God; instead, have a relationship with God. We will find meaning in that relationship.

If I do not have a purpose and a meaning, my life will become reckless, hopeless, and Nihilistic. I have a moral obligation to find meaning in my life, and not just search after happiness in life. If I tend to only pursue happiness, I may not attain it. I find meaning in my family relationships. I found meaning in my life when my two sons were born, and also when my three grandchildren were born. Furthermore, I have found meaning in my life with my relationship with Jesus. This I call the ultimate meaning.

When life becomes meaningless, we humans fall into a state of despair, and the desire to live becomes hard, which may even lead to ending life itself. The suicide rate is climbing in the Western world and in many countries. In India, suicide rates increase during and after final examinations. These particular students in colleges and universities, who strive hard to achieve high grades in their final examinations as expected by their parents, tend to kill themselves, if they get lower grades than expected. They do this because they believe that they have violated their purpose in life for themselves and for their families. They think that they have brought shame to their families. Failure in examinations made them think that their lives had no more meaning and purpose.

I was perplexed when my friend Sai took her own life. I kept asking the question why? She had two beautiful and educated daughters, she retired from a successful nursing career with a good pension, and she was a practising Christian. Yet, she found living was more difficult than dying. Zacharias stated: "Despair is not just a moment; it is a way of life". Was Sai living a life of despair? Had she lost the meaning and the purpose in life? A man (Jim) who lived with us many years took his own life as he became fearful of his future. Jim was in his 80's, and he was afraid that he might have to move out of our home and go to a facility when he needed assistance to live. Did fear take away his meaning and his purpose in life?

Meaning is fostered during each stage in life, and different experiences bring meaning to life. For example, a sense of wonder and enchantment in childhood is essential for a child to have meaning. The older one gets, the more it takes to fill one's heart with wonder, and more wonder is needed to make meaning. For example, when Mila, our granddaughter, was one year old, a picture of a puppy made her wide-eyed. At the age of two, she saw a real dog and heard it bark; , she was thrilled and excited.

A child who is filled with wonder is also filled with gratitude. Where there is no wonder and gratitude, there is boredom and emptiness. G.K Chesterton, a British journalist, warned us that if you take the sense of wonder, mystique, or enchantment away from a child, we take away gratitude. Thus, the loss of wonder results in the loss of gratitude.

As children grow, visual images become a powerful mode of making meaning for them. For example, photos, videos, paintings, YouTube, television, and movies have invaded the minds of our youth. Thus, pornography is a problem as many young people have become addicted to their visual pleasures. Do we parents know what our youths are watching on the internet? Do our youth recognize pornography is wrong?

As the youth grows to be an adult, love and belonging become essential to have meaning in life. I was sad to learn how Princess Diana longed for love and belonging in her married life. Bertrand Russell, the well known Atheist, conceded that the one thing he missed in life was love. Women and men who have lost their spouses in life, often find life meaningless. What can fill that void? Old age can be a difficult time as we may lose our spouses and become lonelier. So, how do we keep our lives meaningful in our old age? We can lose hope in such times, and life can become meaningless.

Responsibility in life is also gives meaning to life. For example, both my sons are married now and have children. Having wives and children have given them additional responsibilities. It seems that these additional responsibilities have brought meaning and purpose to their lives. As parents, they have to love their children and also instil a sense of courage. The parental goal is to make children competent and courageous. Jonathan Haidt stated, "We are to prepare the child for the road and not the road for the child."

A sense of courage is helpful when tragedy strikes; if not, we become resentful. When we are resentful, we become bitter. A bitter person can be cruel to others and add to the suffering in this world. We must participate in stopping the unnecessary suffering in the world. One way to achieve this is by pursuing meaning rather than pleasure. If the purpose in our life is to pursue pleasure, we become disappointed.

Moreover, the worldview we hold is influential in making meaning. For example, in Modernism, reason influences making meaning. Whereas, in Post-modernism, where there is no objective truth, no absolutes, no reason, and no purpose, making meaning is merely the meaning that is chosen by the person without a purpose. A life without purpose is meaningless. In a Christian worldview, sin is the violation of purpose.

In the Gospel message, joy is central, and sorrow is peripheral. I have observed this in many Christians who are suffering with illness; yet they seem to find solace in praying, singing to God and finding joy. My sister Rachel was an example. She would come home after renal dialysis, weak and tired; yet she would sing and praise God. I am not saying that she never had times of desperation, she did, and those times, she also cried out to God.

Our life's big lessons are learned through suffering and hardship and not through pleasure and achievements in life. This lesson has been an important lesson for me in learning humility. However, we are living in a pleasure-seeking society, and we human beings are basically pleasure-seeking beings. Different people find pleasure in different things. Some may seek pleasure in what makes them feel good, for example, pornography, alcohol, drugs, and sex.

In 2018, the deaths of two famous TV personalities made me realize that achievements and pleasures did not bring meaning to their lives. One was the celebrity and gifted chef, Anthony Bourdain, who committed suicide by hanging at the age of 62. He left behind a young daughter. Bourdain claimed; "His body was a fun-house". Viewers and fans of his well-publicized TV shows saw him as an accomplished chef who seemed to have everything in life. Was he just seeking pleasure in his life and had he lost the real meaning to life?

The same year, another celebrity, Kate Spade, a fashion designer, also committed suicide. She was only 55 years old. Apparently, she left a note for her 13-year-old daughter stating that it was not her fault that she committed suicide and told her daughter to ask her dad. Had Kate lost her meaning and purpose in life? I wonder what would have prevented both Bourdain and Spade from committing suicide?

If there is a real purpose to our life, then there is a right way to live our lives. Morality will help us to follow that right way.

234

Morality: Is There Objective Morality? My conception of morality has consisted mainly of what I thought was right and what I thought was wrong. I knew some things were either right or wrong for me to do. For example, I knew that telling a lie was wrong, and that I was expected to tell the truth. There were times I lied out of fear of punishment for something I had done wrong, and I knew that it was wrong for me to lie. I also learned that it was the right thing for me to do to obey my parents and my older siblings, and to respect older people.

In my upbringing in India, I valued loving relationships and a family life where both parents were present in raising the children. The marriages were between a man and a woman, and most marriages that I had witnessed were arranged by parents. Divorces were not common, even if the marriage was rocky with abuse, as the societal expectation was for the husband and the wife to live together and work it out.

Dating was not a common practice in my community when I was growing up; thus, if there was love between a boy and a girl, it was kept secret from the parents. I heard of many tragic incidents occurring, including suicide, resulting from parents not allowing the couple in love to get married, but forcing the boy and the girl to marry a boy or girl as arranged by the parents. I grew up with the belief that dating was wrong.

However, I was drawn to the cultural norm of dating in Canada when I met Ranjit, and I justified that it was all right for me to go out on dates with Ranjit. Similarly, I grew up with the belief that drinking alcohol was wrong, and I never drank alcohol in India. This was the norm for girls who grew up in my era. In Canada, I have a glass of wine with a meal and that is fine with me. My moral code has shifted. Was this a cultural shift or a change in my morality? However, certain moral beliefs are foundational; for example, my faith in God and Jesus as my Lord and Saviour is an Objective Morality.

What is an Objective (Absolute) Morality? If God does not exist, there is no Objective Morality. The existence of a moral absolute is a pathway to God. It is where one gets one's ethics from. Ethics are moral principles which govern our behaviours, for example having respect for colleagues you work with.

Immanuel Kant (German Philosopher) claimed that morality could be deduced from reason alone, and God was unnecessary for ensuring morality. Sam Harris, an American Philosopher and Neuroscientist, had been trying to show evidence in his writing on the "Moral Landscape", that morality could exist in humans as part of human flourishing. He claimed that Objective Morality could exist without God and that we learned our Objective Morality from our parents, teachers, society, and our conscience.

On the other hand, Dawkins (2006), the Atheist guru, claimed that there was no good and no evil; we all danced to our DNA. Key Neilson, a Canadian Atheist, also asserted that there was no God, and there was no morality. However, he admitted that morality was a difficult problem for Atheists to deal with because moral law guided one to act meaningfully.

Those who do not endorse an Objective Morality resort to moral relativism. Objective Morality and moral relativism differ in their foundational premises.

In Moral Relativism, no objective or universal moral principles exist, but individuals make their own moral choices based on their beliefs and culture. If morality is relative, we would have a world in which nothing would be wrong; nothing would be evil or good. Justice and fairness would be meaningless. Moreover, each individual would construct his/her own truth, and there would be no right or wrong. Geisler (2004) argues that in Moral Relativism: "There are no differences between Mother Teresa and Hitler, freedom and slavery, equality and racism, care and abuse, love and hate, or life and murder" (p.179). In a pluralistic culture with Relative Morality, everything is permissible. In such a worldview, there would be no sin or evil. Can such a society survive?

For me, some things are absolutely wrong for example, torturing an innocent baby purely for pleasure is wrong and an evil act. However, in Moral Relativism, this act can be considered right or wrong, depending on the choice made by the individual. I learned that the animal world is immoral. For example, if a lion kills a zebra, we do not say that the lion committed a murder, and the lion is not charged with murder. It is we human beings who contemplate the issue of morality, moral law, and a moral law giver.

Is there a Moral Law Giver? I believe that the moral law giver is God, and the moral laws are given to humanity as commandments that give us a moral framework. Moses was given the Ten Commandments by God. Jesus reduced these commandments to two that he said were the most important: Love your God; Love your neighbour. These two laws are the foundation of all other Christian laws. God exists as our foundation of Objective Moral laws and values. Thus, morality guides us as to how we should live, and the moral laws are our obligations as Christians.

For a Christian, the Sermon on the Mount is moral law giving on a higher plane. Through the Sermon on the Mount, God transcended the law. For example, the commandment of love is to love God and then, love your neighbour. We are commanded to love others as we love ourselves. . Where there is love, there is freedom to love or not to love. Where there is only freedom, there is evil. Where there is evil, there is a need for forgiveness and justice. Jesus has proclaimed love as the supreme ethic. Jesus has come to fulfill the law and not to destroy it.

Accountability (Conscience) means that there is an expectation for us to be answerable for our actions. I believe that there is an eye beyond the human eye, God's eye. If we do not have to be accountable to God, then we can cheat without others seeing us, and we do not care if God is watching. If we do not have a sense of accountability, we do not have a conscience. The feeling of remorse comes from being conscious of the crimes we commit. There are those who do not feel remorseful. They are without a conscience. They are not accountable to God.

In conclusion, a God has dictated a moral framework and moral laws that laid the foundation for Christianity. Now, in the 21st century, the New Atheists are promoting the moral liberation of people. They claim that there is no moral accountability or judgment. G. K. Chesterton, a British Journalist, reminds us that "before you move a fence, ask, why it was put there in the first place." He goes on to say that: "When you stop believing in God, you may believe in anything". Believing in anything is worse than believing in nothing.

I am thankful for the opportunity to learn about morality as it has been a guide to living a morally responsible life.

Destiny: Is Jesus My Destiny? Destiny is concerned with the question: "Is there a life after death?" There can be different parameters for this question; for example, is there a heaven and a hell? Do I have a soul? Answers to these questions are difficult and controversial. My focus will be on Jesus as my destiny.

However, I have learned about the concepts of heaven and hell. My conception of heaven and hell include that there is a deep chasm between us and God. The chasm is too steep for us to get to God and heaven. So, God has come down to us by sending His own son Jesus to be born as Man, to suffer, and to die on the cross to redeem us from our sins. He rose from His death on the third day, and whoever believes in Jesus will be redeemed and have the hope of an eternal life with Him.

This eternal life with Jesus is my destiny. Who is Jesus to me? The quote below is one way to describe Jesus.

The greatest Man in history is Jesus. He had no servants, yet they called Him Master. He had no degree, yet they called Him Teacher. He had no medicines, yet they called Him Healer. He had no army, yet kings feared Him. He won no military battles, yet He conquered the world. He committed no crime, yet they crucified Him. He was buried in a tomb, yet He lives today. (Author unknown).

Who is Jesus to me? Everyone has an opinion about who Jesus is. Historians, poets, philosophers, and others have regarded Jesus as the centerpiece of history. Jesus has been talked about, debated, loved yet hated, controversial figure on this Earth. Different religions have beliefs about Jesus as to who He is. For example, Islam calls Him a prophet, and the Hindus acknowledge Him as one path to God among the many paths. Jesus is worshipped and revered; yet, his name is used as a swear word.

Recently, I was in a supermarket to buy groceries, and I heard a woman scream "Jesus". She certainly got my attention and the attention of many others in the store. Apparently, a man had accidently hit her ankle with his grocery cart. It seemed to have hurt her badly. Her sudden reaction was to cry out the name of "Jesus" to express her anger and frustration. Was she using His name as a swear word?

Many consider Jesus as a prominent historical figure, a great moral teacher, a prophet, and even a sacrificial lamb; yet, they may not believe He rose from His death. Atheists ridicule those who believe in the resurrection of Jesus, as they claim it is in violation of the natural laws.

In answering "Who Jesus is", I have focused on aspects of Jesus and His message that have been significant in my learning. For example, the "Trinity" has been a difficult concept for me to understand and explain to others. Similarly, "Jesus is the son of God" is a controversial concept to try to convince others of. "Jesus is the Truth" is refuted by many, and I have been eager to understand it. The belief of some that women are degraded in the Gospel inspired me to examine Jesus' regard for women. I have also included "The Suffering of the Servant King" & "His Resurrection".

How do I explain Trinity to others? The doctrine of Trinity is a core belief of Christianity; yet, I found it to be difficult to comprehend and to explain to another person. I have found the explanation given by Nabeel Qureshi, in his book: "Seeking Allah, Finding Jesus" (2014) simple and easy to comprehend.

Qureshi explains the Trinity as the concept that God is three persons in one being, in which "Being'" is different from "person". For example, each one of us is a human being and a person. Qureshi explains that the "Being" means the quality or essence that makes something what it is; whereas the "Person" is the quality that makes someone who he is. "The doctrine of Trinity teaches that God is one being with three persons: Father, Son and Spirit" (Qureshi, 2014, p. 196). God is one being but exists eternally with three persons (Trinity) living in relationship with each other. Jesus is the second member of Trinity. Jesus said: "He who has seen me has seen the Father" (John, 1:3).

It is said in the Bible, "God is love". Love happens in a relationship. Thus, love is manifested in the three persons of God. This makes it easier for me to understand how love is manifested in God. The Trinity means that God is relational-in relationship. I need humility to believe in the Trinity because humility gives me the heart to accept God as greater than I am, much greater. I cannot know everything about God, and nobody has seen God, the Father. If I have the humility, I will trust Him and believe what He has revealed about Himself in the Bible. The doctrine of Trinity confirms that Jesus has been with God from the beginning. He is the creator and the saviour. He is co-equal with God. This is the core Christian belief; yet, many find it hard to believe this truthful claim. Similarly, the belief that "Jesus is God" is denied by many, including Christians.

Is Jesus God ? Many believe in Jesus, but not as God. I believe that "Jesus is my Lord". This has been my belief in my growing-up years. I have no reason to question it. In Canada, I am surrounded by people who question "Who is Jesus really?" Even some who call themselves Christians are also questioning if Jesus is God. Many consider Jesus as a moral teacher and a prophet, but to acknowledge Jesus as God is far more difficult.

Jesus was also called the Son of God and the Son of Man. I have searched for clarity between these names in relation to believing Jesus was God. Jesus was called the Son of God as He was identified with the logos, the Word of God. The Word was formed into order at the beginning of time. "In the beginning was the Word, the Word was with God and the Word was God" (Genesis 1:1).

Throughout the prophesies in the Old Testament, Jesus' life was predicted as the Son of God. One example was in Isiah 53, where the Messiah was depicted as Jesus who would suffer for the sin of all people. The Messiah's strength was shown by humility, suffering, and mercy. In the New Testament in John's gospel, John described Jesus as fully human and fully God. This was the truth about Jesus and the foundation of all truths.

Jesus was also called the Son of Man, a counterpart of the Son of God. The Son of Man affirmed His humanity, and the Son of God affirmed His divinity. By the power of the Holy Spirit, He became incarnate from the virgin Mary and was made Man. For the Son of Man came to save that which was lost. He came to serve humanity; yet, He lived on this earth as a homeless person. And Jesus said: "Foxes have holes, and the birds of the air have nests, but the Son of Man has nowhere to lay His head" (Matthew 18:20). As the Son of Man, Christ sacrificed himself on the cross. His death proved that He was human. As the Son of God, he was resurrected on the third day. His resurrection revealed that He was God.

Did Jesus claim that "He was God"? In Mark 14:55-64, Jesus was brought to the high priest and the Sanhedrin for His trial for blasphemy. The high priest asked Him: "Are You the Christ, the Son of the Blessed? Jesus answered: "I am, and you will see the Son of Man sitting at the right hand of power and coming with the clouds of heaven". The high priest understood what he meant and condemned Him for blasphemy. What Jesus said was in reference to the apocalyptic vision of the prophet Daniel (Daniel 7:13): "There before me was one like a Son of Man, coming with the clouds of heaven". The Son of Man was given everlasting dominion, and all people were to serve Him. The Son f Man was divine; He was Yahweh, the Hebrew name of God in the Bible. Jesus was fully human and fully divine. He lived as an ordinary man; yet He brought salvation and healing to all. He was rejected and despised by many. Jesus, himself, had claimed; "I am the Way, the Truth, and the Life".

Is Jesus the Truth? As I have stated before, in our current Postmodern culture, truth is subjective and relative, and there is no absolute truth. Moreover, truth is exclusive to each religion. Jesus' claim of: "I am the way, the truth and the life, no man come to the Father except through me" is a claim of exclusivity. Jesus is exclusive. For example, Buddha was born a Hindu, but rejected Hinduism's fundamental doctrines. Every religion at its core is exclusive. Truth cannot be all inclusive. Truth, by definition, is exclusive (Zacharias, 2000). Christ is the symbol of truth. It is a transcendent ideal. Christ is the highest Good.

Jesus understands the human condition. Only on the Cross does evil, forgiveness, love, and hope, all converge together. No other religion offers the forgiveness of sin that Jesus has offered by his sacrificial death on the Cross. In Hinduism and Buddhism, one must pay for one's sins through karma. In Islam, one's good deeds must outweigh one's bad deeds to attain paradise. A person is never sure if he or she has attained it. Whereas, in Christianity, I believe that I am promised forgiveness through the grace of Christ. That is the "Truth".

For me, Truth is not an ideology; it is personal. If I am truthful, I cannot live a double life. My character is defined when I am faced with temptations. My public proclamation of faith must be practiced in my private life. Living a double life will deny God's omnipresence (present everywhere) and omniscience (all knowing).

I am called upon to be a steward of Truth, especially for my children and grandchildren. They are watching me. I do not underestimate what they notice when they watch me. I understand that telling the truth makes relationships stronger as truth builds trust. I must tell the whole truth, and I must not hide the truth. For example, I must share the truth of a living God, including the truth that Jesus is God, and I can trust Him. Truth is the light in the darkness. Truth is personal.

Did Jesus Display a Regard for Women? I grew up with the belief that Jesus cared for me as a child and now he cares for me as a woman. As a child, I learned the verse in Luke 18:16: "Let the little children come to Me, and do not forbid them; for such is the kingdom of God". What a confidence boosting promise! Such a promise surely gave me confidence to do my best in what I did. Now that I am a grown-up woman, I have the assurance that Jesus loves me and cares for me.

Throughout history, claims have been made about how women have been oppressed by men. It is still a claim in our current Postmodern culture that women are oppressed by men, and that we live in a "patriarchal tyranny". The Apostle Paul has also been accused of treating women without respect. Yet, Jesus treated women with high regard; for example, Jesus listened to His mother Mary regarding the need for more wine at the wedding in Cana. In addition, Mary of Bethany sat at His feet to learn from Him and called Him Rabbi (teacher) as His disciples did. Jesus defended this woman's right to learn and stated that Mary had chosen education and that could not be taken away from her. This practice was a violation of Judaism as Rabbis did not teach women.

Jesus had a serious long conversation with the Samaritan woman at the well and told her she was like any other thirsty soul needing the living water. Jesus revealed to her: "I am the Messiah". Although she was the least valued and most dishonoured of her day, she became an evangelist.

Jesus trusted women, as, after His resurrection, he revealed himself first to the women. Mary Magdalene was the first witness to the resurrected Christ. Jesus commanded Mary to go and tell His brothers and disciples. This was the time in history when a woman's testimony was not even acceptable in a court of law. Jesus sent Mary to proclaim the good news: "He is Risen". Another example was when Jesus was walking with the cross, He told the weeping women not to weep for Him, but that they should focus on their futures.

Jesus treated women with more care beyond the norms during His time on this earth. One example was a woman with the alabaster jar who poured expensive ointment on Jesus' feet. I am citing this example from the Gospel of John, Chapter 12; Mary (Martha's sister) poured a bottle of expensive oil over the feet of Jesus and wiped His feet with her hair. People were not happy that Mary spent that kind of money to buy expensive perfume to pour on the feet of Jesus rather than spending it on the poor. Jesus responded by saying that you have the poor with you always; do not condemn Mary for what she has done. Mary might have been filled with joy that Jesus showed love and kindness to her. Jesus told those who complained that what this woman had displayed would be preached as part of the Gospel everywhere.

Another example of His caring was when Jesus healed a bleeding woman, showing His compassion for a woman. According to Gospel of Matthew (9: 22 & 23), a woman who had suffered from twelve years of bleeding was healed. She had been considered unclean and an out-cast, so she had not been able to live a normal life. She snuck up behind Jesus and touched his garment. She had believed that if she touched Jesus, she would be made well. But Jesus turned around, and when He saw her, He said: "Be of good cheer, daughter; your faith has made you well". And the woman was made well from that hour. This woman, who was an untouchable, and who was forbidden to enter inside a temple, and not touch another person, "touched Jesus". Yet, Jesus did not condemn her but, He showed love and kindness and healed her. Sadly, we humans often tend to give up hope and give up on others.

Jesus' compassion for women was also shown when He forgave an adulterous woman. According to John's Gospel (8: 3-11), the Jewish leaders brought a woman to him who was caught in an act of adultery. They asked Jesus that according to the law of Moses: "This woman should be stoned, but what do you say?" They asked this question to test Jesus and find a way to accuse Him of "wrong-doing". But Jesus stooped down and wrote on the ground with His finger. Then He raised His head and said: "He who is without sin among you, let him throw a stone at her first". Those who brought the woman to Him left one by one, being convicted by their conscience. Then, Jesus said to woman: "No one has condemned you, neither do I condemn you; go and sin no more."

I was interested to note that the Jewish leaders brought only the woman and not the man who had also committed adultery with the woman. According to the Jewish law, they both deserved the punishment. The Jewish leaders were trying to trick Jesus; yet Jesus neither condemned the woman nor condoned her action, but He gave an opportunity for the leaders, including the woman, to examine their sinful hearts. Jesus came to the Earth to show His love for us sinners and to give us an opportunity to examine our sinful natures.

The regard that Jesus showed for women in these Bible stories instills in me the responsibility to live a life that is pleasing to Jesus. Sometimes, I feel that I am lukewarm in my faith in professing the love of Jesus to others. I am reminded of the verse in Revelations 3:15-16: "I know your works, that you are neither cold nor hot, I could wish you were cold or hot. So then, you are lukewarm, and neither cold nor hot, I will vomit you out of My mouth". I have asked myself that if I believe in my heart that Jesus is my Lord and that I reflect His love in my actions, should I be all right? No, I must act out my beliefs which include sharing my beliefs with others. I must grow in this regard.

Jesus' Crucifixion: The Ultimate Suffering has widely been described by scholars and theologians. In addition, movies have been produced to show the intensity of the suffering of Jesus on the Cross. For example, the movie, "Passion of Christ" has tried to depict the ultimate suffering of His death on the Cross. It was difficult for me to watch the movie and the suffering of Jesus on the cross. Jesus drank the cup of God's wrath, so we do not have to experience it.

Jesus' crucifixion is the ultimate in voluntary suffering. I realize my inadequacy in describing the suffering on the Cross. Yet, His suffering is central in answering the question of who Jesus is. So, I have copied the vivid description by Truman Davis, M.D. from the book "I Don't have Enough Faith to Be an Atheist" by Geisler and Turek (2004, p 381-383). I was quite emotional when I read it, and I could not read it a second time. It is like watching the movie, "Passion of Christ". I could not watch it a second time. Yet, I believe this is a must read to be read at least once.

The Suffering of the Servant King:

"The whip of the Roman soldiers used on Jesus has small iron balls and sharp pieces of sheep bones tied to it. Jesus is stripped of his clothing and his hands are tied to upright post. His back, buttocks and legs are whipped either by one soldier or by two who alternate positions. The soldiers taunt their victim. As they repeatedly strike Jesus' back with full force, the iron balls cause deep contusions, and the sheep bones cut into the skin and tissues. As the whipping continues, the lacerations tear into the underlying skeletal muscles and produce quivering ribbons of bleeding flesh. Pain and blood loss set the stage for circulatory shock.

When it is determined by the centurion in charge that Jesus is near death, the beating is finally stopped. The half fainting Jesus is then untied and allowed to slump to the stone pavement, wet with His own blood. The Roman soldiers see a great joke in this provincial Jew claiming to be a king. They throw a robe across his soldiers and place a stick in his hand for a scepter. They still need a crown to make the travesty complete. A small bundle of flexible branches covered with long thorns and plaited into the shape of a crown is made, and this is pressed into his scalp. Again, there is copious bleeding (the scalp being one of the most vascular areas of the body). After mocking him and striking him across the face, the soldiers take the stick from his hand and strike him across the head, driving the thorns deeper into his scalp.

Finally, when they tire of their sadistic sport, the robe is torn from his back. The robe had already become adherent to the clots of blood and serum in the wounds, and its removal-just as in the careless removal of a surgical bandage- causes excruciating pain, almost as though he is being whipped again. The wounds again begin to bleed. In deference to Jewish custom, the Romans return his garments. The heavy horizontal beam of the cross is tied across his shoulders, and the procession of the condemned Christ, two thieves and the execution party walk along the Via Dolorosa. Despite his efforts to walk erect, the weight of the heavy wooden beam, together with the shock produced by copious blood loss, is too much. He stumbles and falls. The rough wood of the beam gouges into the lacerated skin and muscles of the shoulders. He tries to rise, but these humans have been pushed beyond their endurance. The centurion, anxious to get on with the execution, selects a stalwart North African onlooker, Simon of Cyrene, to carry the cross. Jesus follows, still bleeding and sweating the cold, clammy sweat of shock.

The 650 yard-journey from the fortress Antonia to Golgotha, is finally completed. Jesus is again stripped of his clothes except for a loincloth which is allowed on the Jews. The crucifixion begins. Jesus is offered wine mixed with myrrh, a mild pain killing mixture. He refuses to drink. Simon is ordered to place the cross beam on the ground, and Jesus is quickly thrown backward with his shoulders against the wood. The legionnaire feels for the depression at the front of the wrist. He drives a heavy, square, wrought-iron nail through the wrist and deep into the wood. Quickly, he moves to the other side and repeats the same action, being careful not to pull the arms too tight, but to allow some flexibility and movement. The beam is then lifted, and the title reading "Jesus of Nazareth, King of Jews" is nailed in place.

The victim Jesus is now crucified. As he slowly sags down with more weight on the nails in the wrists, excruciating, fiery pain shoots along the fingers and up the arms to explode in the brain-the nails in the wrists are putting pressure on the median nerves. As he pushes himself upward to avoid this stretching torment, he places his full weight on the nail through his feet. Again, there is the searing agony of the nail tearing through the nerves between the metatarsal bones of the feet. At this point, another phenomenon occurs. As the arms fatigue, great waves of cramps sweep over the muscles, knotting them in deep, relentless, throbbing pain. With these cramps, comes the inability to push himself upward. Hanging by his arms, the pectoral muscles are paralysed, and the intercostal muscles are unable to act. Air can be drawn into the lungs, but it cannot be exhaled. Jesus fights to raise himself in order to get even one short breath. Finally, carbon dioxide builds up in the lungs and in the bloodstream, and the cramps partially subside. Spasmodically, he can push himself upward to exhale and bring in the life-giving oxygen. It is undoubtedly during these periods that he utters the seven short sentences that are recorded.

Now begin hours of this limitless pain, cycles of cramping and twisting, partial asphyxiation, searing pain as tissue is torn from his lacerated back as he moves up and down against the rough timber. Then another agony begins. A deep, crushing pain in the chest as the pericardium slowly fills with serum and begins to compress the heart. It is now almost over- the loss of tissue fluid has reached a critical level; the compressed heart is struggling to pump heavy, thick, sluggish blood into the tissues; the tortured lungs are making a frantic effort to gasp in small gulps of air. The markedly dehydrated tissues send their flood of stimuli to the brain. His mission of atonement has been completed. Finally, he can allow his body to die. With one last surge of strength, he once again presses his torn feet against the nail, straightens his legs, takes a deeper breath, and utters his seventh and last cry: "Father, into your hands I commit my spirit." (Geisler 2004, 381 - 383)

This was the ultimate suffering. The ultimate sacrifice was when Jesus offered himself to God and the world to be betrayed, tortured, and crucified. Jesus pleaded: "My God, My God, why has thou forsaken me?" (Matthew 27:46). Jesus gave all of Himself for my sake and for the sake of the world. No one experienced suffering more than Jesus Himself through His suffering and death on the Cross.

Jesus came to Earth in the flesh. At the time of His crucifixion, people did not recognize Jesus and did not receive Him. They rejected Him, and they killed Him. The world had become devoid of God, and it was amoral. Jesus was more than persecuted; He was murdered. After Jesus was crucified and buried; He rose again on the third day. Jesus was resurrected.

Jesus' Resurrection is the core message of Christianity; yet, this message is rejected by many, including those who claim to be Christians. Many say that the crucifixion can be historically accepted: however, the evidence for the Resurrection is not convincing enough for others. Can a Christian reject the message of Resurrection? For me, the Gospel message that Jesus died on the Cross and that He was resurrected on the third day is the foundation for my belief system. What do I tell those who are seeking evidence for the Resurrection?

I would say that Biblical scholars and historians have provided three significant pieces of evidence that the Resurrection of Jesus occurred. The first was the "empty tomb"; Jesus' tomb was found empty soon after His interment. The second piece of evidence was the "eye-witness testimony of Jesus' physical appearance to individuals and groups after His Resurrection". The third piece of evidence was the persecution and death of all of His eleven disciples; this also pointed towards a Resurrected Jesus. The disciples proclaimed the Resurrected Jesus until their deaths. They lived lives of hardship for 30-40 years. They all died as martyrs, testifying for the Resurrected Jesus.

I believe that the spread of Christianity worldwide is also pointing towards the Resurrected Jesus, not a Jesus that just died on the Cross. It is His resurrection that gives me hope. It is His Resurrection that makes Him my destiny. Now, the hope I have in a Resurrected Jesus gives me meaning and purpose to live a morally responsible life.

It has been an amazing and a rewarding learning experience to explore Christianity and the Gospel of Jesus as my Worldview in comparison to other Worldviews. It gave me a greater appreciation of the teaching of Jesus with regard to Love as the supreme ethic, God's forgiveness as a gift, and the hope of an eternal life. I am truly grateful for this opportunity.

This takes me to the final section,

## Tenets of Postmodernism and its Impact on my Beliefs

The current context in North America seems to me to be that the culture war of Postmodernism is winning. The year 2020 has been an extremely challenging year. The following reasons give one a glimpse of these challenges.

In recent months, since mid-March 2020, we have been faced with the global pandemic of COVID-19 that has locked down all of us for months now (a life of seclusion, masks, and hand sanitizers). We still do not know when this lockdown will be fully lifted. We are now experiencing the second wave of COVID-19. This has been a very difficult year for most of us and worse for the poor. I am broken hearted to know that poor people in many parts of the world have no job, no income to buy food and are locked down in their little huts. They are starving and some dying. Many are lonely in care homes as visitors are restricted. Ranjit and I have been blessed to have our son Ajay, wife Joyti, and their two precious children living in the same house. We are grateful to have them around during this period of lockdown.

Moreover, in June, the brutal murder of George Floyd in the US, resulted in both peaceful and violent protests. The looting, and rioting in the aftermath, for the cause of Black Lives Matter (BLM) added confusion and fear across North America. The spread of COVID-19 is global; the unrest and uncertainty are global. The world economies are floundering. In addition, during the 2020 US election, the hatred between the Republicans and the Democrats has been quite palpable in the news media. These events gave me a pause to look up to God and realized the importance of spending more time in prayer.

I have learned that the ideology inherent in Postmodern culture has been challenging to my beliefs. For example, the Objective truth (unchanging truth) I believe in is replaced by relative truth (subjective truth). The Scripture I have read with reverence is being deconstructed, and new meaning is being created. In this concluding section, I am presenting the tenets of current Postmodern culture and its impact on my Christian beliefs.

The ideologies inherent in Postmodernism have been spreading fast in North America and the West. Currently, the Millennials (Generation Y) and Centennials (Gen Z) have been the two generational cohorts most impacted by these ideologies. I am concerned for my three grandchildren who are Centennials. Millennials (Generation Y), born between 1980 – 1995, have grown up in an "on-line and a social net-working" world. They have become the largest users of social media (Face-book, Texting, and Tweeting).

Centennials (Generation Z) were born between 1995 – to the present. This period has been tarnished by the attack on the Twin Towers in the US in 2001. Gen Z's share many characteristics with the Millennials; for example, they constantly use technology and social media. However, Centennials have become more aware of the ill-effects of technology. There are two billion of them world-wide. Our three grandchildren (Mila, Alea and Loic) are Gen Z's. I am concerned about the impact of Postmodern culture on their education and life in general. The challenge for parents is to raise their children to be technically savvy while keeping them safe from the ill-effects of technology.

In learning Postmodernism, I found it vague and complex. I have chosen the following tenets as I believe that these ones have had the most impact on my Christian beliefs.

- Deconstruction of Objective Truth
- Identity politics: Individual vs Groups
- Critical Theory / Critical Social Justice

I am examining these tenets in relation to their impacts on my beliefs.

## Deconstruction of Objective Truth

This is a dangerous tenet because it deals with the question, what is truth? Postmodernists claim that there is no Objective Truth. The existing truth is destroyed by individuals constructing their own truths from their lived experiences (Phenomenology). Thus, truth becomes relative to the experience of each individual and it is socially constructed. Whereas, Jesus claims, "I am the Truth". Thus, the truth that is proclaimed in the Scripture is objective.

If truth is constructed by individuals, it is relative to who is constructing it, and each person constructs his / her own truth. So, does Subjective Truth replace Objective Truth? If Subjective Truth is the preferred truth, what will happen if these truths are in contradiction to each other? Whose truth is the accepted truth? The Postmodernists try to discredit truth through an ideology called, "Deconstruction of the Met-narrative".

Deconstruction is the process by which Meta-narratives are taken apart, and the existing truth is destroyed. Jacques Derrida, a French Philosopher is considered the founding father of deconstruction. Derrida used deconstruction as a strategy to interpret Western thought and tear down its foundation. For example, in reading a book, the author's intentions are dismissed, and Subjective Truth is established by the reader. This has implications for children in the school system, and it is of concern to me because the Postmodernists' Relative (subjective) Truth may become the truth for our children in schools, in universities, and in public arenas.

Furthermore, the Bible is a grand narrative with objective meaning. In Postmodernism, it is dismissed in relation to its foundational interpretation. Thus, the real meaning of the Bible narrative is dismissed, and the underlying truth is destroyed or replaced with the Relative Truth of the person interpreting the Bible. For example, a Bible narrative is: "Life is sacred"; however, this is dismissed in Postmodernism by discrediting the sanctity of the individual.

I have also learned that Postmodern Christians welcome different interpretations for the Bible narratives and tend to deconstruct Bible verses. Individual interpretations are validated and accepted. I believe this would pave the way for moving away from the original intended meaning in the Scripture. I read the Bible with reverence, and I praise God for His message through the Bible. The claim of the "death of truth" is in violation to those who believe in the Bible, which contains the teachings of Jesus. As a Christian, I believe what the Bible says is true and trustworthy, a guide to salvation.

## Identity Politics: Individual vs Groups

I see myself as an autonomous individual and believe in the sanctity of life. In Postmodern culture, the sanctity of the individual and life is violated. The individual is persuaded to belong to an oppressed victim group. This ideology has divided people into identity groups. It is violating one's identity. What defines my identity? I am a woman, a wife, a mother, a grandmother, a sister, an aunt, and a friend. However, none of these titles defines me. Does my colour and my ethnicity define my identity? I do not belong to a specific identity group. I am a nurse, but that is my profession. I am a woman of colour, and I do not believe that my colour defines my identity. I see myself as an individual with essential worth, made in the image of God. That defines my identity.

Identity politics is when people of a particular group form an exclusive alliance with another group with a similar ideology or traits. By forming such groups, people are divided into groups based on their race, sex, gender, and class.

In race, people are divided into two groups, Whites against Blacks with the claim of racism. In sex, groups are men against women. This division has resulted in the domination of women by men, and it has been called patriarchy. In gender, people are divided into straight against LGBT (Lesbian, Gay, Bisexual, Transgender). This has led to conflict between straight and LGBT groups. In class, people are divided into the oppressors against the oppressed. This has resulted in the perception of oppression.

In such a division into groups, individual identity and autonomy are rejected for the group identity. The group is given priority over each individual in the group. Moreover, the idea of the autonomous individual is demolished, and there is no place for individual rights and responsibility. Individuals can be accused of the crimes of their group. The identity group claims that no one else understands the group other than the group itself. This group phenomena began with the Millennial generation, and it is reverting to Tribalism which is dangerous.

Identity politics is inconsistent with my belief in the sanctity of the individual. Moreover, salvation takes place at the individual level, not at the group level. Similarly, responsibility is placed at the individual level. Groups cannot be held responsible for action or inaction. In addition, suffering also takes place at the individual level; it is not the group that suffers. If my identity is my group, it takes away my right to do what I wish to do. Instead, I am forced to do what the group wants me to do. I am reminded here that Jesus did not place the adulteress woman in a group of "prostitutes"; he was concerned for her personal story. I have also noted that free speech is devalued in groups because sovereignty of the individual is denied. Individuals become the mouthpieces of their identity groups.

In the Gospel message, the sanctity of each individual is emphasized, and the message of love, grace and forgiveness is presented as personal. Such a personal message gives me essential worth. I am saved by His grace. My identity is defined by God who created me. Because God created me, He owns me, and He has authority over me; yet He also loves me. Thus, I am obligated to love Him and obey His commands. Because He is a living God, I am privileged to have a personal relationship with Him.

Since individuals are merely the mouthpieces of their group in Identity politics, they see themselves as victims and part of an oppressed group. They could become nihilistic, miserable, and even malevolent, with no gratitude. I have observed in schools the goal of Postmodernists is to give students a social identity and make them sensitive to racial, sexual and class identities. In university settings, people are silenced when they express any dissenting views on identity groups.

Some of the movements related to identity politics on campuses and across North America are the LGBT (Lesbian, Gay, Bisexual, Transgender) movement, the Black Lives Matter (BLM) Movement, the "Me Too" movement, and the Alt-Right Movement. In the US, with the recent brutal murder of George Floyd, BLM has become a forceful group, responsible for violent protests. On the other hand, looking back at history, peaceful protests have been successful in moving change forward, an example was, Martin Luther King Junior and his March on Washington.

## Critical Theory (CT) & Critical Social Justice (CSJ)

As I have explored the constructs of CT and CSJ, I have learned that Critical Theory is one of the fastest growing theories with its sub-theories and unique terminologies, in Postmodernism. I have only included here those that have a direct impact on Critical Social Justice. These are the following: Critical Race Theory, (a sub-theory of Critical Theory), Diversity, Inclusion, and Equity.

In my exploration of Critical Social Justice, I have observed that Christians are divided on the issues related to Social Justice. I have soon realized that Social Justice has been interpreted in two separate paradigms: one is the Marxist-based Critical Theory paradigm, and the other is the Gospel-based Biblical paradigm. So, I explored Social Justice from both paradigms to differentiate Social justice based on the Gospel message and Critical Social Justice based on Critical Theory.

Critical Theory originated from the Frankfurt School in Germany in 1930s as part of Social Research by a group of German philosophers. The founder of this Social Research group was Max Horkheimer, a German philosopher, and a sociologist. These philosophers were Marxist sympathizers. They were interested in finding out why Marxist prediction of the working class overthrowing the capitalists, failed. Many of these scholars left Germany and established themselves in Columbia University in New York. More recently, Critical Theorists were interested in not merely understanding the society. They were interested in finding out how the systems in society were failing people and how they could change the society. They focussed on systemic power and oppression in society with the goal of Social Activism.

Although Karl Marx did not coin the phrase "Critical Theory", the Marxist theory of class divisions was foundational to Critical Theory. The class division of rich versus poor was initially based on wealth distribution. It was later translated to oppressor versus oppressed based on power. A branch of Critical Theory focused on race, and it was called Critical Race Theory.

Marxist-based Critical Theory and Critical Race Theory were based on a secular worldview with no God or religion. In fact, Karl Marx denied the existence of God and coined the phrase: "Religion is the opiate of the masses". However, the foundation of the Biblical paradigm is God. The goals for Social Justice in these two paradigms are different.

In Critical Race Theory, the goals were the liberation of all oppressed groups and the eradication of oppression and racism at all levels. It also dealt with homophobia, income inequality, human rights violations, LGBTQ rights, child poverty, the criminal justice systems, access to abortion for the disadvantaged groups, promotion of Islamic immigration, and participation in the "Me too Movement". Critical Social Justice in Critical Theory also meant distributive justice, which was distribution of resources.

I believe oppression, domination, and racism are bad, and they are opposed to the Gospel message. Racism is real and pervasive. In the past, the Blacks suffered a great deal as a result of slavery in America. Similarly, Indigenous people also suffered a great deal in residential schools in Canada. Although slavery was abolished in America and all residential schools were closed down in Canada, its impact on Blacks in America and Indigenous people in Canada still remains.

In general, racism is defined as believing in the superiority or inferiority of groups of people. However, racism is redefined in Critical Race Theory based on two main constructs: White Privilege and White Fragility by Critical Race Theorist, Robin DiAngelo. She redefined racism as marginalizing people of colour within a system which results in inequality (DiAngelo, 2018).

Robin DiAngelo (2018) in her book "White Fragility: Why It's So Hard for White People to Talk about Racism" has defined the concepts of White Privilege and White Fragility. She presents racism as a system in which the Whites are raised and socialized in a white culture. As a result, the Whites have a racist worldview with racist biases and have a distorted view of "what it means to be a racist". She portrays the Whites as mentally fragile, morally deficient, and ethically inferior and claims that they must repent for their "whiteness". She argues that White people lack the "racial stamina" to deal with racism, and she calls this White Fragility.

I have found this book to be a true depiction of Postmodern ideology as what is presented in this book is what the author professes as her subjective truth. Yet, she is propagating it as truth for everyone else.

In Critical Race Theory, a stark division has been made between Whites and Blacks and has made the claim that all Blacks are identified as victims of systemic racism. All structures, orders, and authorities are oppressive, and Whites are the oppressors while Blacks are the oppressed. It has further claimed that "whiteness" makes the Whites more "privileged". This is called White Privilege. One way to deal with the White Privilege is to be "antiracist". The purpose of being "antiracist" is to elevate the Black voice.

I am dismayed to learn of DiAngelo's claim that Black people who work with White people suffer from "microaggressions" resulting from indirect, subtle, or unintentional discrimination. So, she suggests that White people must be on guard always to prevent "microaggressions". Moreover, Whites can never be free of racism; thus, the claim "I am not a racist" prevents them from critically examining their "white supremacist culture". She suggests that the Whites do antiracial work to "become woke" (woke refers to becoming aware of racism and injustice), which would help them to see through the lens of oppression. She further advocates that the Whites undergo a life-long program of "race conscious education" to minimize racism in them. DiAngelo has strongly described the Whites as not only racists, but as, "incurable racists" because of their white skin colour.

I reject DiAngelo's theory of White Fragility. My rejection is based on DiAngelo identifying all White people as racists because of their white skin colour. This is dangerous and playing Identity Politics. In fact, as a woman of colour, my experience with White people has been quite different. Many White men and women have been kind, respectful, helpful, understanding, and loving in their relationships with me. I have identified many White people in my life story who have sacrificed their lives for the poor and the disadvantaged, the Blacks, and the people of colour. So, we must celebrate their contributions also.

In addition, according to Critical Race Theory, all White heterosexual men are privileged, morally bad, and oppressors, while all Black women are victims of white-male oppressors. In the West, Straight White Men are hated collectively. The only way a cisgender (sex is same as gender), White, heterosexual man can escape his White Privilege is by becoming an ally of a "victim group" and becoming "woke" on an ongoing basis. The death of White culture is seen as liberating. For me, such thinking is divisive, racist, and dangerous.

More recently, during the Black Lives Matter (BLM) protests, I saw a four-year old girl holding a placard with an apology for "being white". I also saw a young White woman on bended knees on the road apologizing to a Black person for "being White". This was absurd to me. How could a person be held responsible for "being White"? The underlying message was that White people were born as racists, they lived as racists, and there was no forgiveness for their White Privilege.

I also watched "group humiliation" in the cause of realizing White Privilege, where a group of White people were kneeling down on the floor and apologizing to the Blacks for "being White". They also washed the feet of a group of Black people. Was this a symbol of "group humility" from the White race? I believe being humble or having humility should happen at an individual level, not as a group phenomenon. They were made to apologize for the wrongdoings of their White ancestors. This was against what Jesus taught. Sin, redemption, and salvation occur at the individual level.

Moreover, White people are accused of having "unconscious or implicit biases". Stereotypes are one kind of "unconscious bias". In organizations, "unconscious (implicit) bias training" is offered to reduce unintentional discrimination. Also, there are Bias Response Teams in organizations, especially in universities to which employees and students can report "biased speech" or "speech as violence".

The role of Social Justice Advocates is to identify the victim groups who are oppressed and in minorities. Commonly identified victim groups are Blacks, women, LGBTQA (lesbian, gay, bisexual, transgender, queer, and allies), people with disabilities, immigrants, and other minority groups. Although women are not a minority group, they are identified as an oppressed group; therefore, they are also considered to be victims.

Some groups belong to more than one victimhood. This is phrased as "intersectionality", a construct inherent in Critical Theory. The phrase "intersectionality" was coined by Critical Race Theorist, Kimberle Crenshaw in 1989. It means adding other struggles of victimhood to a particular disadvantaged group. For example, women being Black, lesbian, and poor leads to multiple disadvantages. Thus, they belong to multiple victim groups. These disadvantaged groups are victims of oppression, so the privileged cannot blame them for their shortcomings. If a person does get blamed, it is called "victim blaming", which is a concept inherent in Critical Race Theory.

I saw brutal injustices in India in how the "untouchables" were treated by those belonging to higher castes. It was not the White skin colour that caused oppression and injustice towards the "untouchables". It was caused by sin in the human heart. What needed was a transformation of the human heart to embrace the "untouchables" without discriminating them as outcastes.

In the Gospel message, the focus is on helping the individual who is in need, whereas, in Critical Social Justice it is about group rights. The Gospel message also emphasizes that racism, oppression, and domination are manifested as a result of evil acts by people. It is the sin that leads to evil acts and not the colour of one's skin. In God, we all are equal as we all are made in His own image. However, there is evil in this world and in our hearts.

In the Gospel message, both victims and victimizers need forgiveness. Both the oppressors and the oppressed need a saviour. One cannot repent for the sins committed by someone else. We must acknowledge that racism exists and confront the structures of racism in existence. Racial superiority or inferiority is in contradiction to the Gospel message as, in God, we all are equal. God demands justice; it is not optional in the Gospel. We must be about justice because injustice is a sin.

The Bible verse, Micah 6:8 states: "He has shown you, O man, what is good; and what does the Lord require of you, but to do justly, to love mercy, and to walk humbly with your God". Christians must stand for justice. God also demands of us acts of kindness, charity, justice and generosity as stated in Isaiah 58:7; "Share your bread with the hungry, and that you bring to your house the poor who are cast out; when you see the naked, that you cover him and not hide yourself from your own flesh". The Gospel message is, "in God we all are equals".

In Critical Theory, the constructs of Diversity, Inclusion, and Equity took on a different meaning than one I have been familiar with. These words do not mean what I think they mean. Constructs of Diversity, Inclusion, and Equity are constructs inherent in Critical Theory.

Diversity, according to traditional theory is, recognizing individual differences, considering alternate viewpoints, and respecting other perspectives. I believe that each one of us is unique in our way of being and be given the opportunity to make individual contributions.

Growing up I saw people around me as belonging to one ethnicity with different belief systems. However, there were class distinction based on wealth (rich vs poor) and of course there were differences in sex, men vs women. I have believed in the value in diversity in that individuals bring different perspectives and knowledge that can be enriching to the group and organization. I have now learned that diversity is interpreted differently in Critical Theory.

In Critical Theory, diversity sets one individual apart from another based on, ethnicity. It recognizes individual differences in relation to race, ethnicity, gender, sexual orientation, belief systems, and physical disabilities. Thus, people are divided into various groups based on the above individual differences. However, in Critical Race Theory, the main focus is on ethnicity (colour of the skin).

People are divided into groups based on the premise that people belonging to a particular ethnic or racial group think alike. For example, all Black people think alike. Thus, they must be appointed to committees and boards to speak on behalf of the Blacks. Implied in this belief is that a Black person is needed to speak for the Blacks in general. I believe that it is not a person's ethnicity or colour that makes a person qualified to represent another person. A non-black could very well know more about the plight of the Blacks than another Black person. Many examples come to mind where a White person has pleaded for the rights of a Black person or an Indigenous person.

For example, when I was working in Hazelton, I witnessed Dr. Whiting, a White man, pleading and working on behalf of the Indigenous population in Hazelton and its surrounding villages. I observed how genuinely and tirelessly Dr. Whiting worked to improve living conditions for the Indigenous people. He employed mostly Indigenous people in various hospital departments. I was touched by his love for the Indigenous people, and I saw him as a person who could fairly plead on behalf of an Indigenous person. Moreover, I am a woman of Brown colour and I do not see myself as qualified to speak on behalf of Brown people because my perspective is not based my Brown skin colour. I think I have integrated perspectives from different cultures.

In Canada, the majority White population is making changes to accommodate minority groups. Universities are setting aside seats in programs with selective admission for non-white students, e.g. Black and Indigenous students. For example, in the Nursing program with selective

260

admission, we set aside a certain number of seats each year for Indigenous students, despite the fact that more qualified students would have applied for admission to the program. This is done to provide opportunities for Indigenous students to become Registered Nurses.

Inclusion, in traditional sense, means everyone is accepted without discrimination by others regardless of their race, gender, religious beliefs, or sexual orientation. It means openly "welcoming" a person to the group. Inclusion gives the person a sense of connection and belonging to the group or organization.

However, in Critical Race Theory, I have learned that Inclusion means restrictive speech. In a diverse group, one has to be cautious about saying anything that may potentially hurt another's feeling. It is one way of protecting the feeling of a person who is "oppressed" or a "victim." For example, a white person may keep silence as there is the possibility of that person being racist towards the Black person.

In Critical Race Theory, even the presence of a white person can cause "microaggression" towards a Black person. Keeping silence is more acceptable than saying "I am not a racist". By Inclusion, the "victim" is given a voice and power to speak up. Increasing power to the "victim" is a goal in Critical Race Theory. Moreover, Critical Race Theorists advocate that organizations set aside segregated safe spaces for Blacks to recover from "microaggressions" resulting from unconscious biases a White person. I believe such thinking is divisive, promoting racism.

Equity: I have learned that the construct of equity is interpreted differently in different context and is usually addressed along with equality.

Equity is commonly understood as the equality of outcome and it is different from equality of opportunity. I have observed that inequity and inequality exist in the world. I often ponder if we could ever eliminate all inequalities and inequities in this world. Inequality exists at different levels. For example, people are unequal in relation to economic status (wealth) and social privileges (ethnicity, age, height, IQ, good health, attractiveness, sexual orientation etc.).

"All inequities and inequalities must be eliminated" is the slogan for Social Justice warriors. Can we eliminate all inequities and inequalities? How can we achieve equality of outcome? If equity is meant as fairness in treating everyone equally despite their colour, creed, or ethnicity, then it is achievable. However, if equity is meant as equality of outcome, I am skeptical that we can achieve it. How do we encourage and reward excellence? If we do not reward excellence, the incentive for striving for a higher outcome is taken away.

Is achieving equity and equality for everyone, a utopian vision? The countries who tried it failed miserably. For example, Stalin in Socialist Russia had promised to bring about utopia through bringing equity and equality for all. He failed miserably with the loss of millions of lives. Even equality itself is hard to achieve in many situations. I believe that we must strive for the equality of opportunity for all. There is a move towards trying to achieve equity in organizations (the school system, municipal organizations) through adopting policies.

Postmodernists advocate that society must be altered and that bias must be eliminated until all the outcomes are equitable. I understand that we can measure outcomes, but can we achieve equality in outcomes for everyone? Every individual is unique with different capabilities, strengths, talents, and acumen and may vary in their achievements.

Equity is practiced in children's sports. The same medals are given out to every child on a particular team to celebrate equity. Each player is given a trophy for participation; there are no champions or prizes for those who excelled in the game. We cannot reward excellence because it is in violation of the Postmodern ideology of equity. Whereas my athletic son who played professional hockey told me that competing was essential even at a young age to play your best and to have fun in playing. Competition results in inequitable outcome.

Back to the topic of Critical Social Justice: the question still remains, does Critical Social Justice mean what I think it means? Justice is doing what is right. In Critical Social Justice, the focus is on a group or groups. Whereas the Gospel message is aimed at the individual. Two central Gospel messages are the love of God and His forgiveness of our sins. God loves each one of us individually and forgiveness is granted on a personal basis. In the Biblical paradigm, the individual is the focus, not a group. Also, salvation is granted to the individual; there is no group salvation. It is the individual who is responsible, not the group.

Another aspect of Critical Theory that deals with sexuality is also worth examining here. It has been asserted that being gay and transgender is hardware-related, which means one cannot change; whereas being a woman is software, which means one can change. It is argued in Critical Theory that "being woman" is not biological, but it is a role that is socially constructed. Thus, anyone can play the role of a woman. This has implications for the roles of fathers and mothers in a family and in parenting.

I have observed a real change in the roles of fathers and mothers in parenting children watching my two sons as fathers. They are a lot more involved in actually caring for their children compared to my father's role in caring for his children. It is great to see more domesticity in males today, as opposed to when I was growing up.

Justice is to set things right. God is just. Jesus is our standard who has lived a perfect and sinless life and died a sacrificial death. As a follower of Christ, I am called to do justice. However, injustices are everywhere in the world. For example, child abuse, family violence, sex trafficking, and sex trade are real injustices. How do we deal with these injustices? Slavery is still prevalent in many countries in the world. How do we deal with the existing brutality of slavery in the world especially in African countries?

Learning the history of slavery is important. For example, the Jim Crow Laws and the suffering involved in lynching has given me insight into the injustices that occurred during slavery in America. I was devastated to learn about the suffering of the Black slaves as a result of lynching. Such suffering should have never happened. However, blaming the whole White race now for the atrocities committed by the evil human beings who were slave owners is not doing justice. To bring about justice, there has to

263

be a change of heart from evil acts to loving acts. We must have a heart to love one another. That is the Gospel message.

Social Justice warriors advocate for the state redistribution of power and wealth (advantages and resources) to disadvantaged groups. For them, the issue of Social Justice cannot be debated. Social Justice warriors claim that their identity is inseparable from their group identity. No debate or dialogue occurs, but the opposing party has the right to remain silent.

On the other hand, the Gospel message emphasizes the need for justice and peace. God hates unkindness and injustices: yet, God is willing to pardon the sins of those who repent. Both victims and victimizers need forgiveness and need a saviour. However, one cannot repent for the sin committed by someone else. God demands that we have mercy, as mercy triumphs over judgment. As a Christian, I must stand for justice. We are image bearers, so, we have to live in truth. As Christians, we are obligated to help the poor and the needy. As per Isiah 1:7: We are to do good, seek justice, rebuke the oppressor, defend the fatherless, and plead for the widow.

Jesus also teaches us to give cheerfully and freely. He never forces us to give. "Each of you should give, not reluctantly or under compulsion, for God loves a cheerful giver" (2 Corinthians, 9: 7). The message of giving in the Bible is based on the premise that we, as Christians, must care for the poor, the hungry, and the disabled. Jesus also despises those who love money and hoard wealth: "The love of money is the root of evil" (Galatians 2:10). Matthew 19:2 reads: "If you wish to be perfect, go sell your possessions and give the money to the poor and you will have treasures in heaven". The Bible reveals two perspectives in this regard: money and wealth are evils to be avoided, and prosperity and well-being are blessings from God. The need for wealth is also seen as a resource to foster a good life.

For me, to be able to give is a blessing, and I cherish the freedom of choice that I have in my giving. I reject the Socialist philosophy of forcefully taking what I own and giving it to others against my will. As I understand it, the shared wealth is distributed to identity groups, for example, groups based on race, sex, gender, and class. Not everyone in the group may need the help. Here the group is the prime target, not the individual. However, I do believe that I have an obligation to give to the poor who are starving and suffering. I thank God for placing me in a position to be able to give, rather than to receive. The Gospel message is personal to each individual. The individual is the one who is oppressed and is suffering. How can I show the love of Jesus to others? This takes me to the conclusion of my story.

## CONCLUSION

## What Can I Say?   What Can I Do ?

Within the current Postmodern culture, how can I share the message of Jesus? I have faith in God, but faith is a difficult concept to explain to someone who does not believe in God. For example, Dawkins (atheist) asserts that faith is for those who do not seek evidence. However, the Bible states: "Faith is the confidence in what we hope for and the assurance about what we do not see" (Hebrew, 11:1).

The new Atheists and the Secular Humanists have demanded that God and religion are kept out of the public arena. This has had an impact on Christianity in secular nations. Yet, Gospel message is growing while Christians are being persecuted in many countries. Iran plays a lead role in this persecution, while the message of Christ is spreading in Iran. I often wondered whether I would be courageous enough to suffer persecution for the sake of Christ. I must admit, I have been timid in sharing my Christian faith openly. However, being a Christian I have an obligation to live by the Gospel message.

What Can I Say? I know I have a story to tell, the story of Jesus. I have heard people say, faith and religion should be kept as a private matter. This has been my dilemma. So, I kept my faith as a private matter. Political correctness has stifled me from openly talking about God in public. As a woman of colour, I wanted to integrate myself into the mainstream and immerse myself in the academic culture. I wanted to be a part of the big group, to be accepted, and to be respected by my colleagues. I wanted to advance in my career. Academic culture is mostly a Godless culture. So, I refrained from talking about my faith in God at my workplace.

I do share my beliefs with those whom I feel comfortable. However, I have been hesitant to speak and share my beliefs with non-believers. I recall, when Jesus was captured by the Romans, the young woman told Peter: "You are one of them". Peter was afraid and denied this claim. Fear made Peter deny Jesus three times. What is keeping me from sharing my beliefs with others?

I go to church, read the Bible, pray to God, but I seldom share my beliefs with others. I am reminded of how Dawkins ridiculed those who believed in God as deluded or insane. For Atheists, God is a delusion. I do not want to expose myself to such groups. I do not want to offend anyone. I do not want to be ridiculed by anyone.

On the other hand, as a Christian, I have an obligation to share the love of Jesus to others. I have learned that people can change their worldviews. However, they need to hear the story of Jesus. Fear and shame are stumbling blocks. How can I get past such stumbling blocks? Keeping Jesus in my heart as my Lord is the beginning step. I have learned that the antidote to fear is setting Jesus apart in my heart. I must rely on God to give me courage and strength.

I should always be ready to give an answer to those who ask. I think I have grown in this aspect as my spiritual journey has been a journey of learning. Yet, I ask, am I ready to share the message of hope with others? Sharing the message of hope must be a dialogue, and I must listen to the person. I must be prepared to admit it if I do not know the answer to a question. I know I have so much more to learn. If I am answering a question, I need to be sensitive to what the questioner holds valuable and try to answer the questioner, rather than merely focussing on the question and the content. My tone is more important than my content. Never forget the Cross as it is the central message of the Gospel.

What is the message of hope? Hope is a virtue. I have the Hope that God loves me. My Hope also brings me joy in my life. It helps me to stay positive in times of hardship. I have the assurance that God will be with me through turbulent times. I do have the Hope of an eternal life, and it helps me to tackle today with courage. My Hope is in Christ Jesus.

I have come to realize that spending quality time to learn the message of Hope keeps me grounded. The Word of God gives me wisdom to differentiate false doctrines from the Gospel message. I have come to believe that a firm foundation in the Gospel is essential during this uncertain and turbulent time in the 21st century and within a Postmodern culture.

The world around me is filled with fear, conflict, and hardship. The future looks uncertain. There is pain and suffering around me. I must try to place myself in the place of the person who is hurting. I must act in a way that demonstrates empathy, humility, and grace. I must be willing to share in the pain of others. In addition to sharing the message of Hope, I must act out my beliefs; if not, I am an empty vessel.

What Can I Do? Upon reflecting on my beliefs, I have identified the following areas as important ones for me to act upon:

Love my God with all my heart,

Love my neighbour and also love my enemy

Forgive others as I forgive myself

Show humility in my day-to-day life.

I find it easier to "act out" my beliefs than "speak out" my beliefs. However, it takes courage, discipline, and commitment to act out my beliefs on a day-to-day basis. I am sure it is a lot easier to live a life not believing in God, because then a person is free to do what he/she pleases. Fuoco, the French Postmodern philosopher, told us to live without boundaries. Jesus told us to love God, love our neighbour, and love our enemy.

Loving God with all my heart: I believe the central message of the Gospel is "to love". The famous chapter in 1 Corinthians, Chapter 13, is dedicated to describing love as a gift from God and its characteristics. It is also written in the Bible that "God is Love": "For God so loved the world He gave His one and only Son that whoever believes in Him shall not perish but have everlasting life" (John 3:16). This verse proclaims His utmost sacrificial love for us all. We are also told to: "Love your God with all your heart and mind and all your might". In fact, this is the first commandment. Putting God first in everything I do is not easy. I need His constant guidance to do this.

268

Jesus told the famous parable of the "prodigal son", which showed the ultimate love of a father for his son. The father loved his son without any condition and forgave him for what the son had done in the past. The son came to ask for forgiveness. He was already forgiven. Loving God and loving one another was greater than any other commandment. Love triumphed over hate.

Loving my neighbour as myself and loving my enemy: Loving my enemy is a revolutionary idea. It is a difficult commandment to follow. Love and forgiveness are the central messages of the Gospel. Jesus said that if someone hits you on one cheek, turn your other cheek. C.S Lewis asserts that an unpopular Christian virtue presented in the Bible is this one: "Thou shall love thy neighbour as thyself". He goes onto say that within Christian morals "thy neighbour includes thy enemy" (Lewis, 1980, p153).

Lewis is trying to make sure we understand "what loving your neighbour as yourself" means. Lewis poses the question; how exactly do we love ourselves? Loving oneself is based on the principle that "hate the sin, but not the sinner". Lewis asserts that we do this when we apply this to ourselves; "We hate our actions, yet we love ourselves". He wants the same rule to be applied to dealing with our enemies, in hating their actions and yet loving them as persons.

It is not enough to love our parents, children, siblings, and those who love us. I am to love those who are lowly and who are different from me. It is easy to love those who are of a high status. I see this trend in families. I must reach out to those who are in need and lowly, "the least of these". Reflect the love of Jesus to all persons around us. The Good Samaritan, out of compassion and love, helped a stranger who was beaten and left on the roadside. This was love in action. One example of showing my love to the needy is to open my home to share a meal with a poor family. I am grateful that now I understand what it means to be "loving your enemy" means.

Forgiving others as I forgive myself: Like love, forgiveness is demanded of us by Jesus. Forgiveness is a deliberate decision to release feelings of resentment or vengeance towards a person or a group who has harmed me.

In relation to forgiveness, I have two choices: one is to forgive the person(s) who harmed me; two is to keep the anger and hatred toward the person(s). If I forgive, I am better able to move forward without bitter feelings. On the other hand, if I cannot forgive, I am keeping resentment and hatred in my heart. Jesus tells us to "forgive seventy times seven" (Matthew, 17:21). This seems to be an impossible act. However, I can do anything with God's help and guidance.

I have heard people ask how can we forgive Hitler for the atrocities he had committed and in exterminating six million Jews? Based on the principle above, Hitler hated the Jews and enjoyed murdering them, thus he deserved punishment. It was up to God and the law of the land to punish him.

I was also reminded of the Louisiana prison where the prisoners on death row heard the message of Jesus and repented of their sins that they had committed. Yet, they awaited the day of their execution under the law of the land. However, they had peace and hope in their hearts. I had struggled with this principle in the past and it made sense to me now. Those who had committed crimes and were deserving of punishment repented of their crimes, but they still had to face the punishment according the law of the land.

Showing humility in my everyday life: Being humble is such a significant part of being a true follower of Jesus. The life of Jesus is a true model of humility. The opposite of humility is pride. C.S. Lewis has identified pride as the great sin, the essential vice, and utmost evil. Pride is manifested when one ignores and patronizes others; they want to be the big noise at a party. Pride leads one to be greedy and selfish. Pride and the greed for power and money can cause people to cheat others, including one's own family members.

Power is what pride really enjoys. Wanting power reminds me of the existential philosopher Nietzsche, a German genius, who rejected the message of humility in Christianity. He talked about the superman with power, and he wanted to be above God. Pride is the enmity to God. Lucifer wanted to be more powerful than God. Similarly, Adam and Eve wanted to be like God and listened to the serpent rather than obeying what God had instructed.

If I am proud, I would be looking down upon others, but if I am humble, I would be looking up. My greatness would come from humbling myself and looking up to God. Jesus left His crown to pick up the Cross. That is humility in heaven. I have come to the realization that I must have a life steeped in prayer to show humility, to love God, to forgive others and to love my neighbour. I am not able to do it alone, just by relying on my knowledge and strength.

Jesus has called Christians who are proud and self-righteous, hypocrites. The Christian hypocrites look down on others and tend to judge them. Here I am reminded of the following Bible verse: "Thou hypocrite, first cast out the beam out of thine own eye, and then shalt thou see clearly to cast out the mote of thy brother's eyes" (Matthew 7:5). As Christians, we are to live a life of humility, a significant moral virtue.

My desire is to live a life of "more than me" by knowing Jesus deeply and making Him known. I want to tell my story of joy, peace, and blessings that I have in my life. I look at my three grandchildren and ask the question, do I really deserve the joy they bring to me in my life? How do I make my life count? I must pray for help to make me a storyteller about Jesus. I need to get used to asking the question, what is the intent of my actions? Is it to promote myself or to glorify God? I need to act in a way that demonstrates empathy, humility, and grace. I need to feel compassion that leads to action, which leads to sharing the pain of others. Doing good to others is also my moral obligation.

As I have come to end of my story, I am concerned that in the 21st century, people are in a disarray. Fear and uncertainty are causing depression and anxiety in people. Suicide rates among the young are on the rise. Our young people do not know where to find meaning in life. The average person does not know who Jesus is. Have we violated the purpose of life? A car is made for transportation, and if it is used for killing people, it is a violation of purpose. We have turned away from that which we are made for. How can we reconnect? How can I live out my beliefs?

I have a responsibility to express my gratitude for what God has done for me in my life. I look at myself and see how blessed I am. God has given me health to live a fulfilling life. I am grateful for keeping Ranjit and me alive to enjoy our grandchildren. God has blessed me with a loving family. Above all, I have been privileged to experience the love of Jesus. I must express my gratitude in having all that I am blessed with.

I came to Canada with very little, to a country of freedom and opportunity. I was naïve and single. I was far away from my parents and my siblings. I had the freedom to love God or reject God. I had the freedom to live a morally responsible life or live a life without boundaries. However, I knew I was accountable to God. Although I have made mistakes in my life, I am grateful to God that He has guided me to stay on His path.

Fast forward to 2020. Fifty-six years later, I am even more convinced that my Christian beliefs gave me the best answers to life's big questions of origin, meaning, morality and destiny. The Gospel message of love, forgiveness, and the hope of an eternal life gave me courage to face dark times in my life. I have also learned that we have the free will to make our own choices. With wisdom from above and a life steeped in prayer, we can make the right choice. This is the message I leave for my children, grandchildren, family, and friends.

Alea and Mila 2019

Dear Mila:

You are our first-born grandchild. We had waited for a long time for a grandchild, so when you were born, your Dada and Ammachi were so happy. I thanked God for giving me such a precious granddaughter.

Mila, you are almost four years old now. I remember so well the day you were born. Because you were born few days earlier, you were tiny (only 4 pounds and 11 ounces). So, your doctor kept you in the intensive care unit for the first day. You had to be fed milk in a small cup. I just loved feeding you and watching you how you were sucking with your tiny lips. You were so good and drank milk drop by drop from a tiny cup. Gradually you gained enough strength to drink milk from a bottle. You slept most of the time for the first few days.

I was so happy when you smiled the first time, you looked beautiful. Then you began to say few words. Once you began to speak you were so clear and then you learned to sing songs. You loved watching the movie Frozen. I was amazed when you told Alexa to sing, "into the unknown from Frozen two". You loved us watching you perform by singing and dancing. You loved books being read to you. Your mom and dad took you to library and signed out books for you. You also had a collection of your own books. You loved the stories, the elephant, and the tailor; the boy and the wolf were your favorite ones.

You can count now and know the alphabets too. You can also write your name. You love colouring and really good at doing puzzles. You also love going to Sunday school. I will tell you one story about you: one day you came upstairs after dinner and told me that your stomach was hurting and needed medicine. You said, "Ammachi give me a Lindor for my stomach-ache". That was your tricky way of asking for a treat. When your brother, Loic was born, you loved watching him and later playing with him. Loic just loves playing with you. You are his loving big sister.

Ammachi and Dada love you so much. I know you will be good in your studies. Love God and listen to mom and dad. Ammachi

Dear Alea:

I could not see you when you were born as you were in Vancouver. I was in Kamloops. Your Daddy called us right after you were born and told us you were a beautiful healthy baby girl. We were filled with joy to have our second granddaughter. Your mom and dad were happy to take you home on the third day. Your daddy called us when he was driving you home from the hospital. It was late at night. He said, "Alea is crying without stopping and don't know what to do". He found out later you were hungry, and they had no milk to give you. Most stores were closed. You cried until your dad got milk for you from a drugstore. We all were relieved. I was so thrilled to see you as a chubby baby, a bundle of joy.

Alea, you are growing to be a big girl now, three years old. You are so active and full of energy. You are strong and could go up and down the stairs before you were two years old. You learned to count up to ten in both in English and in Mandarin. That is amazing. It is great your mom is teaching you Mandarin. You have so many toys and your favorite toy is Robert. You also love reading books. You love singing "O Canada", our National Anthem. Your second birthday was lots of fun. You were the star and we all had fun. Enjoyed watching you play with your cousins and friends. We loved watching the video of your school Christmas concert, you loved dancing.

Dada and I love whenever you came to Kamloops with your mom and dad. I wish you lived closer, then we could see you more often. You love playing with Mila and sometimes you both have fights. Alea, you are strong and tough and love riding your bike. I was surprised to see you driving your bike along with your dad for a long way. You did not get tired. You had so much energy.

You are a precious gift. Dada and Ammachi love you very much. Come and visit us in Kamloops.

With lots of love and blessings: Ammachi

276

Dear Loic:

Loic, February 2020

The day you were born was the happiest day in our family. How precious it was to have a healthy grandson. You were born on February 23rd, and I have been noticing changes each day in you. We are so fortunate to have you in the same house that we can see you every day. It is such a blessing. Your smile is so precious, and it makes all of us think how precious a gift you are. You are such a good baby, you drink milk when hungry, play and sleep and seldom cry. Your big sister Mila loves to play with you. Sometimes she is little rough, and we tell her to be gentle with you.

Just few days after you were born, there was an outbreak of a viral infection called COVOD-19 (Coronavirus Disease 2019). We just thank God, when you were born in Kamloops hospital n February there was COVID 19. However, it started spreading fast. Loic, we are following the guidelines to keep you and the rest of the family safe. So, the first four months after your birth, we had no one visiting us. Your Mamy came when you were born. That was a great help. Then your Nana and Nany came to see you. Your Thaya and Mama had to wait patiently for few months before they could see you. This was a very unusual time for us. When you grow bigger you may hear about this pandemic.

Dada loves playing with you and look forward to spending time with you each day. We long to see you grow up and hear you talk and see you walk. This morning you gave me a big smile. You looked at me when I called your name. You have a smart and beautiful sister, Mila who is very protective of you.

You are getting heavy for me to carry you around now. You love being outside and you watch the with eager eyes what is going on around you. You are curious when I take you around.

You are the happiest baby and make us all happy too, a precious gift from God. Everyday, we see difference in you, the way you smile and your expressions. You are so gentle mannered and content. You wave now and say bye. Just can't wait to hear you talk and also walk.

May God keep you safe and healthy. Ammachi will be praying for you.

Ammachi and Dada love you so much. With lots of love: Ammachi

## Appendix A: Learning Sources

Christian Apologists

Ravi Zacharias, (Born and raised in India, lived in Canada, now in the US) is a Christian Apologist and Founder of RZIM (Ravi Zacharias International Ministry). He is a renowned speaker (travels to many countries), writer and author of many books.

Book: Can Man Live Without God (1994)

John Lennox, an Irish Mathematician, a philosopher of science, Christian apologist, and Emeritus professor of Mathematics at Oxford University and a great speaker.

Book: Seven Days That Divide the World (2011).

Stephen Meyer, Director of the Center for Science and Culture at Discovery Institute in Seattle, Received PhD in philosophy from University of Cambridge. He presented and debated his 'Intelligent Design' argument.

Book: Signature in the Cell (2009).

Frank Turek, speaker, author, President of CrossExamined.org, dynamic speaker, a great defender of Christian faith.

Book: Stealing from God (2014).

Tim Keller, Pastor of the Redeemer Presbyterian Church in Manhattan, New York, writer, and author. Has planted many churches in the US.

Book: Reason for God (2008).

Nabeel Qureshi, Christian Apologist, Medical Doctor, a devout Muslim, who became a follower of Jesus. He was diagnosed with stage four stomach cancer and died in 2016, at age of 34.

Book: Seeking Allah Finding Jesus (2014), New York Times Bestseller.

C.S. Lewis, One of the intellectual giants of the 20th century, and most influential Christian writer of his day. He was a fellow and tutor in English literature at Oxford University, chair of Medieval and Renaissance English at Cambridge University.

Book: Mere Christianity (1952, 1980)

Dinesh D'Souza, an Indian-born American Conservative, political commentator, author, filmmaker, a speaker, and a great debater. Book: The Big Lie (2017).

James White, Director of Alpha and Omega Ministries, a Christian apologist, writer, and author.

Book: The Forgotten Trinity (1998).

William Lane Craig, An American Analytic philosopher, a Christian theologian, on Faculty at Biola University, Renowned scholar, writer, and author.

Book: Philosophical Foundations for a Christian Worldview (2003).

David Sharpe Wood, A former atheist, now an American evangelical missionary, a critique of Islam, and head of the Acts 17 Apologetics Ministry. A member of the Society of Christian Philosophers. A close friend of Nabeel Qureshi.

I have relied on his sermons and debates and not his books.

Hugh Norman Ross, A Canadian Christian apologist, Old Earth Creationist, with a Ph.D. in Astronomy from University of Toronto. Book: Creator and the Cosmos (1993).

Abdu H. Murray, an attorney by training is the North American Director of RZIM, a devout Muslim became a devout Christian, an apologist, speaker, and author.

Book: Grand Central Questions: Answering the Critical Concerns of the Major Worldviews (2014).

I have also learned from speeches by Christian preacher, Michael Ramsden, and Christian scientist, James Tour.

New Atheists

Richard Dawkins is an English ethologist, evolutionary biologist, and author. He was a professor at Oxford University, now an emeritus fellow of New College, Oxford. He is known as the 'guru' of the four horsemen of New Atheists: (Sam Harris, Late Christopher Hitchens, Daniel Dennett).

Book: The God Delusion (2006).

Sam Harris is an American author, neuroscientist, philosopher, blogger and podcast host and a critic of religions. His field of study is in philosophy and Neuroscience. Educated at Stanford, his thesis: Moral Landscape, how science could determine human values (2009).

Book: The End of Faith (2005).

Daniel Dennett is an American philosopher, writer, and cognitive scientist. Educated at both Cambridge and Oxford universities,

Speaker, debater, and author of many books.

Book: Consciousness Explained (1991).

(Late) Christopher Hitchens was an English, author, columnist, orator, journalist, and social critic, speaker, and debater.

Book: God is not Great, Religion Poisons Everything (2009).

Lawrence Krause, cosmologist, taught at Yale and Arizona State Universities, author, speaker and debater.

Book: A Universe from Nothing (2012).

Michael Shermer is an American science writer and the founder of the Skeptic Society. He was a Christian and is ow a skeptic.

Book: The Moral Arc (2015).

Peter Singer is an Australian moral philosopher, a professor of Bioethics at Princeton University, he is influenced by Karl Marx, speaker, and author.

Book: Animal Liberation (1975).

Other scholars

Jordan Peterson, who has become a popular figure recently, when he published his book, Twelve Rules for Life, in 2018. He is cited as one of the most influential Canadian thinkers of our times. He does not call himself a Christian apologist or an atheist, but says he lives as though God exists. I have found his presentations inspiring and his book, offering a lot of practical wisdom and critique of ideologies.

David Berlinski is known as a secular Jew and a skeptic. He is a Mathematician and a philosopher. He wrote the book: A Devil's Delusion (2013) as a rebuttal to Richard Dawkins' book: 'The God Delusion'.

Listening to presentations, debates and interviews on You Tube by both Christian apologists and atheists listed in Appendix A is my main learning source and my main mode of learning. I am amazed at how easy it was to access presentations and debates on You Tube.

The Holy Bible

However, the most meaningful learning source for me was and still is, the Holy Bible. I was fortunate to have a copy of the 'Life Application Bible', the New King James Version.

The Bible was written between BC 1500 and AD 100 and it took 1600 years to complete both Old and New Testaments. It was written by 40 authors. The 66 books in the Bible were initially written in Hebrew, Greek, Latin, and Aramaic and later translated to English and other languages. Moses wrote the first five books in the Bible. John wrote the last book (Revelation). The Bible is identified as a conversation between

God and human and is a Book of God's words that answers the 'why' questions in life. Whereas, science is the book of nature that explains the 'how' questions. Science does not talk about what is reality, good and evil, love and suffering. Science does not deal with purpose and meaning in life. I go to the Bible for answers to such questions.

# ACKNOWLEDGEMENT

I would like to sincerely thank Jan Petrar for her generosity in helping me with formatting and bringing this work to life. Thank you, Jan.

My special thanks to Sharon Frissell for taking the time to read the book and helping me with making some necessary changes. I know it was a tedious task and I deeply appreciate your help.

Marilyn White, thank you so much for your feedback especially in asking me questions that helped me to include my perspectives on major concepts in Part III of the book. Really value your feedback.

Thanks to Molly and Jose for reading my final draft and giving me feedback. Thank you, Molly for reading the book on behalf of my extended family. I appreciate you taking the time to read it. Thank you, Jose for your feedback, specifically on part 3. I value your expertise in Biblical knowledge.

I thank each one in my family (Anil, Joyti, and Janice) for supporting me and being patient with me while I was writing this book. A special thanks to Ajay, for taking the time to read the hockey section and Part III and challenging me with questions. Thank you also for your help in selecting the relevant books to read. You have been an inspiration to me throughout.

A special thanks to my husband, Ranjit for his ongoing support from the beginning to completion of this challenging task. I really appreciated when he brought me a hot cup of delicious tea while I was struggling with words in front of the computer. Thank you for revising and giving me feedback on the parts referring to your story. Ranjit, you have been my supporter and critic at the same time. Thank you.

A special thanks to Heather Mewhort for doing the final editorial changes and making my book an easier read.

Above all I thank God for His guidance from the beginning to the end.

## BIBLIOGRAPHY

Berliski, Davud. *The Devil's Delision Atheism and Its Scientific Pretensions.* New York: Crown Forum, 2008.

*Bhagat Singh.* January 10, 2020. https://en.wikipedia.org/wiki/Bhagat_Singh.

C.S.Lewis. *Mere Christianity.* Harper Collins, 1980.

Dawkins, Richard. *The God Delusion.* Boston: Houghton Mifflin, 2006.

DiAngelo, Robin. *White Fragility: Why It Is So Hard for White People to Talk About Racism.* Boston: Beacon Press, 2018.

Frankl, Viktor. *Man's Search for Meaning.* Boston: Beacon Press, 2006.

Geisler, Norman and Frank Turek. *I Don't Have Enough Faith to Be an Atheist.* Wheaton: Crossway, 2004.

Harris, Sam. *The End of Faith: Religion, Terror, and the future of Reason.* New York: Norton, 2004.

—. *The Moral Landscape.* New York: Free Press, 2010.

*Hinduism.* January 10, 2020. https://en.wikipedia.org/wiki/Hinduism.

Keay, John. *Into India.* Cambridge: University Press, 1999.

Keller, Timothy. *The Reason for God Belief in an Age of Skepticism.* USA: Penguin Group, 2008.

Krause, Lawrence. *A Universe From Nothing Why There is something Rather Than Nothing.* New York: Atria Books , 2012.

Lapierre, Dominque and Larry Collins. *Freedom at Midnight.* New Delhi: Tarang Paperbacks, 1991.

Mangalwadi, Vishal. *India: The Grand Experiment.* Surrey, UK: Pippa Rann Books, 1997.

Meyer, Stephen. *Signature In the Cell DNA and the Evidence for Intelligent Design.* Harper Collis, 2009.

Murray, Abdu. *Grand Central Questions Answering Critical Concerns of the Major Worldviews.* USA: Green Press, 2014.

Peterson, Jordan. *12 Rules for Life.* Random House Canada, 2018.

Quereshi, Nabeel. *Seeking Allah, Finding Jesus A Devout Muslim Encounters Christianity.* Grand Rapids, Michigan: Zondervan, 2014.

Qureshi, Nabeel. *No God But One A Former Muslim Investigating the Evidence for Islam & Christianity.* Grand Rapids, Michigan: Zondervan, 2016.

Scott, Melrose. *Seventy Years 1904-1974 A History of the School of Nursing at Royal Inland Hospital.* Kamloops: Clow Printing LTD, 1974.

Shields, Elizabeth Lindsey and Laurene. "Collaborative Curriculum Guide." Curriculum Guide, Victoria, 2002.

*Sikhism.* January 10, 2020. https://en.wikipedia.org/wiki/Sikhism.

Simpson, Sharon and Karen Abbott. *Traditions and Transitions: History of the Nursing Program at Thompson Rivers University, 1973-2003.* Quebec: Gauvin Press, 2010.

*Subhas Chandra Bose.* January 10, 2020. https://en.wikipedia.org/wiki/Subhas_Chandra_Bose.

Turek, Frank. *Stealing from God.* USA: NAVPRESS, 2014.

*Udham Singh.* January 10, 2020. https://en.wikipedia.org/wiki/Udham_Singh.

*William Carey.* January 10, 2020. https://en.wikipedia.org/wiki/William_Carey_(missionary).

Wilson, Dorothy Clarke. *Dr. Ida Passing on The Torch of Life.* Chennai: Bhawana Printers, 1985.

Wolpert, Stanley. *India.* Berkley: University of California Press, 1991.

Yancey, Doroth Clarke Wilson and Philip. *Ten Fingers for God.* Grand Rapid, Michigan: Zondervan Books, 1989.

Zacharias, Ravi. *Jesus Among Other Gods.* Nashville: Thomas Nelson, 2000.

—. *The End of Reason.* Grand Rapids, Michigan: Zondervan, 2008.

—. *Walking From East to West.* Grand Rapids, Michigan: Zondervan, 2006.

—. *Why Jesus? Rediscovering His Truth In an Age of Mass Marketed Spirituality.* New York: Hachette Book Group, 2012.

—. *Why Suffering Finding Meaning and Comfort When Life Doesn't Make Sense.* New York: Hachette Book Group, 2014.

Manufactured by Amazon.ca
Bolton, ON

19491330R00160